We Wear the Mask

ᴈ❧

AFRICAN AMERICANS WRITE AMERICAN LITERATURE,

1760–1870

Rafia Zafar

COLUMBIA UNIVERSITY PRESS

New York

Columbia University Press
Publishers Since 1893
New York   Chichester, West Sussex
Copyright © 1997 Columbia University Press
All rights reserved

Library of Congress Cataloging-in-Publication Data
Zafar, Rafia.
    We wear the mask : African Americans write American literature, 1760–1870 /
Rafia Zafar.
        p.   cm.
    Includes bibliographical references and index.
    ISBN 0-231-08094-8 (acid-free paper). — ISBN 0-231-08095-6 (pbk.)
    1. American literature—Afro-American authors—History and criticism.
    2. American literature—Colonial period, ca. 1600–1775—History and criticism.
    3. American literature—Revolutionary period, 1775–1783—History and criticism.
    4. American literature—19th century—History and criticism. 5. American
literature—1783–1850—History and criticism. 6. Afro-Americans in literature.
    I. Title.
    PS153.N5Z34   1997
    810.9′896073—dc21   96-53974
                                                                              CIP

An earlier, shorter version of chapter 2, "Capturing the Captivity," appeared in
MELUS 17:2 (Summer 1991–1992); chapter 4, "It is natural to believe in great men,"
appeared in altered, briefer form in *Frederick Douglass: New Literary and Historical
Essays,* ed. Eric J. Sundquist (New York: Cambridge University Press, 1990).

∞

Casebound editions of Columbia University Press books are printed on permanent
and durable acid-free paper.
Printed in the United States of America
c 10 9 8 7 6 5 4 3 2 1
p 10 9 8 7 6 5 4 3 2 1

**FRANCIS CLOSE HALL
LEARNING CENTRE**
Swindon Road Cheltenham
Gloucestershire GL50 4AZ
Telephone: 01242 532913

UNIVERSITY OF
GLOUCESTERSHIRE
at CHELTENHAM *and* GLOUCESTER

NORMAL LOAN

44706 03/05

FOR NATHANS PAST AND PRESENT

CONTENTS

৵

CONTENTS

ACKNOWLEDGMENTS

How many scholars can say that a book manuscript took less time to complete than they originally planned? Scholarly books, like renovations on a house, take far longer than initial estimations. This book was no exception to such wisdom, but I have been wildly fortunate in friends and colleagues. As individual after individual willingly assisted me, I discovered how extensive and strongly spun a web of supporters I possessed: perhaps that is the greatest result of this undertaking.

Dana Nelson, Deborah McDowell, Nellie Y. McKay, and Susan Bernstein helped me greatly by reading and commenting on the earliest incarnations of these chapters. Their tough, good, and extensive remarks proved invaluable, especially as I began shaping the final manuscript. Sandra Gunning and Wendy Motooka provided crucial feedback late in the revision process. Of all the above-named colleagues, Sandra has suffered the most from puzzling over unfinished sentences in rushed-through drafts to allowing me to bend her ear on sundry crises of life in Treetown: she should know by now how very much her friendship means to me. And early on, of course, Werner Sollors and Sacvan Bercovitch provided the initial push for this book by directing its first incarnation, as my 1989 Harvard dissertation; in the process, they have gone from advisers to friends.

Beyond those who logged in hours wrestling with my prose and ideas, there have been a remarkable number of people who have graced me with their friendship, encouragement, advice, and examples. They are the late Nathan Huggins; Nellie McKay, whose help began before a word of this project was written; the Spungs and the Fett Rogerses; Robin Kilson, both for her long-running friendship and "Defending Our Name"; Earl Lewis; Lynn Weiss; Val Kivelson; Sue Juster; P. A. Skantze; Julie Ellison, who pointed me to Ann Eliza Bleecker; Bob Weisbuch; John Saillant and Elizabeth McHenry, fellow toilers at Harvard in the thickets of early African America; Phil Richards; T. Susan Chang; Teresa M. Hunt; Linda Bjork-Terrell; and others whom I hope will forgive me for omitting their names. At this juncture, it seems remarkable that I can remember how to type. My folks, Elizabeth and Jim Havens, and my sister, Maryam Zafar, know too well how long this project has stayed with me. My husband, Bill Paul, another Columbia author, urged me on at those depressing times when it seemed I would never finish: I am lucky not only in my choice of mate but in his having published two books before I did. Last, but never least, my son Nathan will probably count himself lucky to have lived only through part of this book's gestation: when things got bleak, he always reminded me that a hug can work wonders.

My editor, Jennifer Crewe, kept the faith even when I had lost it. I am grateful to Columbia University Press for the opportunity to work with her. The anonymous reviewers for the press read the manuscript not once but twice, providing advice at the beginning as well as the long view that comes from having seen an entire work at two disparate stages of its creation. Thanks as well to my two research assistants, Nish Saran at Harvard University and James Crane at Michigan, who charged and recharged books, ran down citations, and struggled to find missing sources. However much the writing of a book is solitary, its appearance depends on teamwork.

Most profoundly I owe the Charles Warren Center for Studies in American History at Harvard University and the Ford Foundation Postdoctoral Fellowship for Minority Scholars. They provided financial assistance as well as a supportive work environment, giving me an entire year free from teaching and advising responsibilities. Ernest May, Akira Iriye, and the all-wise Susan Hunt gave me an academic home at Harvard few could rival, and I appreciate their support and counsel. Christine O'Brien and Jennifer Rodriguez of the National Research Council, which administers the Ford Fellowships, answered my many questions, even the obvious ones. My fellow Warren Center fellows, the infamous "wild bunch," aka Class of 1996, made me laugh, taught me about professionalism, and got me in gear when I needed a push. Thank you, Tom, Daniela, Petra, Phil, and Tim.

The University of Michigan helped speed this book's progress: Dr. Lester Monts and the Office of the Vice Provost for Academic and Multicultural Affairs offered much encouragement, as well as a Faculty Award for Research; the Horace H. Rackham School of Graduate Studies and the Office of the Vice President for Research granted me a Faculty Recognition Award. The English department, as well as the Center for Afroamerican and African Studies, especially Michael Awkward and Sharon Patton, offered support, collegiality, and a multitude of friends and cheerleaders. I have been fortunate in my institutional affiliation, for Michigan has contributed in so many ways that I doubt I could recall them all. For the ones here enumerated and all the others at the U I have inadvertently omitted, many thanks.

Whatever its faults, *We Wear the Mask* will always be my first book. Well I might say, with Anne Bradstreet, that

> . . . being mine own, at length affection would
> Thy blemishes amend, if so I could:
> I wash'd thy face, but more defects I saw,
> And rubbing off a spot, still made a flaw.   *("The Author to Her Book")*

If my readers acknowledge its inevitable missteps, I hope they will also find its merits. Should they do that, this book and I will have achieved our goal.

Rafia Zafar

OCTOBER 1996
ANN ARBOR, MICHIGAN

We Wear the Mask

❧

ॐ

INTRODUCTION
Of Masks, Mimicry, and Invisibility

This book began to take shape during my graduate studies, when I asked myself at what point did Americans of African origin begin to see themselves as African American writers. It seemed to me, even in the nebulous early planning stages, only common sense that writers of African descent did not immediately see themselves as African American writers. I thought early black authors did not write a self-consciously black literature in the way we now understand it—with a sense of themselves as creators of an African American literature and the resultant expectations and intentions of both the audience and the artists. Although it seems almost tautological, writers of African descent did not, until after a certain historical point, write as African Americans. Certainly, many of us who study African American literature have touched upon this issue, implicitly alluding to an earlier, different phase of the tradition. But sufficient attention to the complex movement toward a modern African American literature, to the rhetorical experiments of antebellum writers building up to a self-conscious literary tradition, has not yet been paid. These antebellum writings have yet to receive their due, as the work of either "Americans" or "African Americans," in large measure because of the difficulty twentieth-century readers have in

1

drawing connections between an eighteenth-century colonial New England poet like Phillis Wheatley and a twentieth-century southern-raised, then Chicago-based novelist like Richard Wright.[1] This book represents my attempt to understand two parts of the African American literary tradition that can appear almost discrete.

In fact, forty years ago Richard Wright anticipated my conjectures: "you may feel that we [contemporary Negro authors] ought to write like Phyllis [sic] Wheatley, Alexander Dumas, or Alexander Pushkin. Well, we simply cannot; our world is not their world."[2] Reading his essay, "The Literature of the Negro in United States," one sees that Wright romanticizes the status of Wheatley, Dumas, and Pushkin as writers of African descent, asserting that the three were true inhabitants of their surrounding national cultures—the United States, France, and Russia, respectively.[3] Yet he is not so off the mark to ask, and answer, if the Wheatley poem he quotes is "the writing of [a Negro]? No, not by present-day American standards" (115). Explaining that "being a Negro has to do with the American scene, with race hate, rejection, ignorance, segregation, discrimination, slavery, murder, fiery crosses, and fear" (115), Wright locates the modifier "African American" as a cultural marker dependent on social situations:

> As the Negro merges into the main stream of American life, there might result actually a disappearance of Negro literature as such. If that happens, it will mean that those conditions of life that formerly defined what was "Negro" have ceased to exist, and it implies Negroes are Negroes because they are *treated* as Negroes   *(148; emphasis mine).*

Analogously, we consider certain writers producers of African American literature because we read their works that way—looking for evidence of those tell-tale "conditions of life." Again speaking of Wheatley, Phillip M. Richards formulates this transformation of writer into black writer differently:

> The combination of an emerging African consciousness and the ongoing adaptation to American society make up the central paradox of what might be called the black process of Americanization. As African Americans entered the social fabric of the new nation, they emphasized their newly generalized ethnic identity as Africans.[4]

African American writers are not just born in America of black parents. Rather, their African American literary consciousness has been developed through the literary experimentations of African-descended residents of what would become and what was the United States.

Recently, other scholars of the origins of African American literary history have helped me to understand more completely the transformations of antebellum black writers and their links to "white" literary culture. Critics of African American literature such as Frances Smith Foster, Carla Peterson, William L. Andrews, and Hazel Carby, as well as American "comparativists" like Werner Sollors, Eric Sundquist, and Sandra Gunning have confirmed my comparative approach. In the following discussion I hope to complement and expand upon their scholarship by situating the work of early African American writers (that is, men and women publishing in English) in close and parallel relation to the work of their European-American contemporaries, and by demonstrating how various moments within seemingly traditional texts mask identity-defining and persuasive strategies of black authors that show their simultaneous allegiance to both American letters and an African identity. In addition, the important discursive exchanges among African Americans, the intragroup signifying, will also open up this critical discussion. Eric Sundquist has said of black and white United States literature that "the two traditions can be seen as both one and separate," and points out that what hardly worked in the legal sphere can be difficult to argue for in literature.[5] While adding to the growing body of criticism in early African American letters, We Wear the Mask contributes to a discourse on Anglophone-American literature increasingly inflected by questions of race, marginality, and center, for although this manuscript focuses on black American writers, I cannot look at their work alone. I will therefore identify instances of appropriation from and accommodation to the European-American literary mainstream as trials and experiments in the development of an African American literary consciousness. As such experimentation did not take place in a vacuum, so several of the chapters herein interweave discussions of "black" and "white" American texts.

To understand the ways these authors have appropriated pre-existing genres to propound an emerging African American literary consciousness, I have sometimes used the word "mask" or "veil" to describe how authors as disparate as Olaudah Equiano and Eliza Potter sought a rapprochement with an essentially white audience. If, as Paul Laurence Dunbar wrote, to wear the mask that "grins and lies" is to efface evidence of struggle and sorrow, and to "mouth with myriad subtleties," then an exploration of the ramifications of such literary acts seems necessary in any discussion of early African American literature.[6] I do not believe that

3

black writers before 1870 saw themselves as tragic in the way that Dunbar encapsulated in his most famous poem. Caught in the double conscious-ness of a late nineteenth-century African American, raised with the ever-present specter of the failed Reconstruction, Dunbar railed against his lack of acceptance in the mainstream. His predecessors, understanding from the outset that they could not be part of the white literary world to which Dunbar's national career gained him only partial admittance, saw themselves and their writings less plangently. As Saunders Redding remarked some time ago, "Almost from the very beginning the literature of the Negro has been literature either of purpose or necessity."[7] To a large degree this may indeed be considered the case, for writers prior to, during, and immediately after the Civil War did figure racial justice as a primary motive for writing.[8] That political or didactic motive, however, had to be sweetened, veiled, or otherwise masked to be acceptable to a white audience. Nathan Huggins, writing on performance and masking in African American culture, has noted that the mask functions as a way to "move in and out of the white world with safety and profit," and suggests further that "the trick had been too perfect; *legerdemain* had undone itself in a disappearance act where the self had vanished, but also the incantation to call it back again."[9] Yet there was an advantage in these lit-erary strategies: by writing in "whiteface" these early black writers reached an audience familiar with their literary styles, if not their social objectives. Certainly, as Huggins believed, they ran the risk of disappear-ing into their own performances. Sometimes the disappearing act itself was precisely what was aimed for.

By interpolating a single word into one of the most often-quoted sen-tences of African American literature, I can foreshadow for my readers the theme of this book: "the problem of the Twentieth Century *scholar* is the problem of the color-line."[10] In these closing days of the century identi-fied as so pivotal by Du Bois, interpretations of U. S. literature must con-sider the textual ramifications of that color line—how and why a writer of African descent places him- or herself within the larger American setting, and how the resulting texts are studied. Early African American literature, I have found, is not so different from the literature that has been deemed "mainstream." Yet a world of difference hides in their similarities.

Not very long ago, to grant African American letters any consonance with American literature as a whole was seen as a kind of cultural treach-ery. In some quarters, perceived "whiteness" still functions as an occasion for the deepest opprobrium. Once an insult, the adjective "black" was made over into a point of pride during the 1960s by a generation devoted to providing Americans of African descent with a raison d'être and an artistic and critical aesthetic of their own. But such an aesthetic, as Phillip Brian Harper has suggested, contributed to a growing divisiveness among African Americans.[11] Similarities between African American and non-black American writers were downplayed; apparent attempts on the part of a black author to ally him- or herself with mainstream society were castigated as racially unconscious at best, traitorous at worst. Early black writers were thought to have accepted "the techniques of the sentimental novel, rather than the devices of Black oratory, narrative, and folklore, [and that] indicates both the weakness of their conception and the distance between these early writers and the masses of their people."[12] More recently, literary historian Elizabeth McHenry has asserted that, in contrast to previous beliefs that such writers were distant from their compeers, "free blacks in the urban North formed literary societies as a place in which to read and experiment with rhetorical strategies. . . . They sought effective avenues of public access as well as ways to voice their demands for full citizenship and equal participation in the life of the republic."[13] Readings of works by early African Americans as both publications from the United States and productions by members of a minority group have been relatively rare.[14] An identifiably black literary tradition had to be delineated to demonstrate to white doubters the significance, if not existence, of an African American expressive art.

The difficulties of defining and interpreting "Black Literature and Literary Criticism" per se are shown in the writings of two highly influential critics.[15] Throughout their ground-breaking writings, Houston A. Baker Jr. and Henry Louis Gates Jr. address the specificity of works generated by Americans of African descent. Baker once announced his intention to identify "the distinctive, . . . culturally specific aspects of African American literature and culture."[16] In *The Journey Back,* Baker notes American whites "could look to a Puritan ontology and sense of mission . . . [to aid their] definition of self," whereas black Americans were barred from such a societal or philosophical grounding because "white externality [offered] no ontological or ideological certainties."[17] In this formulation of American culture as without positive meaning for those of African descent, the early African American use of the dominant society's genres appears anomalous at best and racially self-effacing at worst. In later studies, such as *Workings of the Spirit,* Baker does acknowledge "my own orientation," that of "a theorist who began work under the aegis of the Black Aesthetic and whose nationalist orientation remains strong."[18] However strong this *caveat emptor*, to proclaim the "blackness" of African American literature before the Civil War presents some problems. On his part, Henry Louis Gates Jr. has argued for the "two-toned" nature of black literature, asserting that the combined strands of African or black vernacular and Western classical traditions comprise the tradition's inherent duality, the "double-voicedness," of such works.[19] Aiming for a nonessentialist conception of "blackness," Gates argues for a black identity as but one trope among others in the African American writer's bag of tricks: "There can be no transcendent blackness, for it cannot and does not exist beyond manifestations of it in specific figures."[20] But his own criticism sometimes contradicts this assertion, for he does indeed posit the existence of an identifiably "black" expression. This apparent double-voicedness, to use Gates's own locution, of black expression may well be a stylistic maneuver employed by an artist, *along with* whatever racial consciousness she or he chooses to exhibit: blackness can be a trope, a political position, a phenotypical difference, or none of the above.

Critics of African American literature must at some point wrestle with the question of what makes a writer, or her texts, black. Can African descent alone establish a writer's membership in the canon of African American writers? Not if "African American consciousness" in its literary manifestations post-dates those writers. Early black writers wrote poems, fiction, and autobiographies, but these documents are not, in the twentieth century, automatically recognized as "African American literature." Racial identity is fluid and changeable, and might even be said not to exist at certain points: "the simplistic view that geographical and social isolation have been the critical factors in sustaining" racial and ethnic categories should, as one sociologist has said, be dispensed with.[21] For the purposes of anthropologists and literary historians alike it may be the racial boundary, or rather the maintenance of such a barrier, that is important—not the phenotypical difference or the cultural content it encloses.[22] Although many of us can now agree with Theodore W. Allen and others that race is socially constructed, the reader's desire to codify and classify remains. For Phillis Wheatley and John Marrant "blackness" per se may have been something of a nonissue, at least as far as most of their *texts* were concerned. Without a doubt they were aware of themselves as people of African descent; such markers appear throughout their writings, as do their repeated, positive self-identifications as Africans. Nevertheless, Wheatley, Marrant, and other eighteenth-century "Africans" were not writing a literature constructed as African American. They were "Africans" writing American literature, participating in a particular discourse without necessarily seeing themselves as African *Americans*. Sterling Stuckey has noted in a discussion of "the names controversy" that "Afro-Americans" as a term did not become dominant until the 1890s; "African" was the designation preferred by those of African descent through at least the first third of the nineteenth century.[23]

If the very African Americanness of an author demonstrates an essentially un-American vision, as has been implicitly stated in American literary histories written before the present time, where does that leave analyses of black writers in the United States? Writers themselves may think in either/or terms and later contradict such remarks in other statements: consider Toni Morrison's comment, "at no moment in my life have I ever felt as though I were an American," with her later assertion of the essential Africanness of America.[24] Decades earlier, W. E. B. Du Bois propounded the essentially, perennially divided and doubled nature of African American consciousness, questioning the place of the black in North America. Literary expression by one physically designated as African American should be un-American as well. But within a "dominant" literature that hyphenates, and therefore in some manner incorporates and/or co-opts alternative expressions, the two terms cannot be mutually exclusive. By designating a work "African American" a reader makes a distinction that in some ways militates against a text's inclusion within the pale of "American" literature and erases similarities with parallel texts worth exploring. The placement of a text within the parameters of "white" or "black" must be examined carefully, as should the issue of whether and why African American writers would consider themselves either American or African American, or both.

Until approximately the last third of the nineteenth century, African American writers adopted many of the ideas and genres of the white dominant culture in order to declare themselves part of it. Not witless imitators, many of these African Americans exhibited a positive attitude about themselves: "African" as an appellation was well regarded by those considered "black"—why else choose the name *African* Methodist Episcopal Church? Many of the African Americans thinking and writing before Reconstruction attempted in their works a literary "transculturalization," whereby they as individuals became part of the host society.[25] From a broadly African perspective the borrowing of alien cultural markers or methods made sense; the forced laborers might, after a time, be accepted within dominant American culture.[26] If one proceeds on the assumption that many African cultures see conformity as a positive rather than a negative attribute—that belonging to a group, or Turnerian *communitas*, strengthens one's sense of self and security—it then follows that adoption of white genres does not mean, to someone of African culture, mere imitation. "If the African, therefore, places a high value on conformity, as does the American, he does so as a result of different sets of considerations. His actions are based more upon the positive rewards of conformity than upon the [American] fear of nonconformity."[27] Thus, a negative interpretation of genre adoption by African Americans may illustrate entrenched European and white American ideas about the superiority of individualism and exceptionalism, rather than reflecting African attitudes. And while a theory of "Afrocentricity"[28] may not be aimed at explaining black adoption of white forms, to conceive of an African identity willing to adopt and expand upon pre-existing elements would be to concede, at least in theory, the possibility that these writers took up the words and forms of their host society first to find a place in it, and only later to create an African American culture. That the earliest African American writers were seeking "communal empowerment through personal conformity"[29] may at first seem an oxymoron. In colonial and nineteenth-century America the fact that artists such as Wheatley and Douglass insisted on their participation within a national discourse was indeed radical—if only because they were saying they too could use certain genres and methods, and wield them well.[30] Furthermore, if one considers such efforts in the light of voluntarism—in the words of Werner Sollors, basing one's identity on consent rather than on descent—then writers in this first century of African American literature were indisputably American, even as their loyalties were divided.[31]

Reasonably, some may question whether my primary focus on narrative works, without reference to Africanisms, folklore, and the vernacular, is justified. Valerie Smith has advised that "to emphasize the textual dimension is to misrepresent the complex origins and affinities of the black work of literature."[32] In a related warning, Carla Peterson urges that we avoid privileging one genre over others:

> The dominant trend in literary scholarship has been to privilege the slave narrative as *the* African American literary form of the antebellum period. . . . As a result, literary criticism of the late twentieth century has come dangerously close to replicating the historical situation of the early nineteenth century in its valorization of those African American texts produced under the direction of white sponsors for the consumption of a white readership.[33]

I hope not to privilege unduly the literate over the oral, the slave narrative over the poem, the "European" over the "African." The writers discussed here did, however, use particular rhetorical styles for particular reasons, which may explain an apparently old-fashioned emphasis on the "European," rather than the "African" elements of African American literature. I perhaps favor the autobiographical mode because of the link I perceive between telling one's own story and creating one's own literary history. African Americans in the United States wrote in literary forms that were, for the most part, not extant in contemporaneous African societies. I do not apologize for their adoption of these genres, for the writers did not either. Hazel Carby has observed that the concept of a black women's literature is "essentialist and ahistorical . . . [for] no language or experience is divorced from the shared context in which different groups that share a language express their differing group interests." Her conclusion, that "language is accented differently by competing groups, and therefore the terrain of language is a terrain of power relations," says much about how authors like Wheatley, Douglass, and Elizabeth Keckley engaged with the American language, and why.[34] Their writings acknowledge and address—implicitly if not overtly—their largely white audience.

The texts discussed in the following study often fall under the rubric of those "produced under the direction of white[s]," and suffer accordingly, in their estimation by modern critics, from that limitation. Of all the works herein treated, perhaps only Eliza Potter's anonymously self-published book, *A Hairdresser's Experience in High Life*, can escape that ascription—and Potter's work was still a production aimed at white buyers, even if they were subject to her thinly veiled criticisms. Whatever kind of text these artists produced, and in whatever manner their work appeared, the authors' phenotypical "difference" relegated eighteenth- and nineteenth-century African Americans to a maligned minority, and their works to a nearly orphaned status. Natally and artistically alienated, Wheatley and her African American colleagues before Reconstruction have long been consigned to a peculiar no-man's-land, in artistic terms neither black nor white, the gray area of American literary history.

This book is therefore a chronological, yet hardly exhaustive survey of African American literary masks, mimicry, and invisibility. Since the late colonial period black writers have produced a wide variety of written expression, in addition to oral and cultural forms of protest and accommodation,[35] which are less easily accessed. The white literary forms available—captivity and conversion narratives, neoclassic poetry, and so on—

were tried on and out, and intriguing variations on familiar genres began to appear. Again, African American literature is *not* merely a set of changes rung on white genres. Rather, so-called "white" approaches to written expression were taken up and altered by Africans and African Americans, without falling into the trap of "social science fiction."[36] Through literary masking, the use of literary genres and styles familiar to whites, black American writers gained access to an audience that had not previously believed the Negro had any rights worth respecting. Such literary endeavors came with built-in risks and traps, but the limitations themselves are worthy of consideration. As a late twentieth-century literary historian, I seek to define how to read comprehensively these "whitefaced" literary acts, without overprivileging the imitated genres and while contemplating the inescapably limited nature of early black writers' success.

The writings of Phillis Wheatley, John Marrant, Henry Bibb, and Harriet Wilson can all be said to be in some measure transcendent. Although their works may be seen as experiments in literary masking, they changed permanently the meanings of the genres they appropriated. Neoclassic poetry, Franklinian success stories, and sentimental dramas of domestic intrigue are not usually, to readers of the late twentieth century, imagined to be "black" genres; neither do most readers think of black authors as practitioners of these forms. But in adapting genres to craft a particular sensibility, black authors eventually altered our conceptions of "mainstream" America, as other critics have already demonstrated.[37] In part because of this conscious adoption and adaptation of pre-existing literary styles, a body of contemporary African American literature became possible. Practicality and cunning alike dictated that a writer of African descent in America use the forms with which the European-American audience was familiar. Early African American narrative and poetry gained transforming and transformative power from the tension between an author of African descent and her or his preferred European-descended genres.

My first chapter discusses Phillis Wheatley, long acknowledged the first black writer in the United States to publish a book. In a somewhat unusual approach, I compare and contrast Wheatley with two of her European-American peers, Joel Barlow and Ann Eliza Bleecker. Such a placement will be crucial to a reconfiguration of Wheatley's position within literary studies, for we cannot only compare Wheatley to her African American successors. In the late 1770s Wheatley enjoyed international success, traveling to England to promote her work and becoming the protégée of the Countess of Huntingdon. Her supporters in the nineteenth century used her as "proof" of Negro humanity; her critics, following Thomas Jefferson's estimation of her work as beneath remark, deemed her little more than a talented mimic.[38] In our century she has been alternately scorned as insufficiently "African American" in consciousness or slighted as a derivative rhymester; she has also been called supremely talented for her classical allusions and elliptical references to freedom. Wheatley's travels from literary curio to center stage attest to the rapidly evolving status of African/American literary history in the late twentieth century. Any study such as this must begin with an examination of her work.

Puritan captivity and conversion narratives, the first manifestations of New World slave autobiography, provided other venues for early black writers. Some years ago I came across Annette Kolodny's noting of "the structural and stylistic affinities between the captivity narratives and slave narratives—both essentially accounts of captivity amid powerful Others," and I then proposed to expand upon her brief and provocative comment.[39] I found that in the seventeenth century captives like Mary Rowlandson would refer, and defer, to their "masters"; their labor as enslaved whites was forcibly extracted by Bible-spurning pagans. Similarly, in the next two centuries black Christians documented the inhumane treatment they received at the hands of white churchgoers. Blacks and whites could alike be dominated by a white male Protestant ruling class, although their relation to that elite differed mightily. Narrators on both sides frequently related their experiences via another, albeit friendly, "powerful Other" (almost invariably a white male editor). Despite such patronizing direction and editing, African American narrators like the free black John Marrant and the ex-fugitive Henry Bibb began the process of rescripting the American story of bondage. As could be expected, the captives' voices were often muffled, altered, and screened.[40] While many whites authorized or proposed specific types of literary production, as when John Marrant set down his conversion experiences for the Reverend Aldridge, others feared the uses to which literature, and even literacy, could be put.[41]

Frederick Douglass's master, Mr. Auld, exemplifies the classic "resistance to borrowing" when he discovers his slave's reading skills: "Mr. Auld . . . at once forbade Mrs. Auld to instruct me further, telling her, among other things, that it was unlawful, as well as unsafe, to teach a slave to read."[42] Self-reliance openly manifested by a black was unusual and generally undesirable; therefore, Douglass pioneered the African American male's insertion into the American success story. My fourth chapter explores African American success stories' parallels to and departures from this American genre, concentrating on Douglass's appropriation of Benjamin Franklin's role as former indentured servant become successful man. These autobiographical works show how slave and free authors alike reordered the priorities of the genre to fit the teller. Intriguingly, the publication of the Anglo-African Olaudah Equiano's autobiography preceded Franklin's by nearly thirty years, for in 1789 Equiano had already conflated the story of the self-made man with the picaresque tale and the conversion narrative.[43] Franklin and Douglass alone do not set the parameters for the New World success story.

Franklin died two years before the publication of Equiano's best-selling *Narrative*, but Harriet Beecher Stowe readily acknowledged that she had read many slave narratives before writing *Uncle Tom's Cabin*. White Protestant female writers frequently contested male authority without a corresponding comprehension of an American group even more oppressed than they—despite their adoption of the figure of the wronged slave as a stand-in for the injustices practiced against white females.[44] Stowe's ambivalent stance on the black American family in the antipatriarchal *Uncle Tom's Cabin* triggered a wealth of black responses ranging from measured and favorable reception to protest and rejection.[45] In answer to Stowe, William Wells Brown gathered up a number of written genres— slave narratives, newspaper articles, folk stories, and others—to create *Clotel, or the President's Daughter*, an unsubtle condemnation of white liberalism that would in turn be revised by African American women. A discussion of these inter- and intragroup exchanges over the literary representation of African America, specifically the black woman, make up the penultimate chapter. Casting their rejoinders in autobiographical form, whether as slave narratives or indentured servants' horror stories, Harriet Jacobs and Harriet E. Wilson attempted to re-form Stowe's images and attitudes. Jacobs, writing under the pseudonym Linda Brent, combined Stowe's sentimental strategies with techniques of the slave narrative and the autobiography;[46] publishing *Our Nig* anonymously, the free black Wilson traded sentiment for scathing condemnation to expose northern white racism and oppression.

Wilson's and Jacobs's reluctance to reveal their true identities points to a final predicament of the mid-nineteenth-century black woman author, a subject I take up in the final chapter. Like Jacobs and Wilson, Elizabeth Keckley tells a story of bondage, abuse, and eventual escape; like Douglass, Keckley paints herself as one who walks unbowed in slavery and escapes perpetual servitude by her own skill—in her case, by purchasing herself and her son. Yet curiously, Keckley's post-Civil War memoir, *Behind the Scenes; or, Thirty Years a Slave and Four at the White*

House (1868), seems almost to discard its author after a scant three chapters. Although that move toward invisibility is anticipated by the pseudonymous and anonymous self-portrayals of Wilson and Jacobs, the near-total erasure of a black female narrator is not; in this, Keckley is only eclipsed by Eliza Potter, who self-published *A Hairdresser's Experience in High Life* (1859), an anonymous memoir, right before the Civil War. Potter's career as groomer to the rich and would-be rich place her in a highly visible yet unobserved position—that of the personal servant who is everywhere, yet in her employers' eyes nowhere. The hairdresser's acid-tongued comments on white society support her invisibility: in exposing others' lives she shields her own. I thus close this study with the sight of the black writer as invisible viewer, a stance chosen by an African American writing for Americans.

In noting the imitative and contradictory acts of African American writers before 1870, we have often overlooked the possibilities of acculturation and creative engagement. Subversion, resistance, and opposition are not the only indicators of an African American literary identity. To know and understand the range of rhetorical masks, mimicry, and invisibility used by the authors of this period increases the level of sophistication of American literary criticism. Equally important is the recognition of the diverse rhetorical exchanges circulating within this period: the inter- and intragroup dialogue, as well as the innovations by male and female practitioners of similar genres. Somewhat later in the nineteenth century a sea change would lead U.S. authors of African descent to reconsider the appellation of "American" writer and move toward an increasing consciousness of their position as African American writers. Early African Americans wrote American literature, and they meant it to be such. When they begin to write as African Americans, and not as transculturated Africans, an American literary milestone is reached.

1

𝔷❧

SABLE PATRIOTS AND MODERN EGYPTIANS

Phillis Wheatley, Joel Barlow, and Ann Eliza Bleecker

"I scarce could tell them anything
of Africa, though much of Boston
and my hope of Heaven. . . ."

—*Robert Hayden*
A Letter from Phillis Wheatley: London, 1773

Despite Phillis Wheatley's forthright self-identification as an "Afric muse," her command of eighteenth-century literary fashion does not commend her to most modern readers. Her reputation has generally rested on a handful of poems, including "On being brought from AFRICA to AMERICA," "To the University of Cambridge, in New-England," "On the Rev. Mr. George Whitefield," and "On Imagination," along with one or two others. *Poems on Various Subjects, Religious and Moral*, her only book, appeared in London in 1773; it contained some thirty-eight verses. Twentieth-century critics such as Robert C. Kuncio, Mukhtar Ali Isani, and William H. Robinson have unearthed and discussed almost another twenty, but there the record ends (although some two dozen letters round out her literary corpus). The works of Pope and Milton obviously influenced the young poet, and critics have also noted the sway of Mather Byles and other Puritan divines.[1] Elegies were her preferred verse form—about one third of *Poems on Various Subjects* are elegies—and her preferred line was the heroic couplet.[2] Unlike her contemporary Joel Barlow, but like most Americans of African descent before 1900, Wheatley left little in the way of a written estate. When she died, her husband advertised for a second manuscript of her poems to be returned to him, but that collection has not reappeared. Thus her critical standing largely rests on a slim volume of works composed when she was still in her teens, verses in which the poet-self is discreet, restrained, and rarely at the fore. Nevertheless, even with the plethora of classical allusions, invocations to the muses, biblical references, and praise of the hereafter, there is a new, *American* voice present here. Sounding both like and unlike Pope and Byles, Wheatley's voice struck original notes. Although her sound would not be the barbaric yawp of a Whitman, her remarkable performance was that of a writer who was immersed in white colonial culture yet remained apart from it. Whether she gently admonished the careless, privileged students of Harvard or honored the accomplishments of a fellow African American artist, Wheatley addressed exceptional issues in remarkably unexceptional style. She was a lonely first among African American authors.[3]

If she judged from her volume's warm reception in abolitionist-minded England, Wheatley may well have believed the sentiments expressed in her poems would achieve similar success in the United States. Yet the original, British edition of *Poems on Various Subjects* could not appear until the English publisher had in hand the authenticating seal of no fewer than eighteen male colonial worthies.[4] The American edition of Wheatley's works would not be published until months after her death, for even this imprimatur was not enough to guarantee the volume's appearance during her lifetime.[5] Despite her exemplary Protestant piety, lofty sentiments, and professional style, Wheatley would see her publications in British North America limited to newspapers and broadsides. The young poet kept her views on racism and African American oppression within the parameters of acceptable expression, and her more aggressively pro-American poems had been withheld from the 1773 British edition of her poems.[6] Unsurprisingly, then, the protest embedded in such verses as "On Being Brought from Africa to America" has been invisible to many readers because of her oblique argumentation. Readers must always keep in mind the necessity of literary masking, the rhetorical subterfuge with which, one hundred years later, Dunbar would grow so weary. The veil, recognizable as a black literary convention by the mid- to late-nineteenth century, becomes invisible or opaque when combined with conventions of eighteenth-century poetics.[7] Wheatley's dispassionate observations in the face of enslavement, racism, and a constrained future may also be the willed, forced dissemblance of a young black poet.

Saunders Redding's remark that "On Being Brought" shows a "distinct sense of abnegation and self-pity" has echoed for decades in subsequent criticism.[8] The first line and last couplet embody the kind of language Wheatley critics attack for a perceived self-hate. Terrence Collins has flatly stated that it is nearly impossible to dissociate her poetry's images from the cultural equations of black/pagan/evil and white/saved/good: "For Wheatley, the terms of religious escape and racial denial of the self are . . . the same."[9] If we follow that line of thinking, " 'Twas mercy brought me from my *Pagan* land" (line 1) is a self-hating response to enslavement, for "mercy" must be read as a euphemism for white domination. In fact, much proslavery argument did rest on the belief that the forced emigration from Africa and subsequent "paternalistic" bondage provided so-called heathens with the opportunity for Christian salvation. Wheatley's poem has therefore been interpreted as proslavery, or at least regrettably without racial dignity, for its supposed demonstration of the desire to be Caucasian. In light of this interpretation the final two lines, "Remember, *Christians*, *Negros*, black as *Cain*, / May be refin'd, and join th' angelic train" (ll. 7–8), translate into a pitiable plea for acceptance: the foregone conclusion is that the poet's allusion to the biblical injunction against the children of Ham and stated desire for refinement mean a wish to be white. Similarly, the phrase "benighted soul" (line 2) and reference to prevalent white beliefs in the demonic nature of Africans—"Their colour is a diabolic die" (line 6)— have been taken to imply an appalling lack of self-pride. Yet such an interpretation can operate only when the reader has decided in advance against the possibility of Wheatley speaking on more than one level, against what Mae Henderson has termed the black woman writer's—by extension Phillis Wheatley's—"multiple and complex social, historical, and cultural positionality."[10]

Wheatley's multivalence has not been invisible to Sondra O'Neale, who insists that to understand Wheatley one must comprehend also the biblical and spiritual roots of early African American literature. O'Neale notes that to "overlook biblical terminology [is to miss] . . . its implications for slavery" and disregard the strategic significance of Wheatley's "use of biblical symbolism . . . as a poet and an abolitionist."[11] Other eighteenth-century black Americans like John Marrant found the messages of dignity and salvation in the teachings of Jesus Christ empowering, as did their Caucasian fellows.[12] The refusal to recognize the liberating possibilities of Protestant Christianity and the supposition that Wheatley must want to be "white" because she is a confessed Christian have fostered simplistic critiques of her work. The urge for refinement cannot be only a desire to become white, for in another poem Wheatley defines "refinement" as extra-earthly joy: "He welcomes thee [in heaven] to pleasures more refin'd, / And better suited to th' immortal mind" ("To A Lady on the Death of Her Husband," 30). Wheatley equates refinement with the next world and its delights, a point she makes again in her poem about the death of Reverend Whitefield. Circulated first as a broadside-elegy about a charismatic and internationally known divine, "On the Death of Rev. Mr. George Whitefield. 1770" gained her the approval of whites in both colonial New England and the mother country. The genuinely expressed pious sentiment, couched in irreproachable heroic couplets, did not fail to win readers. Addressing the late Whitefield as a "happy saint, on thine immortal throne," Wheatley reminds her audience of the prophet's "sermons in unequall'd accents" and his prayer "that grace in ev'ry heart might dwell" (ll. 1, 5, 20). Whitefield's remembered "strains of eloquence refin'd" puns on the double meaning of "refined": first, as in divesting oneself of earthly concerns and second, as in the commoner meaning of elevated speech (22–23).[13] The poet's recollection of Whitefield's wish "to see *America* excel" is calculated to gain the sympathies of her audience.

Yet along with these sentiments we discern a voice countering the opprobrium cast at Wheatley's fellow African Americans:

"Take him my dear *Americans*," he said,
"Be your complaints on his kind bosom laid:
Take him, ye *Africans*, he longs for you,
Impartial Saviour is his title due.
Wash'd in the fountain of redeeming blood,
You shall be sons, and kings, and priests to God."   *(ll. 32–37; 23)*

Even more than the above lines, a variant version published in England stresses the point of African equality, as John Shields has demonstrated: "If you will walk in Grace's heavenly Road, / He'll make you *free*, and Kings, and Priests to God" (ll. 43–44, 210; emphasis mine).[14] Undoubtedly, either Wheatley or her editor realized the probable reaction of a colonial, slavery-condoning readership and substituted the couplet above; in either case the poet makes her point clearly. Despite the potential ingrained, negative responses of Wheatley's white readership to slaves and their kin, *Poems on Various Subjects* contains positive, if oblique, messages about African Americans.

In the poem "To S.M. a young *African* Painter, on seeing his works," Wheatley goes beyond scripturally delivered affirmations of African freedom and equality to hail the dignity, artistic worth, and future immortality of Scipio Moorhead, a fellow slave.

> Still, wond'rous youth, each noble path pursue,
> On deathless glories fix thine ardent view:
> Still may the painter's and the poet's fire
> To aid thy pencil, and thy verse conspire! (114)

The inclusion of this sentiment within *Poems on Various Subjects* was a bold move, for the only work the "lab'ring bosom" of Moorhead performs is "living characters to paint." The black subject of Wheatley's poetry is depicted neither as a mute hewer of wood nor as a clownish buffoon; Moorhead, an artist of "ardent view" will gain his deserved reward "in the realm above. . . / There shall thy tongue in heav'nly murmurs flow" (115). Along with paying the young artist the supreme compliment of an ode, Wheatley affords him further splendor: "nobler themes demand a nobler strain." By inserting Moorhead into the array of notables apostrophized in *Poems on Various Subjects*—the Reverend Whitefield, the Earl of Dartmouth, the Lieutenant-Governor—she elevates the "*African* Painter" to their level. In hallowing a socially low figure Wheatley breaks with the neoclassical tradition of treating "high" subjects exclusively; Phillip Richards has seen this move as indicative of Wheatley's ability to "elevate the status of the poem's lowly subjects (young Africans) to their proper role in a providential drama in which they are prophets and harbingers of the millennium."[15] For Wheatley to include an African American servant with the highest of white males, to invoke his talents as though he were the most renowned of painters, and to speak of his immortality and spiritual nobility, claims for black people the neoclassical mode in poetry and an equal place in society—and bespeaks an African American agenda.[16] Wheatley participates in a white, Western, largely male tradition at the same time she fashions it into an expressive, "black" vehicle.

"To the University of Cambridge, in New England" also cloaks an admonition to be racially just within respectful lines to the colony's future leaders. What censure she makes is implied, for much of the poem registers as a typical paean to the scions of the dynastic settlers:

> Students, to you 'tis giv'n to scan the heights
> Above, to traverse the ethereal space,
> And mark the systems of revolving worlds.
> Still more, ye sons of science, ye receive

The blissful news by messengers from heav'n
How *Jesus'* blood for your redemption flows.   *(15)*

Wheatley's prefacing these lines with the remark that " 'Twas not long
since I left my native shore / The land of errors, and *Egyptian* gloom" (15)
does not appear calculated to elevate the poet to more than a bard from an
unenlightened land. Yet along with the gentle warning to "Improve your
privileges while they stay," Wheatley injects something more than the
standard, pious injunction to be good: "Ye blooming plants of human race
divine, / An *Ethiop* tells you 'tis [sin] your greatest foe" (16). That this
young "*Ethiop*" tells Harvard men to "each hour redeem" has particular
importance, given Wheatley's place in colonial society.[17] Betsy Erkkila
suggests that in this poem, as well as in the ode to Moorhead, the stress
laid on such words as "Ethiop" and "Egyptian" is indicative of "racial
pride"; I shared this position until Wendy Motooka pointed out that ital-
icization of proper nouns was standard practice in this period. I do think,
however, that Wheatley's repeated interjections of nationality and race,
whether describing a subject's identity or placing a figure, attempt to
denature or make positive commonly held "dark" associations. As she has
done in the poem for Scipio Moorhead, the poet here advances another
African American, in this instance herself, as prophet and spiritual guide.
Such a stance was unprecedented: Christ the redeemer finds in pen-wield-
ing African Americans "messengers from heav'n." Yet even with these
insinuations of African Americans into the literary discourse, the extent
of Wheatley's dissent from the dominant society's principles can remain
somewhat unclear.

The difficulty lies in the Christian rhetoric Wheatley utilizes. One of
Wheatley's oft-quoted thanksgivings—"Father of mercy, 'twas thy gra-
cious hand / Brought me in safety from those dark abodes" ("To the
University," l. 5, p. 15)—encapsulates the problems readers have had with
Wheatley's oeuvre. Again: how could a black woman, a slave, be grateful
for deliverance from her native country? How could she have designated
her childhood home a "dark" land? Bearing in mind her Protestant faith,
we should remind ourselves that conversion to Christianity does not indicate a corresponding or wholesale conversion to belief in white superiority. The two may have been related (particularly in the New England
colonies[18]), but they were not the same. When Wheatley plays on the
adjective "dark," she refers to both brown-skinned people and the unenlightened—that is to say unconverted—people. To say that the poet
implied a lesser status for most (that is, non-Christian) Africans may not

be entirely wrong, for she, like many eighteenth-century black converts, genuinely believed that Christianity was her saving grace. This does *not*, however, mean that she believed the unconverted to be permanently lost—nor that she accepted white supremacy. When used by Wheatley, a writer of African descent, ambiguities are profound and inescapable in a rhetoric that links light with the saved, dark with the damned. When Wheatley's contemporary Ann Eliza Bleecker linked darkness with evil and evil with the brown-skinned Native Americans, she demonized the nonwhites on the margins of her upstate colonial society without a qualm. Wheatley, even while asserting a black's right to Christianity, undercut this espousal of "African" humanity and liberty by linguistic metaphors linking darkness to damnation and lightness to salvation. To be realistic, we must concede that some of her verse stratagems were more successful than others.

In "To the Right Honorable William, Earl of Dartmouth," Wheatley's essential aim was to celebrate Christianity, which could lead her to ambiguous statement: "I, young in life, by seeming cruel fate/ Was snatch'd from *Afric's* fancy'd happy seat" (74). Such wording may well demonstrate an embedded, internalized Eurocentrism, for Christianity, at least in the United States, was seen as a European belief system rather than an African one. That an abundance of elements in her work does assert African dignity and self-worth, even if cast within a Christian framework, amply illustrates Wheatley's essentially positive conception of herself as an African in America.[19] The number of times she refers to herself as African or Ethiopian in *Poems on Various Subjects* confirms this point of view. In the poem to the Earl of Dartmouth, Wheatley's espousal of American independence rhetoric tends to obscure her protests against the oppression of blacks. Her rhetorical question, "Should you my lord . . . [w]onder from whence my love of *Freedom* sprung" (74), precedes the depiction of her own sudden seizure and kidnap; the query that closes the stanza—"And can I then but pray / Others may never feel tyrannic sway?"—links the sanctity of the parent-child bond with the inevitability of future separation. By casting the infamy of African kidnap in familial terms, Wheatley sets up the break between Britain and nascent America in terms of "natural" rights, preceding even the publication of such ideas in Thomas Paine's *Common Sense*.[20] It was precisely the tragedy of her situation in the African diaspora that enabled Wheatley to comprehend and support white colonists' struggle against a perceived enslavement. The political and poetical task she set for herself was to evoke in a white audience empathy for freedom-deprived blacks. Inevitably, the values already embedded in the metaphors and language of her captors would create tension within, if not a subversion of, her own best efforts.

Like her compatriot Barlow, Wheatley drew on the various events and uprisings leading to the revolution. Barlow had pleaded for republicanism and African freedom in *The Columbiad*, as we will shortly see;[21] Wheatley also conflated the struggle for American independence with African freedom. Her patriotic poems regularly include such petitions, as will be shown in the next section of this chapter. Although many of Wheatley's poems have been lost, some of those missing must have touched the twin chords of African American freedom and white American independence. "On the Affray in King-Street, on the Evening of the 5th of March," numbered among the pieces included in a volume proposed in 1772,[22] would almost certainly have been such a poem. That "affray," better known as the Boston Massacre, marked the opening of the hostilities between British troops and colonists angered with repressive taxation measures. As the black martyr of the colonists, the slain Crispus Attucks would have been the ideal figure in whom Wheatley could conflate the aims of black emancipation and colonial sovereignty. Attucks's patriotic death could have been an occasion to state the case for African liberty, much as the accidental shooting of an American child, portrayed in "On the Death of Mr. Snider Murder'd by Richardson" (136), presented a similar opportunity to make political points for the colonists. Fervor for the cause of African American freedom could be combined, through Attucks's martyrdom, with a cause her white compatriots would embrace.

If many dissenting critics, African and European American alike, had closely read Wheatley's thought (in verse and epistolary form), they would have found it difficult to dismiss her as a rhyming Uncle Tom. Wheatley's letters to her friend and fellow slave Obour Tanner, or to the Native American [Mohegan nation] minister Samson Occom, himself caught between the rock of his Methodist faith and the hard place of his racial identity, differ in tone and style from those addressed to whites.[23] Most are concerned with the problems of being a Christian in a secular world, but that Wheatley was a *black* Christian in a *white* world added a unique stress to her quest for enlightenment. Writing to a white minister, Samuel Hopkins, Wheatley stresses the Christianizing influence of Europeans on Africans:

Europe and America have long been fed with the heavenly provision, and I fear they loathe it, while Africa is perishing with a Spiritual Famine. O

that they could partake of the crumbs, the precious crumbs, Which fall
from the table of these distinguished children of the kingdom.   *(176)*

Curiously, Wheatley throws doubt on the worthiness of the Europeans
themselves by stating they "loathe" Christianity, even as she refers to
the "crumbs" falling from their table. She furthermore asserts Africans
"are unprejudiced against the truth" (176), once again intimating that
Caucasian bearers of the gospel have much to learn from their darker-
skinned brethren. Her unquestionably sincere attitude of humble sup-
plicant notwithstanding, Wheatley had no trouble seeing through the
failings of white missionaries.

A letter to a confidante, or a nonwhite compatriot, could raise concerns other than salvation or heavenly refinement: "Wheatley's Christianity is not the Christianity of political quietism and submissive piety,"
as Donna Landry has observed.[24] In the same letter to the Reverend
Occom cited above, Wheatley expresses quite explicitly her feelings
about religion and racism:

> I ... am greatly satisfied with your Reasons respecting the Negroes, and
> think highly reasonable what you offer in Vindication of their natural
> Rights: Those that invade them cannot be insensible that the divine
> Light is chasing away the thick Darkness which broods over the Land
> of Africa ... [revealing] the glorious Dispensation of civil and religious
> Liberty, which are so inseparably united, that there is little or no
> Enjoyment of one without the other.   *(176)*

Referring later to the whites who would enslave others as "our Modern
Egyptians," the young poet delivers a typological interpretation of eighteenth-century society that incorporates Enlightenment beliefs about
natural rights as well as her own African American commitment to black
freedom. (In much the same way, African American spirituals linked the
destiny of the singers with that of the ancient Israelites or other biblical
figures.)[25] Two hundred years before the civil rights activists of the 1960s,
Wheatley declared that Christianity and black freedom were inseparable;
to be a black Christian was not to be unequal. As Cynthia J. Smith has
remarked, "knowing of Wheatley's circumstances as a slave ... [too many
readers accept] unquestioningly the premise that someone in [her] position would have feelings of inadequacy."[26] Any critic who can read the
closing sarcasm of her letter to Occom and still believe her to be without
racial consciousness is a resistant reader: "How well the Cry for Liberty,

and the reverse Disposition for the Exercise of oppressive Power over others agree,—I humbly think it does not require the Penetration of a Philosopher to determine." (177). Hortense Spillers concurs succinctly with Wheatley's prototype of "liberation theology": "Is it too much to say that the African could not *but* have become a Christian in the sociopolitical context of the United States, as a *strategy* for gaining his/her historical ground and humanation here?"[27]

In selecting neoclassical poetry as her preferred genre Wheatley showed continuity of approach, if not style, with later African American writers; they, too, would appropriate the master's tools to dismantle the master's house.[28] But adopting "English" methods of versification also placed her within the mainstream of colonial poets: as Cynthia J. Smith reminds us, in the "eighteenth century . . . imitation was not only the literary fashion of the day but the very means to excellence" (588). To craft a signature at once familiar to her largely white audience yet distinct in outlook, creativity, and identity was the task a very young poet set for herself. Unhesitatingly Wheatley adopted the language and religion of her captors, for she knew they could be used to celebrate other than the usual goals and heroes. Among her coevals Joel Barlow too would write of other gods than Christian ones and heroes of non-European lineage, while a second woman poet, Ann Eliza Bleecker, would stop before drawing a link between freedom and racial equality. Wheatley simultaneously positioned herself as an avatar of African American literature and a key player in early United States literary discourse. Let me then discuss Wheatley in conjunction with two of her fellow Revolutionary-era poets.

By the circumstantial evidence of having already lost her front teeth when she was purchased by John and Susannah Wheatley, Phillis Wheatley was judged to have come into the world around 1754. Joel Barlow, whose fame as essayist and diplomat has also survived, if at a lesser level, and Ann Eliza Bleecker, whose works were published posthumously in 1793 by her daughter, were also born about that time.[29] Wheatley's education was conducted in the home of her owners by their daughter Mary, who was about a decade older. The black poet's upbringing was as different as one could imagine from that of the Yale-educated Barlow and the genteelly raised Bleecker, yet a comparison of these three poets brings a fresh perspective to all colonial literature of the United States—not just African American. Some might call the linking of these three poets forced, but the "race thing" has for too long obscured a useful examination of their similarities. Beyond the accident of their all having been born about mid-century, readers can see that their work shares two significant elements: the choice of a particular style, often referred to as "neoclassic" (which can somewhat reductively be said to include elevated diction, a relatively disinterested speaker, a predilection for heroic couplets, and classical and epic references); and a patriotism often manifest in poetic praise of the colony, and then nation, that Wheatley, Barlow, and Bleecker call "Columbia."[30] My purpose here is not to set out all the similarities in the work of Wheatley, Bleecker, and Barlow, or even to compare their lives; such a mechanistic exercise would do little to illuminate the complexity and congruities of their works. Instead, by examining selected aspects of their writings, I would like to redirect and refocus prior, separate discussion of the three poets. As Americans they shared literary forms; as Americans they reinforced *and* rejected supposedly shared cultural norms.

The African-born Wheatley's assumption of the dominant, Anglo-American literary elements shows her engagement with them as a lyricist writing in English and her attempted reconstruction of them as a member of the black diaspora. Whereas all three of these writers added an American spin to the literary genre they preferred, a style already in decline in Great Britain, Wheatley's racial (self-) consciousness injected a note missing from the other two poets, although all engaged with prevailing notions of racial difference. Wheatley has been much denigrated, and only lately praised, for the veritable tightrope walk she performed when adopting the prevailing standard of poetic discourse and political rhetoric. Phillip Richards, a most insightful Wheatley scholar, has cleared through much of the dust and heat of previous critiques: "To the extent that Wheatley's poetry reflected Anglo-American culture, particularly views of blacks, it was criticized; and to the extent that her poetry resisted American culture, it was praised."[31] She not only successfully navigated the ideological rhetoric of freedom and liberty of her day and made superb use of Protestant typology and oratory, but also, through clever "legitimating functions," created a distinctive African American voice (Richards 177 and *passim*). Wheatley's poetry, as Richards demonstrates, presents a fascinating portrait of the artist as a black—and an American. Her work must be discussed not only in the context of African American literature, in which she can appear anomalous due to her relative chronological isolation and choice of genre, but also as part of a dialogue with other American poets of her day. Resituating Wheatley demands complex narrative-building on the part of the critic, a doubly conscious literary history that echoes and reflects the dual lives of its author, simultaneously an American and a diasporic African. What follows is the beginning of one such literary history that appreciates the competing agendas of its authors and acknowledges their commonly held beliefs. I hope to illustrate the intertextual dialogue that exists among early American writers, whatever their assigned racial category.

Joel Barlow did not wrestle with the racial double-consciousness of Wheatley. Like hers, however, his work derived from more than one cultural source: although he began his career as a conservative, Yale-educated colonial, in later years the diplomat Barlow would include as his friends such figures as Thomas Paine and Mary Wollstonecraft.[32] Wheatley's political opinions must be deduced from not much more than a single book of poems, published when she was not yet twenty, whereas we can see the development of Barlow's political thought over a thirty-year period; a comparison of the two versions of his American epic demonstrates this movement.[33] In its first incarnation *The Vision of Columbus* (1787) "paid high tribute to Louis XVI, took an orthodox view of human history, and was excessively cautious in dealing with such 'new' ideas as those of the Scottish philosophers."[34] Twenty years later, in *The Columbiad* (1807), Barlow's poetic persona has removed all traces of aristocratic sympathy and replaced Columbus's guiding angel with the classical figure of Hesper; references to old systems, be they the Church or the Crown, have been swept away in favor of new, republican ideals.[35] Like many of his compatriots in the late colonial period, Barlow had to forge a creative identity based on both his European heritage and what elements of an American identity he could uncover.

In his introduction to *The Columbiad*, which Barlow believed to be his greatest work, the poet invokes Homer and Vergil while seeking to remake the epic into a form less militaristic and more American: "Much of the fatal policy of states, and of the miseries and degradations of social man, have been occasioned by the false notions of honor inspired by the works of Homer."[36] A sympathetic follower of the French Revolution, Barlow desired by the time of his epic's final version to "encourage and strengthen, in the rising generation, a sense of the importance of republican institutions" (389). As Leon Howard has said, the works of Barlow and his fellow "Connecticut Wits" are significant more for their revelation of contemporary thought than for stylistic niceties.[37] For while Barlow sought to entertain his readers, the overall effect was unabashedly didactic:

Think not, my friends, the patriot's task is done,
Or Freedom safe, because the battle's won,

Unnumber'd foes, for different arms that wield,
Wait the weak moment when she quits her shield,
To plunge in her bold breast the insidious dart
Or pour keen poison round her thoughtless heart.   *(book 8, ll. 79–84; 685)*

Like his avowed model Vergil, Barlow attempted to create a myth of nation-creation. His task was no less than to mythologize the discovery, exploration, and conquest of a continent previously unknown to Western Europe, specifically, the fortunes of the British colonies that would later become the United States. *The Columbiad* would, therefore, be not so much concerned with facts as with eternal verities:

> The desultory parts of the historical action must be brought together and be made to elevate and strengthen each other, so as to press upon the mind with the full force of their symmetry and unity. Where the events are recent and the actors known, the only duty imposed by that circumstance on the poet is to do them historical justice, and not ascribe to one hero the actions of another. But the scales of justice in this case are not necessarily accompanied by the calendar and the map.   *(383–84)*

In Barlow's world the somber mood of the elegy, so prominent in Wheatley,[38] does not reign; his is an optimistic, expansive *Weltanschaung* that sees setbacks in terms of eventual triumphs. Barlow's more sanguine view may be attributed to his outlook as a white American male who can attest to the American Revolution as at least a partial confirmation of youthful ideals. Wheatley, equally patriotic, whose verses elevating the American cause would be tactically deleted from the London edition of her poems[39], could see that freedom for the colonies would not mean liberation for enslaved Africans. In Barlow's epic, Columbus is visited in the King of Spain's dungeon by Hesper, the "guardian Genius of the Western continent" (412). Hesper cheers the dishonored explorer, telling him "thou soon shalt see / That half mankind shall owe their home to thee" (book 1, ll. 475–76; 435). Later, Columbus weeps when the revealed future shows the Spanish slaughter of Indian innocents. Hesper bids him not to mourn:

> While sorrows thus his patriarch pride control,
> Hesper reproving sooths his tender soul:
> Father of this new world, thy tears give o'er,
> Let virtue grieve and heaven be blamed no more.
>
> . . .

Nor think the labors vain; to good they tend;
Tyrants like these shall ne'er defeat their end;
. . .
The mind shall soar; the coming age expand
Their arts and lore to every barbarous land;
And buried gold, drawn copious from the mine,
Give wings to commerce and the world refine.   *(book 2, ll. 371–94; 471–72)*

Rather than being exalted as a sacrifice, as in the *Iliad*, blood spilled in the making of America functions as an epic fertilizer: Columbus should be comforted by the knowledge of the good that will follow colonial carnage.[40] The closing lines of *The Columbiad* emphasize such an interpretation:

Here then, said Hesper, with a blissful smile,
Behold the fruits of thy long years of toil.
. . .
Then let thy stedfast soul no more complain
Of dangers braved and griefs endured in vain,
Or courts insidious, envy's poison'd stings
The loss of empire and the frown of kings;
While these broad views thy better thoughts compose
To spurn the malice of insulting foes;
And all the joys descending ages gain
Repay thy labors and remove thy pain.   *(book 10, ll. 628–42; 779–80)*

In the eighth book, Barlow attacks slavery as a destructive, antirepublican blot on the morally impeccable Revolution. Its infamy is indicated to have but a passing hold. Atlas, identified by Barlow as the guardian of Africa, steps into the narrative to remind the audience of the disparity between republican ideals and chattel slavery:

Enslave my tribes! what, half mankind imban,
Then read, expound, enforce the rights of man!
Prove plain and clear how nature's hand of old
Cast all men equal in her human mold!   *(book 8, 223–26; 691)*

Atlas's paternal reference to "my tribes" reveals Barlow's representation of the deity as African, for the god makes himself a synecdoche of the inhabitants of that continent: those "inthrall'd. . . millions of *my race*" (emphasis mine). Barlow's racialized deity echoes the classical association of Atlas with a mountain range in northwest Africa.[41] Invoking a warning of the fate brought on by such unbrotherly actions, Atlas rages

> if still they dare debase
> And hold inthrall'd the millions of my race;
> A vengeance that shall share the world's deep frame,
> That heaven abhors and hell might shrink to name.
> Nature, long outraged, delves the crusted sphere
> And mold the mining mischief dark and drear;
> Europa too the penal shock shall find,
> The rude soul-selling monsters of mankind.   *(book 8, ll. 263–70; 693)*

Barlow suggests the solution is the instillation of republican pride and virtue—"Men well instructed will be always just" (696). Once counseled wisely, the reader will do the right thing. Depending on his audience's adherence to the ideal of natural rights—"Equality of Right is nature's plan; / And following nature is the march of man" (697)—Barlow need do little more than point to the iniquity of the slave trade: *The Columbiad* itself will help to overturn the system. "[W]ould you not be slaves, with lords and kings, / Then be not masters; there the danger springs" (697).

The poem of Barlow's best-known today, a gastronomical encomium entitled "The Hasty Pudding" (1796), strikes quite a different, humorous tone.[42] A proto-Proustian meditation on an unprepossessing New World dish, this mock epic has upheld Barlow's reputation, for its modest charms far surpass the prolix splendors of *The Columbiad*.

> I sing the sweets I know, the charms I feel,
> My morning incense, and my evening meal,
> The sweets of Hasty-Pudding. Come, dear bowl,
> Glide o'er my palate, and inspire my soul.   *(Canto I, ll. 15–18; 88)*

An homage to the colonial dish of cornmeal mush, "The Hasty Pudding"'s opening invocation of various heavenly figures and procession of heroic couplets, contrasted with its whimsical subject, indicates the poem's obvious debt to Alexander Pope and the English tradition of the mock epic: consider it an American riff on the "Rape of the Lock."[43] With the yoking of lowly subject and lofty meter, Barlow found a level of art attempted, and missed, in *The Columbiad*: the very unexpectedness of the conjunction creates the freshness and wit characteristic of the poem.

But man, more fickle, the bold licence claims
In different realms to give thee different names,
Thee the soft nations round the warm Levant
Palanta call, the French of course *Polante;*
E'en in thy native regions, how I blush
To hear the Pennsylvanians call thee *Mush!* *(Canto I, ll. 83–88;90)*

"The Hasty Pudding," a comic analogue to the work of Phillis Wheatley, juxtaposes a so-called "low" subject with lofty rhetoric and dignified classical allusions. Robert D. Arner has correctly pointed to Barlow's creation of an American identity not through the emulation of courtly European traditions, but through the yoking of that heritage with rural colonial folkways.[44] Even more appositely to his African American coeval, Barlow's conjunction of "white" European speech with indigenous manners outlines the new culture taking shape. Nevertheless, though Arner lauds that poem's original mix of subject matter and tone, his appraisal is colored by surprise:

> Although the effect produced by seeing ["The Hasty Pudding" 's] Indian maiden treated in elegant and classically regular couplets is somewhat similar to our reaction to the anonymous seventeenth-century portrait of Pocahontas sitting awkwardly and stiffly in white woman's clothing, Barlow seems to be in earnest in locating American history in the red man's past. *(88)*

Why should he be less earnest than Wheatley? Humorous, unusual, and unabashedly American, "The Hasty Pudding" is neverthless relegated to minor status, doubtless by similar forces in literary history fostering the long-running undervaluation of Wheatley's work. Barlow and Wheatley, in their own century and in some ways still, are considered to be purveyors of low subject matter, less than high status themselves, or both, in Wheatley's case. Barlow's choice of absurd humor and American folklore placed the "Pudding" beyond the pale of the serious; similarly, Wheatley's status as slave and woman, not to mention her (however gently phrased) references to slavery and undemocratic behavior, put her beyond the purview of literature. One could say then that their relative strangeness to readers links them; they share not only a penchant for the heroic couplet, but also a proclivity for remaining resolutely eighteenth-century in thought, approach, and sensibility.

The obscurity of Ann Eliza Bleecker, the third poet in my triumvirate, far surpasses Wheatley's.[45] Although Bleecker has been referred to by at least one twentieth-century critic as "the best lyric poet of her day," a somewhat more recent estimation ranks her work as "lacking in subtlety and unquestionably derivative."[46] Like the slave-poet, Bleecker was the mother of three children (her daughter Margaretta, the lone child who survived to adulthood, compiled and published her mother's works posthumously) whose works frequently centered on loss—in her case, the personal tragedy of her daughter's and mother's near-simultaneous deaths, and her husband's capture by marauding Loyalist troops.[47] Wheatley too suffered losses; however, she may not have felt sufficient psychic or physical *liberty* to voice her pain.[48] Unlike Wheatley, Bleecker was born into and remained in a position of privilege as a financially secure, white Protestant woman. Her works, as inflected by the swirling currents of the Revolutionary era as her Boston counterpart's, demonstrate a somewhat different locus of sensibility, as Julie Ellison has noted: "the strength of feminine rage and grief which constitutes the most impressive feature of her poetry is persistently motivated by the chaotic violence of the racial other." In Bleecker's universe, that "chaotic" other is invariably Native American, while the nearly absent black Americans appear impotent yet empathic shadows (449, 452). Yet if Ellison is right in asserting that for white women writers of the Republican era, the "conjunction of melancholia and race provided occasions for significant literary achievement" (448), we must consider how such notions play out when the writer is herself a member of a racial minority whose very participation within the literary mainstream demands a certain amount of evasion. Could Wheatley transcend the inherited texts of eighteenth-century poetry any more successfully than Bleecker?

Both poets wrote numerous occasional works—that is, verses commemorating particular events—as well as elegies, pastorals, and lyrics invoking the muses and other classical deities and beings. Although Wheatley was and is better known by far, for she is the more accomplished author, a comparison of their works is fruitful because of the correspondences across apparent "racial" boundaries and the differences that remain despite the works' literary similarities.[49] Three pairs of poems strike me as particularly suitable for comparison: the two "Recollection" poems, two poems occasioned by the battlefield deaths of Revolutionary War generals, and two sets of lyrics on peace. These neat pairings of poems suggest, perhaps, the extent to which they shared a literary culture: Phillip Richards has written that "Wheatley's poetry represents a striking example of the internalization of Anglo-American literary forms by a late eighteenth-century African American . . . [she] assimilated the literary genres inherited from Puritanism, eighteenth-century popular verse, the classics, and the English Augustan age" ("Literary Americanization" 164); those "Anglo-American literary forms" were equally influential on Bleecker and Barlow.

Wheatley's "On Recollection" is a response to a dare: "one of [the parties present] said she did not remember, among all the poetical pieces she had seen, ever to have met with a poem upon RECOLLECTION. The *African* . . . went home to her master's, and soon sent [the poem]":[50]

> MNEME begin. Inspire, ye sacred nine,
> Your vent'rous *Afric* in her great design.
> *Mneme*, immortal pow'r, I trace thy spring:
> Assist my strains, while I thy glories sing.
>
> *("On Recollection," ll. 1–4, Mason 76)*

By invoking a classical deity for inspiration, Wheatley links herself to that tradition: Mneme belongs not only to the classical authors but to Wheatley as well. Readers familiar with Wheatley's homage to patronage, "To Maecenas," will note a comparable signature; there, however, she places herself within a tradition of ancient, and African, authors. Citing the Latin poet Terence, whom she takes care to point out in a note is "*African* by birth," Wheatley chides the muses for what we might call a quota system—"But say, ye *Muses*, why this partial grace, / To one alone of *Africa*'s sable race?" ("To Maecenas," ll. 39–40, Mason 50). When she writes of recollection she refers to an ideal rather than actual memories; this notion of memory speaks in a collective voice, as seen in Wheatley's use of the first person plural: "*Mneme* in our nocturnal visions pours / The ample treasure of her secret stores" (ll. 9–10). Wheatley there begins in general, even universal, terms: "The heavenly *phantom* paints the actions done / by ev'ry tribe beneath the rolling sun. . . . *Mneme*, enthron'd within the human breast, / Has vice condemn'd, and ev'ry virtue blest" (ll. 17–20). Every tribe, every human breast, when ruled by the power of memory, will take care to stay on the path of righteousness—or so it appears. Yet in the third stanza, Wheatley makes a veiled yet nearly unmistakable reference to slavery (her earlier use of the word "tribe" seems deliberately to bring to mind Western conceptions of African nations along with its less specific meaning, a category of people):

> But how is *Mneme* dreaded by the race,
> Who scorn her warnings and despise her grace?

By her unveil'd each horrid crime appears,
Her awful hand a cup of wormwood bears.
Days, years mispent, O what a hell of woe!
Hers the worst tortures that our souls can know.   *(ll. 25–26, Mason 77)*

Both memory and rememory, in Morrison's elegant phrasing, seem to be at work here.[51] The coming "cup of wormwood" for the race "who scorn her warnings and despise her grace," would seem a warning for white Americans; surely memory, in the form of the Bible at the very least, would bring to mind the example of the ancient Egyptians whose slave-owning led to their downfall.[52] The metaphor of race, preceded by a reference to "ev'ry tribe" and further elaborated upon in terms of punishment for "horrid crime," does not seem to require further embellishment: surely to one who had survived the Middle Passage, slavery would take first place in the annals of horrid crime. Furthermore, to speak of "Days, years mispent, O what a hell of woe!" simultaneously balances the decades of colonial slave society with the hell both owner and bondswoman inhabit: "the worst tortures that our souls can know."

The fourth stanza, noting the passage of eighteen years (the poet's approximate age), certainly can be read as the poet's reflection on her younger self's foolishness. Yet the lines also remark on the follies of the late colonial period (roughly the mid-1750s to the early 1770s), a time of increasing agitation for independence from England without concurrent uproar for the liberation of American-held Africans. These foolish acts perhaps were "unnotic'd, but behold them writ in brass! / In Recollection see them fresh return, / And sure 'tis mine to be asham'd, and mourn." Something "writ in brass" could be the engraved tablet on a gravestone; such commemoratives, often overlooked in churches and cemeteries, can come back to haunt—as can the legacy of slavery. As a patriot, Wheatley is ashamed of the diametrically opposed ideologies of liberty and slavery; as a slave, she could feel dishonored by her own stillborn liberty. (Wheatley would not be manumitted until about two years after the publication of this poem.) Like a number of Wheatley's poems, "On Recollection" seems to speak in "universal" language, to be a classically inflected, generally aimed reflection on memory and responsibility. Repeated readings, however, yield more than classic interpretations.

Bleecker's "Recollection," on the other hand, quite specifically recalls an individual: the poet's dead daughter, Abella. Her repeated focus on her daughter, who died during the wartime flight from the Bleecker home, becomes what Ellison calls "the Abella topos," an insurmountable grief that affects all subsequent events (453). Although Bleecker uses the elevated diction that would have been familiar to Wheatley—"Soon as the gilded clouds of evening fly, / And *Luna* lights her taper in the sky,"—she almost immediately shifts from a literally celestial view to the memory of "the softest fair / Who ere respir'd in wide *Columbia*'s air; / A transient glance of her love beaming eyes / Convey'd into the soul a paradise." The child's beautiful gaze here supplants the transports of an implied celestial paradise; tragically, utopia had been on Earth only as long as her daughter drew breath. Memory here is concrete, nearly purged of its abstract aspect. Recollection charges the poet's lines with a remembered "rapture," sharpens the verse to specificity by the alternating references to the "sweet charmer" and "few dry bones" that were and are Abella. No euphemisms here, for the mother-poet, grieving, speaks without a screen of conventional desolation; no dispassionate verse celebrates her daughter's untimely end. Joanne Braxton's archetype of the "outraged mother," suggested to scholars of African American literature as a countermodel and complement to the articulate slave hero, finds its counterpart in Bleecker, a white woman who could express her "rage and grief," albeit in poems that would go unpublished in her lifetime.[53] Ideas about eighteenth-century restraint are equally well dispatched by Wheatley's clever maskings of antislavery sentiment within supposed occasional trifles such as "On Recollection" and Bleecker's self-suppressed laments against the injustice of life.

Each woman was marked by the experience of living through a revolution: Wheatley in the turmoil of the port city of Boston, and Bleecker geographically removed in upstate New York yet still close enough to the war to suffer deprivation and acute loss. As poets, they sought to make sense of the political situation and subsequent military engagements, much as each had tried to sort out personal emotional upheaval.[54] "On the Death of General Wooster," unpublished during Wheatley's lifetime, celebrates the life and martyrdom of Revolutionary hero David Wooster, a man whom the poet also counted as a friend. Bleecker's "Elegy on the death of Gen. MONTGOMERY" similarly lauds the exploits of a worthy fighter. While each poem celebrates the sensibility of its hero, each calibrates its worthy's emotional character differently. The two poems are significant for their revelation of the ways racial difference affects United States nationalism and patriotism—and how the impact of "racial others" on gender may, in Julie Ellison's words, present "vexed, often contradictory possibilities for sympathy" (448).

The ancient trope of beginning a verse with an invocation to the muse appears in both poems. Bleecker asks that one of the goddesses of lyric poetry aid her: "Melpomene, now strike a mournful string, / *Montgomery*'s fate assisting me to sing!" (226). With the lines "From this the Muse rich consolation draws / He nobly perish'd in his Country's cause," Wheatley enlists the supernatural in her attempt to glorify Wooster's exploits, actual and alleged. Significantly, Wheatley does not entreat the aid of a single or particular muse, such as Clio [History], Mneme [Memory], or Calliope ["she of the beautiful voice"].[55] Leaving her spirit mentor's allegiances in doubt allows her to claim simultaneously the imprimatur of History, Memory, and Lyric Poetry. "How shall my pen his warlike deeds proclaim / Or paint them fairer on the list of Fame" the poet asks: with poetic license, the vagaries of memory, or the certainty of knowledge?

"On the Death of General Wooster," written after *Poems on Various Subjects*, appears to be a standard encomium: "From this the Muse rich consolation draws / He nobly perish'd in his Country's cause" (ll. 1–2, 149). With an apostrophe reminiscent of those in Barlow's epic, the fading Wooster addresses the immortal one: "Permit, great power, while my fleeting breath / And Spirits wander to the verge of Death— / Permit me yet to paint fair freedom's charms" (ll. 13–15, 149). Significantly, the dying Wooster suggests that independence will not be won as long as Africans are enslaved:

> But how, presumptuous shall we hope to find
> Divine acceptance with th' Almighty mind—
> While yet (O deed Ungenerous!) they disgrace
> And hold in bondage Afric's blameless race?
> Let Virtue reign—And thou accord our prayers
> Be Victory our's, and generous freedom theirs.   *(ll. 28–32, pp. 149–50)*

"Great" and "virtuous" Wooster's attestation to abolitionist sentiments, espoused even as his life ebbs away on the field of battle, makes him a God-fearing freedom fighter for all, with "martial flames, and Christian virtues join'd." Having elevated the patriot-reader's emotions, Wheatley can combine this deathbed injunction with the emphatic final lines—"He waits thy coming to the realms of light / Freed from his labours in the ethereal Skies / Where in succession endless pleasures rise!" (37–40, 150)—to lift the reader to a positive, new conception of African Americans. When Wooster speaks, however, he does so as a kind of authenticating mask for the poet's beliefs. As is often noted by modern readers, the character of the general, a white male, serves as a cover for the abolitionist sentiments of the poet, a black female slave. Wheatley voices her own concerns through

Wooster in order to connect the patriot's cause and that of the African in a powerful, albeit disguised antislavery statement. Yet she also removes herself from the object, or third person, position for the more powerful first person, subject position: "Be victory *our's,* and generous freedom *theirs*" (emphasis added). Coming from the epitome of Protestant piety and patriotism, Wooster's words, as "recorded" by Wheatley, carry far greater weight than the poet's would alone. The young poet, in the meantime, can take vicarious pleasure in her borrowed elevation and power.

Contrast Wheatley's poem-cum-appeal to Ann Eliza Bleecker's eulogy to another fallen Revolutionary martyr, "*Elegy on the death of* Gen. Montgomery." Although he is not given a voice by Bleecker, Montgomery's recalled "eloquence made the chill'd bosom glow, / And animated them to meet the foe" (227). Bleecker depicts Montgomery as faultlessly sensible. Along with his military skills, "Softer virtues" can be included in the general's attributes, for in addition to being "dauntless" and "Invulnerable to fear," Montgomery resounds with as much empathy as any romantic hero: "He wip'd the eye of grief, it ceas'd to flow, / His heart vibrated to each sound of woe" (227). Like Wooster's, his virtues should be long remembered. However, while Bleecker does not directly refer to literally dark forces, signs of intolerance erupt. An image of blood marks the appearance of Bleecker's inability to distinguish among personal loss, ethnic difference, and nationhood. When her hero falls, Bleecker angrily wishes that in Montgomery's stead, "Had half idolitrous *Canadia* bled!" Here she refers either to the faithless Indians of the middle ground, such as those who kidnapped her husband or the ones who instigated the antiwhite bloodbath she describes in "The History of Maria Kittle,"[56] or the Catholic inhabitants of Canada, Britain's ally against the fledgling United States.[57] Rather than turn her elegy to a wider view of liberty, like Barlow's poem *Columbiad* and Wheatley's "Wooster" ode do, Bleecker makes no larger claims, attempts no healing entente. Grieving deeply the losses of near relatives and of her own privileged life, Bleecker finds it impossible to look to a greater sphere for lessons. Wheatley, a slave for over half of her American life, could more forthrightly and repeatedly draw the connection between her personal loss of liberty and the larger cause of the white colonists.

At the end of her life, each woman wrote a poem on peace. The two verses will serve as a final investigation of the poets' parallel lives. In "Peace," as in "Recollection," Bleecker takes a intimate and specific approach. Her peace is pastorally constructed, entwined inextricably with the verdant setting of a spring amble around her home; although "All hail vernal Phoebus! all hail ye soft breezes!" comprises the first line, the diction immediately shifts to less elevated language: "How green are the meadows! the air how it pleases! How gleefully all the birds sing!" (251). "The visit of spring" announces a personified "*Peace* [that] gives new charms to the bright beaming season" (252). There is a lovely quotidian scene in this pastoral: a walk on the grass with a dog; a dally alongside a stream; a butterfly, seized by an infant, that hides behind it the horror of the past war. That conflict is personified in the "murd'ring banditti, the dark sons of treason ... *Britain's* black ally." While Britain and her ally to the north are invoked, along with Washington (heroism emphasized by his name in small capital letters), there is a curious lack of patriotism connected to an ideal of political affairs. The larger concept of liberty and freedom fades away. Still present, however, is the link Bleecker has shown before between nonwhite peoples and evil: "*Britain's* black ally" must be chased to "*Canadia's* deep woods." As Julie Ellison has said, racial difference and signifiers of "darkness" become metaphors for chaos in Bleecker;[58] her intensely self-focused world admits no overarching view. Because this scene is so circumscribed, irony lurks as she sports jocosely around this charmingly personalized peace. Making a frivolous link between a lack of liberty and fishing (by an abrupt move from "WASHINGTON" carved on every tree to her wanderings by a fountain), she protests that catching the fish that glitter in the stream would be "an evil design. / Sport on little fishes, your lives are a treasure / Which I can *destroy* but not *give*; Methinks it's at best a malevolent pleasure / To bid a poor being not *live*" (253). Likewise, she prevails upon "yon infant" to free a "poor insect, ah! yeild it; / There see the freed bird how it flies!" (253). Peace and freedom are extended to the wild beings that flit through her tamed forest, but not to the poet's servants. Bleecker owned at least two slaves of African descent, and her much-relished freedom of movement is not shared with them.[59] While not feared or hated, blacks, virtually absent in Bleecker's writings, face an erasure from the newly formed United States almost as total as that Bleecker would reserve for Native Americans.

Like Bleecker, Wheatley begins her "Liberty and Peace" with a nod to the classics: "LO! Freedom comes. Th' prescient Muse foretold, / All Eyes th' accomplish'd Prophecy behold" (ll. 1–2). Allegorical figures of Grace, Peace, and War share the stage with personified nations: Columbia, Britannia, Galia, Italia, Hibernia, Scotia, Spain, Germania. No mere upstate woodland glade here; Wheatley canvasses the Western world. While urging England, with "The Sword resign'd, [to] resume the friendly Part!" (l. 20), Wheatley says Hibernia, Galia, and Italia should meanwhile raise arms to force the peace: "From every Kingdom on *Europa's* Coast, /

Throng'd various Troops, their Glory, Strength, and Boast" (ll. 35–36). Her "Peace" is international, with no swipes at "idolatrous" nations or demonized allies. The devastation of Boston Wheatley saw was by 1784 echoed in part by her own losses of two children. Yet despite the "Treasures plunder'd, and her Towns destroy'd," despite the ruin of Charlestown with its columns of "Smoak," a "celestial *Peace*" will resuscitate the generous spirit of America (ll. 46–52). Columbia, in turn, will generate realms of peace. Yet it is the word "Freedom," rather than "Liberty and Peace," that begins and ends this poem. Both the opening couplet, noted at the beginning of this paragraph, and the last—"To every Realm shall *Peace* her Charms display, / And Heavenly *Freedom* spread her golden Ray" (ll. 63–64)—indicate that for Wheatley at least, Peace is but a synonym for Freedom. Strikingly, Wheatley uses the word "freedom" four times within the poem and "peace" five times, whereas "liberty" is found only in the title. Does her repeated substitution of "freedom" for "liberty" refer covertly to manumission for American's captive Africans, much as the injunction "Perish that Thirst of boundless Power" (line 27) might carry a veiled abolitionist import? Is Wheatley slyly substituting for a politically freighted term one perhaps more associated with the natural rights of America's most unfree laborers? Truces can be agreed upon and arms laid down; Wheatley further proposes that genuine peace depends on freedom for all. Manumitted about ten years before this poem was published, the poet knew well the meaning of liberty.

So let us close with the image of Phillis Wheatley that prefaced her book of poems. The slender girl in frilled cap and modest dress takes up pen, paper, and book, a slight smile on her lips, her eyes fixed firmly ahead as though searching for the perfect word—indeed *le mot juste*. That contemplative, girlish countenance announces to her readers, then as now, that Phillis Wheatley has resolved to take on the ghosts and models of European culture: that picture, as Walt Nott has written, "is the emblem of the book as a whole and . . . the public manifestation of her participation in the discursive sphere [of America] itself."[60] An equitable evaluation of Wheatley grants her the subtlety of purpose afforded other poets. We must acknowledge her artistic intentions, just as we must admit that she could not always evade the implicit stereotypes in her choice of words. Doing her work of praise and subterfuge, she donned a mask of generic "whiteness" that sometimes camouflaged too well her own position. If Wheatley believed she had both a white readership biased by definition and an ideal black audience extremely limited in numbers and power, then she had to balance competing sets of reader expectations. Speaking as a black and an American simultaneously, she stands as a worthy predecessor to the writers who follow her, whether of African or European descent. Working in two modes, Wheatley reimagined the identity of the patriotic American even as she gave voice to a nascent African American consciousness. To those like her,

> the lonely outsiders who exist precariously
> on the clifflike margins of many cultures—men who are
> distrusted, misunderstood, maligned, criticized
> by Left and Right, Christian and pagan—
> men who carry on their frail but indefatigable shoulders
> the best of two worlds—and who,
> amidst confusion and stagnation,
> seek desperately for a home for their hearts:
> a home which, if found,
> could be a home for the hearts of all men[61]

Richard Wright dedicated one of his last books. From the vantage point of the present, we shall see how Wright's encomium speaks for African Americans writing American literature in the century and more before ours.

2

⁊❧

CAPTURING THE CAPTIVITY

African Americans Among the Puritans

In the century before Phillis Wheatley published *Poems on Various Subjects* the British colonies had already produced a "simple indigenous American prose" form: the Indian captivity narrative.[1] Straightforward accounts of the capture, trials, and eventual liberation of Anglophone settlers, these narratives provided early colonists with their first native genre. Pamphlets celebrating the horrific trials, exploits, and Christian forbearance of women like Mary Rowlandson or Elizabeth Hanson went through numerous editions, both entertaining and enlightening avid readers. To contemporary [white] audiences, these "read to pieces" stories were as heroic as Icelandic sagas.[2] By the end of the eighteenth century, African Americans had also discovered the utility of this earliest American form. Like their Puritan predecessors, "captivated" blacks like Briton Hammon and John Marrant told the story of their encounters with frightening, godless attackers, torture, and death. Such genre-bound narratives, whether penned by black or white Americans, were designed to engage the reader in the narrator's own experience of captivity and/or conversion. Both sets of narrators desired to impress their audience with their appreciation and direct experience of the supreme being as well as to elicit sym-

41

pathy for their bondage in the grasp of alien, incomprehensible captors. For African American storytellers and their white amanuenses, a signal importance of the narratives stemmed from their similarity to the pamphlets and broadsides that had appeared before.[3] Yet unlike their immediate literary models, African Americans who wrote of their captivity shared "nonwhite" status with the captors of their authorial predecessors. That irony of inversion infuses the ordeals of the colonial African American Christians with an often unexpressed, if perhaps privately acknowledged, racial ambiguity. Quite a paradox emerges with the adoption of a Puritan genre to express the civilization and humanity of "Africans."

Significant similarities exist between the captivity and conversion narratives written by black authors and those by whites. Black Americans, however, whether enslaved by whites or Indians, were unlikely to espouse a primary goal of the white captivity narrative—the advocacy of white social and political hegemony—although, as we will see shortly, at least one black narrator did just that, intentionally or not. In general, as African Americans began to possess their own voices, when they moved from "as related by" narratives to "written by him/herself" autobiographies, they transformed the genre they had adopted. White slave owners could be depicted in much the same unflattering light as "savage" Indians had been earlier portrayed by whites. For African Americans, the function of a captivity tale—specifically, its use as propaganda—did not necessarily follow form. As Nellie McKay has observed,

> eighteenth- and nineteenth-century blacks who told their own stories forced a different relationship between Afro-Americans and the dominant culture. Escaped slaves who condemned the "peculiar" institution by indicting its atrocities in writing, and spiritual narrators who claimed equal access to the love and forgiveness of a black-appropriated Christian God could not be nonpersons in the eyes of the white world.[4]

The earliest black narrators adopted, adapted, and finally subverted the genre, first by seeming to endorse the white captivity's aims of exalting Christian civilization, then by taking the premise of captivity a step further to express outrage and sorrow at the hands of Christian captors. As we will see in the following chapter, many nineteenth-century authors would deploy this strategy to its fullest.

In the seventeenth and eighteenth centuries the captivity narrative and its precursor, the conversion narrative, were the main forms of written entertainment for Anglophone settlers in the New England colonies. Novels were still in their infancy, and as a pastime novel reading was looked upon as a pleasure-seeking and immoral practice. Therefore, people read what was available—generally uplifting narratives of Christian life, conversion experiences, or their close American relatives, the captivity tales. (James Albert Ukawsaw Gronniosaw, a kidnapped African who converted to the Protestant faith during his American adolescence, writes of reading both Baxter's *Call to the Converted* and John Bunyan.[5]) Accounts of religious redemption in the New World came to be spiced up with tales of Indian uprisings, psychological and physical torture, adoption into a strange ethnic or racial world (often viewed as "demonic"), and exotic travels. Narratives such as Mary Rowlandson's *The Sovereignty and Goodness of God* and the *Narrative of the Uncommon Sufferings and Surprizing Deliverance of Briton Hammon* combined purposes, doing double duty as entertainment and spiritual guides.

Conversion to Protestant Christianity, specifically Congregationalism, had proved to be a potent status symbol in the New England colonies. Proof of election—membership in the elite group of souls preordained as saved—required a public recital of one's conversion.[6] Under the first Massachusetts Bay Charter, voting privileges were extended only to these elect, and the majority of colony dwellers were not church members but church attendees. A conversion experience, detailed in front of the church membership, could confirm or deny election. These experiences were not only delivered orally, but could also be written down and published to encourage the less confessional and provide edifying reading to the elect. If one then considers the near-constant state of war with the native population, it should not be completely surprising that these narratives of conversion metamorphosed into the popular captivity narratives. The historical accident of the Puritan diaspora, combined with the presence in the New Canaan of an alien, heathen culture, created a new kind of conversion narrative, one that took as its subject both spiritual seeking and secular strife.[7] Whereas a chief purpose of the captivity narratives was to illustrate "God's providence," another, equally important element of the captivities written by North American whites (as opposed to those later written by African Americans) was the espousal and physical (if not actually violent) establishment of a white Protestant ruling class.[8]

These narratives did not function solely as vehicles of religious instruction or political indoctrination. Richard Slotkin and Daniel Cohen have both called attention to the increasing importance of such narratives as entertainment, noting that as the colonial period advanced toward the early national era, a shift in literature from religious to secular reflected the trend toward a separation of church and state. As New Englanders moved away from the early ideal of separatism from an impure society, so too did American literature mirror the increasing disengagement with a Puritan heritage not wholly their own. The view of "heathenish" Indians was transmogrified from horror at the cruelty of the unsaved to a simpler, voyeuristic reveling in their wickedness. Though that all-too-human delight in the profane and the evil informed the earlier narratives, later tales tended to dwell more on the earthly horrors and less on the godly, in good measure because American society became increasingly more secular.[9]

To publish the story of a white former captive was therefore to accomplish at least two ends. The primary purpose was to prove conversion, or election; to confess one's "surprizing" experience of the higher authority was also to be admitted into the circle of citizenry, those whose words and deeds had weight in colonial society. Also, by writing conversion documents that also detailed captivity and enslavement at the hands of the horrifically un-Christian, white narrators conflated the public announcement of conversion with the racial ideology of an elect, ruling class; this published elite, then, was largely composed of middle-class "saints." This second objective, which might be termed literary imperialism, reinforced white views of Indians as inhuman (i.e., non-white)[10] by stressing the Indians' unnatural behavior and horrifying acts; the conclusion to be drawn was that of the rectitude of Puritan rule. Mary Rowlandson's observations about the Narragansetts were echoed by many of her fellow settlers: "This was the dolefullest night that ever my eyes saw. Oh, the roaring and singing and dancing and yelling of those black creatures in the night, which made the place a lively resemblance of hell. . . . Little do many think what is the savageness and brutishness of this barbarous enemy." [11] Ann Kibbey rightly argues that "prejudice was rationalized by religion in Puritan society . . . to a great extent prejudicial and religious beliefs were indistinguishable"; although speaking of earlier events, she asserts that "motives [for the Pequot War], the way it was fought, and the rationalizations that followed all imply that Puritan men created a consistent, coherent structure of meaning for themselves and systematically denied it to those whom they believed to be their enemies."[12] By making capture and redemption in some measure divinely ordained, the captivities bolstered a belief in the American story as scripted by white writers. The trials with and triumphs over the Indian nations could and would be viewed as evidence of European American, Christian superiority. All events were predestined; the social order, as limned by God and the Puritan hierarchy, was unassailable. Any setbacks, be they capture at the hands of the Narragansetts or agonizing droughts, were viewed as chastisements and scourges against a people insufficiently following the letter of God's law.

Mary Rowlandson's *The Sovereignty and Goodness of God, Together, with the Faithfulness of His Promises Displayed* (1682) began some two centuries of English-language North American captivity narratives. During an engagement in "King Philip's" war, the forty-year-old minister's wife was kidnapped from her frontier village of Lancaster, Massachusetts, by a raiding party of Narragansetts. Her little book—written at the behest of her friends and for the "benefit of the Afflicted"—set forth her personal trials and misfortunes, Christian fortitude and forbearance, and eventual deliverance from "the howling wilderness." From the outset, things did not bode well for Rowlandson: "On the tenth of February 1675 came the Indians with great numbers upon Lancaster. Their first coming was about sunrising. Hearing the noise of some guns, we looked out; several houses were burning and the smoke ascending to heaven" (33). Divided into twenty "removes" (the advances, retreats, and encampments of the Narragansetts while Rowlandson was in their keeping), Rowlandson's minor epic paints a portrait of a Christian among heathens, a white woman among red men, a believer cast into a furnace of faithlessness.

> When we are in prosperity, oh, the little that we think of such dreadful sights, and to see our dear friends and relations lie bleeding out their heart-blood upon the ground! . . . It is a solemn sight to see so many Christians lying in their blood. (35)

Rowlandson's book successfully conflates the proof of election with an ideology of domination and power.[13] If we examine the anonymous ("per amicum") preface, the purposes of the printer/publisher, if not of Rowlandson herself, become clearer.

> I may say, that as none knows what it is to fight and pursue such an enemy as this, but they that have fought and pursued them: so none can imagine, what it is to be captivated, and enslaved to such Atheistical, proud, wild, cruel, barbarous, brutish (in one word) diabolical Creatures as these, the worst of the heathen.[14]

Whereas Rowlandson herself may eventually have come to an ambivalent understanding of her captors (following her befriending by her master's first and oldest wife), the white male establishment that urged her to publish her story brooked no such ambiguity.

> That God is indeed the supream Lord of the World: ruling the most unruly, weakening the most cruel and salvage: granting his People mercy in the fight of the most unmerciful: curbing the lusts of the most filthy, holding the hands of the violent, delivering the prey from the mighty, and gathering together the out-casts of Israel. Once and again, you have heard, but here you may see, that power belongeth unto God: that our God is the God of Salvation: and to him belong the issues from Death. That our God is in the Heavens, and doth what every pleases him.[15]

The God of Rowlandson was a white, Protestant, patriarchal deity, and he worked in not-so-mysterious ways. Rowlandson noted "the strange providence of God in preserving the heathen" (44), beings evidently placed on earth to test the faith of His Chosen (i.e., members of the fledgling Bay Colony's settlements). One way to test the fortitude and belief of Rowlandson and the other captives was to prevent part of the English army from crossing a river to rescue Rowlandson: "God did not give them courage or activity to go over after us; we were not ready for so great a mercy as victory and deliverance" (44). Her anonymous editor explains, "the Lord hath made this Gentlewoman a gainer by all this Affliction, that she can say, 'tis good for her, yea better that she hath been, than she should not have been, thus afflicted."[16]

The idea of God's punishing those he loves best runs throughout the Judeo-Christian tradition, and the transplanted Puritans translated that belief into a succinct exegesis of Indian attacks. In a passage toward the end of her narrative, Rowlandson "take[s] leave to mention a few remarkable passages of providence which I took special notice of in my afflicted time." Citing as proof the inability of the British army to rescue the captives, Rowlandson notes the seeming prescience of her captors, who say the British will not be near them before May of that year (Rowlandson was captured in February 1676 and ransomed eleven weeks later), and the sheer fortitude of the Narrangansetts in surviving on famine rations. The marveling ex-captive

> can but admire to see the wonderful providence of God in preserving the heathen for further affliction to our poor country. . . . And yet . . . did the Lord preserve them for His holy ends and the destruction of

many still amongst the English! . . . God strengthened them to be a
scourge to His people. *(68–69)*

As God strengthened the Indians' "barbarous" nature in order to test the
belief of his followers, so did these outbreaks of wartime cruelty "show"
the inescapable eventuality of white Puritan rule. Proof of the Puritan
hegemony lay in the continued attacks:

> I could not but be amazed at the numerous crew of pagans that were on
> the bank of the other side. When I came ashore, they gathered all about
> me, I sitting alone in their midst. I observed they asked one another
> questions and laughed and rejoiced over their gains and victories. Then
> my heart began to fail and I fell a-weeping, which was the first time to
> my remembrance that I wept before them. . . . But now I may say as
> Psal. 137:1, "By the rivers of Babylon there we sat down; yea, we wept
> when we remembered Zion." *(46–47)*

The more she is attacked, vilified, and martyred—read her detailed
descriptions of tortured Christians (42, 54)—the stronger grows Rowlandson's belief in the correctness of the analogy between the Puritan exodus
and that of the ancient Israelites.

If the God of Rowlandson and later captivity authors was white, then a
split between white Protestant dissenters ("His people") and Native Americans of an indeterminate, "heathen" religion could be rationalized. Such a
dichotomy would ease and hasten the imperialistic designs of the capitalist
enterprise called the Massachusetts Bay Company—as opposed to the religious enterprise called the Massachusetts Bay Colony—and similar char-
ters in the North American colonies (ironically, such companies' policies
were often at odds with the theological agenda of the Protestant purists who
ran their day-to-day business). Rowlandson presumptuously and ethno-
centrically labels "our God" *the* "supream" deity, paving the way for generations of belief in the inferiority of Native American religious systems
and its corollary, belief in the inferiority of those peoples. "It was but the
other day," she writes in closing, "that if I had had the world I would have
given it for my freedom or to have been a servant to a *Christian*" (75;
emphasis mine). With those words she draws a line between white Christians and nonwhite "pagans," a demarcation that would gain added, omi-
nous weight with each generation of captivity tales.

"Infidels" and "bloody heathen" (34), "ravenous beasts" and "barbarous
creatures" (35); "black" (36), "inhuman" (37), "merciless" (38), "hideous"

(40), "hellish" (42)—such are the words Rowlandson uses to describe her captors. In order to establish the righteousness of prevailing measures against native peoples, as well as to lay the foundation for institutionalized measures to come, highly charged language was employed to depersonalize and dehumanize the "enemy." (Kibbey assigns the use of such violent rhetoric to *male* coevals of Rowlandson, gliding over the issue of Puritan women's wielding such discursive violence.)[17] Once tagged with such imagery, Indians who fought back could be turned into the "creatures" of narrative. Without such linguistic depersonalization, colonial attacks on neighboring Indian nations would have been difficult to justify. The "Afflicted" for whom Rowlandson wrote were most definitely not the Narragansetts, who had been pushed to their limits by continued white depredations.

Nevertheless, in the course of her removes Rowlandson may have come, if only subconsciously, to appreciate the hard lot that was her captors' as well as hers. Her distaste for the "filthy trash" that was the diet of her hosts fades noticeably:

> The first week of my being among them I hardly ate anything; the second week, I found my stomach grow very faint for want of something; and yet it was very hard to get down their filthy trash. But the third week, though I could think how formerly my stomach would turn against this and that and I could starve and die before I could eat such things, yet they were sweet and savory to my taste. *(44)*

The getting and eating of food occupies a prominent position in the narrative—no surprise when one considers that the Narragansetts were constantly on the move, unable to forage in their usual manner due to wartime conditions, and supporting various captives in addition to their usual number. Hunger so worked upon Rowlandson that by the eighteenth remove she reports that when one of the captured English children was unable to chew a boiled horse's foot, "I had quickly eat up mine . . . [so] I took it of the child and ate it myself and savory it was to my taste" (60). Just weeks before, she would have turned from such fare in horror. Breitwieser has noted Rowlandson's ability to eat such "trash" as an instance of "extremity [likable to religious conversion] driv[ing] her to discover something in herself that she did not know or perhaps fearfully suspected"; such dire straits led to her discovery of an "Indian heart."[18] Acceptance of Narrangansett food, the move from viewing it as disgusting to viewing it as savory, does indeed mark a sea change: a gastronomic boundary has been crossed, for "taste is an *acquired* disposition . . . [that works] below the level of consciousness and language, beyond the reach of introspective scrutiny or control by the will."[19] Rowlandson's acquisition of an "Indian" palate marks a nearly imperceptible change in her attitude, unremarked perhaps by her contemporaries but visible to us three centuries later. Sheer survival strategies too might direct her responses, for she finds benefit in the death of her mistress's papoose, noting there would be additional room in their dwelling (60, 55). This cold-heartedness seems a far cry from the grieving mother who sat up all night with her daughter's corpse, although Rowlandson might justify her response by asserting that the Narragansetts were themselves inhuman. The Puritan captive could find scriptural explanation for her every action: "Then I may say [as] Job, chap. 6:7, 'The things that my soul refused to touch are as my sorrowful meat.' Thus the Lord made that pleasant refreshing which another time would have been an abomination" (60). On the most basic level, the deprivation of nourishment, alien quality of what food she did have, and rough living conditions represent the extraordinary nature of her trials. Whether or not she recognized her own movement toward adaptation, and her own discovery of an inner wilderness, Rowlandson made some adjustments before her release. Not merely physical dis-ease appears to stay with her, but the upending of her ordered Puritan world:

> I can remember the time when I used to sleep quietly without workings in my thoughts whole nights together, but now it is other ways with me. . . . I remember in the night season how the other day I was in the midst of thousands of enemies and nothing but death before me. It [was] hard work to persuade myself that ever I should be satisfied with bread again. *(74)*

Elizabeth Hanson's narrative, written in the next century, demonstrates a shift away from Rowlandson's absolutes by her conscious attempt at understanding her captors, even if many of the prejudices of Rowlandson appear nearly unchanged. Reprinted in successive editions in both the colonies and England from 1728 into the late eighteenth century, Hanson's text, like *The Sovereignty and Goodness of God*, begins with a surprise attack and random murders.[20] Unlike Rowlandson, whose daughter died as a result of a bullet wound suffered during the attack, Hanson witnesses the instantaneous killing of two of her children.[21] Strikingly, her comments on this massacre seem mild—or perhaps disassociative: when she reports the first child's murder, she acknowledges such an act "strike[s] in us the greater terror and . . . make[s] us more fearful of them [the Indians]" (231). When the second child's crying brings on a swift death—the attackers fear the noise will alert nearby whites—Hanson again surprises the reader with an eerie and apparent lack of rancor: "I bore this as well as I could, not daring to appear disturbed or show much uneasiness lest they should do the same to the other" (232). One reason Hanson may have remained calm, at least in the retrospective telling, might be found in the length of her captivity: as opposed to Rowlandson's eleven weeks in captivity, Hanson spent five months with her captors. This greater time perhaps allowed her sufficient time to comprehend, if not condone, their objectives.[22] Perhaps too Hanson was able to see these conflicts as struggles between human beings, rather than as eschatological battles between the followers of a Calvinist God and humanoid demons. This difference of attitude may have been due, as her modern editors suggest, to her Quaker convictions, which contrast with Rowlandson's Puritan orthodoxy.[23] Or she just simply could have been more perceptive. Still, Hanson's more "balanced" account, with what Mary Louise Pratt might call a Mungo Park-like "reciprocal vision," never contradicts a European hegemony.[24]

Hanson's account of the return of her Indian master with his captives underscores this difference in outlook: "many of the Indians came to visit us, and in their way, welcomed my master home. . . . I suppose, in their thoughts [such acts as dancing, feasting, beating on hollow trees] was a kind of thanks to God put up for their safe return and good success" (236). She attributes her master's ill humor to a lack of success in hunting, and attendant shame and hunger, rather than Satanic influences (237).[25] Poor rations, slaps, and separations from children bring from Hanson remarks that impress the modern reader with their honest grapplings between proper piety and human exasperation: "I found it very hard to keep my mind as I ought under the resignation which is proper to be in under such afflictions and sore trials as at that time I suffered" (236). Despite her evident, justifiable disaffection with the man who kidnapped her and murdered two of her children, Hanson can read the motivations behind his "barbarous hands" (239) and "very hot and passionate temper" (238):

I now saw the design of this journey; my master, being, as I suppose, weary to keep us, was willing to make what he could of our ransom. Therefore, he went further towards the French and left his family in this place where they had a great dance, sundry other Indians coming to our people. . . . I was exposed to sale, and he asked for me 800 livres. But the French [did not comply with his demand], offering him but 600. He

said in a great passion if he could not have his demand, he would make
a great fire and burn me and the babe in the view of the city.   *(241)*

Contrast Hanson's remarks with the following passage from Rowlandson,
when she discovers that a Narragansett who has fed and sheltered her has
also killed two English men:

> I looked behind me, and there I saw bloody clothes with bullet holes in
> them, yet the Lord suffered not this wretch to do me any hurt. Yea,
> instead of that, he many times refreshed me; five or six times did he and
> his squaw refresh my feeble carcass.   *(64)*

Rowlandson sees the kindnesses received at the hands of an Indian as evidence of God's workings, rather than paradoxical but human kindness to
an enemy. Hanson's clarity of vision may stem from her ability to perceive her captivity, and the white-Indian wars, as a conflict between peoples rather than between a people and a subhuman tribe.[26]

In her portrayal of her enemies as human rather than monstrous,
Hanson's narrative prefigures the slave narratives of the mid-nineteenth
century. Like her fellow captives of a century later, Hanson comprehended
the other in a way some might find extraordinary. Black slaves similarly
knew the value of knowing the master better than the master knew them.
Placed at the absolute bottom of the social hierarchy, slaves, domestics,
and sharecroppers read every wink and intonation of the race in power,
wielding what force they could by influence rather than outright direction. White female captives like Hanson or Rowlandson experienced *individual* powerlessness, not a *group* disempowerment. Whatever their
unique status as hostages, white Puritan women still were members of a
group that saw itself as being in control. Slave authors knew themselves
to be oppressed as individuals and as a group. The first black narrators had
to subtly subvert prevailing Protestant genres by a seemingly wholesale
endorsement of their aims. Nineteenth-century writers would take the
premise of captivity a step further, substituting depictions of savage heathens with portraits of equally savage Christians. In fact, narratives of the
national and antebellum periods are characterized in part by their inversion of the implicit structure and moral of those written in the century
and a half before. Autobiographers like Frederick Douglass and Harriet
Jacobs depict their fiendish enemies as figurative, if not actual, descendants of the white Christian captives. Black autobiographers would come
to view their narrative selves as literally individual *and* representative.

Although profoundly different motives underlie the colonial-era narratives of white women captives and those of nineteenth-century black autobiographers, both contain a subtext of powerlessness. How that powerlessness gets construed, reconstructed, then deliberately inverted by early African American narrators comprises an important step in the genesis of black literature.

Thousands of slaves and free blacks left written testaments of their sufferings within a slavery-condoning nation. In the eighteenth century, African Americans began a struggle that continues to the present day: the effort to re-script the texts of slavery and oppression in their own words. To "Native Americans and enslaved blacks . . . writing and print may have appeared most clearly as technologies of power."[27] To gain access to that power, literate slaves and free blacks like Wheatley and John Marrant appropriated a variety of literary genres, including the popular captivity and conversion narratives. At first, adaptations of white generic strategies to African American goals proved ambiguous. Such narratives tended to confirm and justify white domination. There were exceptions, as John Saillant has noted: the Reverend Lemuel Haynes, a black Calvinist minister of Vermont, uses the story of two wrongfully imprisoned *white* men "as a symbol of the enslavement of American blacks . . . [merging] the language of the captivity . . . with the language of slavery and emancipation."[28] Imperfect as it was for conveying the degradation and hopes of the African American author, that previously whites-only genre of "captivities" had to be utilized. In the eighteenth century there were few other textual vehicles.

Annette Kolodny has pointed to "the structural and stylistic affinities between the captivity and the slave narratives—both essentially accounts of captivity amid powerful Others."[29] Both blacks and whites spin stories—lurid, Christian, popular—of enslavement and enforced estrangement from their respective cultures by non-Christians. As Richard Slotkin has commented, "like the white Puritan captive to Indians, the slave is in an alien environment, a Christian in hell."[30] Writers in both genres call on God for assistance in bearing the trials He has seen fit to place upon His servant, and for assistance in making an escape. In both captivity and the later slave narratives, the writer addresses the reader directly and/or through the mediation of an authenticator—a clergyman, an abolitionist editor, or perhaps even a slave-holder.[31] Each text attempts to enlist the sympathies of the reader so that justice, or a new order, may be served.

In a political and cultural system where a man's inability to write meant being not physically but politically and ideologically incapable of actual script, black literacy was an oxymoron. By the end of the eighteenth century, English-language literacy in the southern United States had become a "whites-only" dominion.[32] For the earliest African captives, acquiring English meant more than survival; it meant life as a people. In Benedict Anderson's estimation, the spread of "print-capitalism," a logical extension of literacy, enabled European ethnic groups to think of themselves as nations or distinct peoples, an idea that had merit for more than Europeans.[33] Flung together with Africans from other language groups, the kidnapped could barely communicate with one another. With English as a *lingua franca*, however, the enslaved found a means of connecting with their fellows in misery, ending their linguistic isolation.[34] Although later African Americans took oral proficiency in English to its inevitable conclusion by composing their own stories, the first African-American narratives were dictated to, or co-written with, whites.

How successfully could a black, slave or free, possess the captivity narrative? Most could not even use a pen. Literacy was almost unthinkable, much less attainable; more to the point, it was illegal, either by actual statute or common practice. Until well into the nineteenth century, a large percentage of slave narratives took the form of "as-told-to" autobiographies. The crucial difference between present-day celebrities who hire their amanuenses and the colonial autobiographers is that the former have final creative control. Though a dictated narrative can have all the liveliness and verisimilitude of one actually written by a former slave, it has been refracted through the lens of another individual, invariably a white, and that refraction alters its character and intent. Subtly or not, the mixed purposes of white editor and black would-be author compromise and complement each other.

Co-authorship in these early texts reveals an interesting divergence from the more familiar slave autobiographies. They are not African American in the way we twentieth-century readers tend to think of the term—again, remember Richard Wright's assertion that "Negro" literature "has to do with race hate, rejection, ignorance, segregation, discrimination, slavery, murder, fiery crosses and fear."[35] The works of early black writers do not scan all that differently than their white compatriots' texts (as indeed Wright noticed, and not disapprovingly, about Wheatley's poetry). These texts occupy a curious position, or nonposition, in African American letters: they are narratives written by black men that fully adhere to, or seem to adhere to, the model provided by earlier, white

American narratives of conversion and deliverance. Those stories of "sur-prizing" events essentially existed to showcase the episodes leading up to a conversion experience as well as to depict the details of capture by Indian heathen and the road back to Christian civilization. As a framework, the captivity/conversion tale would turn out to be surprisingly useful for the black captive-author, whether "servant" or free. Nonetheless, the white precedent calls into question the authenticity of the black successor.

The legitimacy of the earliest black narratives has long been one of the thorniest issues facing the critic of African American letters.[36] The admissibility to the African American literary canon of such "plain, artless, and factual" texts as the earliest versions of John Marrant's and Briton Hammon's autobiographies has been doubtful, because they have been filtered through the ears and pen of a white "amanuensis-editor" and subsequently beyond the authorial control of the black narrators.[37] In critic John Sekora's opinion, such narratives are

> not an African American genre . . . not black recollection, but white interrogation brings order to the narration. . . . In each instance the meaning, relation, and wholeness of the story are given before the narrative begins; they are imposed rather than chosen.   *(509)*

In fact, this "Anglo-American genre may claim black authors but not black authority" (511).[38] That early narratives like those of Marrant and Hammon may be co-authored is axiomatic: yet when an editor announces, as the Reverend William Aldridge does in Marrant's preface, that he has not changed the facts of a life but merely their relation, the reader must be on her guard.[39] For two very good reasons, these African American narrators are not so helpless as other critics have assumed. Those "plain, artless" facts have been *told* to the editor; even though that editor may choose to leave out parts of the story and rearrange others, the telling itself marks a decision by the early narrator.[40] The facts selected by the black tellers may be suspect, for the same reason that a slave's smiling face and tuneful whistle did not necessarily indicate happiness, simple-mindedness, or unconcern.[41] Additionally, the narratives themselves, because of their original status as a white-controlled form, have in fact been captured by black Americans; domination by the white editor, no matter how significant, can never be complete. Whether or not the black narrators or their white editors meant to do so, the inclusion of slaves within American captivity narratives marked an inroad into and adaptation of white literary and popular culture. By using a genre familiar to and popular with

European American readers, African Americans could convey previously unwelcome antislavery and antiracist sentiments in an acceptable format.

The *Narrative of the Uncommon Sufferings and Surprizing Deliverance of Briton Hammon* is therefore worthy of notice for its black narrator's apparently un-ironic relation of Indian and Spanish captivity.[42] In this picaresque tale of a servant's trials and travels, the issue of Hammon's narrative freedom becomes questionable, for it was Hammon's amanuensis who set the tone of the autobiography. William L. Andrews has written that white "editors . . . solicited these stories *because* they conformed or were conformable to cultural myths and literary traditions of an already established audience appeal, such as Indian captivity or evangelical conversion narratives . . . black self-portraits were cropped and framed according to the standards of an alien culture."[43] Nevertheless, the black self can materialize in a white frame, however incompletely. Deliberately or not, Hammon's comments provide an ironic counterpoint to a formulaic story intended to demonstrate the benign rule of "General Winslow of *Marshfield*," whose "Negro Man, —-Servant" is the ostensible narrator.[44]

In the opening address, Hammon and his amanuensis set up the limitations of his story.

> As my Capacities and Condition of Life are very low it cannot be expected that I should make those Remarks on the Sufferings I have met with, or the kind Providence of a good God for my Preservation, as one in a higher Station; but shall leave that to the Reader as he goes along, and so I shall only relate Matters of Fact as they occur to my Mind— (3)

Hammon cannot give anything but the "Matters of Fact as they occur" to him. Perhaps his editor/ghost writer pointed out the folly of Hammon's trying to say more than just the facts; the audience would not expect more from him, and indeed might even resent it.[45] (In the 1840s, Frederick Douglass would be counseled by his white abolitionist colleagues to give "only" the facts; due to his literacy and secure sense of self, Douglass was able to reject such patronizing advice.) This lack of editorial or human speculation on the part of Hammon tantalizes, especially in light of the Indian attack that comes just two pages later. When the narrator throws himself overboard, "chusing rather to be drowned, than to be kill'd by those barbarous and inhuman Savages," he is spared.[46] He does not speculate on why he is not killed, and we can only guess: the Indians' decision to spare Hammon could not have been based on sympathy derived from like color, for they do slay one "Moses Newmock, Molatto" (6).

Hammon nonetheless finds his captors "us'd me pretty well, and gave me boil'd Corn, which was what they often [ate] themselves" (5). In other historical accounts we find Seminoles and members of other Indian nations taking blacks prisoner, reserving them for their own use or selling them in turn to other Indians or whites. Unlike whites, Indian nations adopted captured whites, blacks, and Indians, so it was entirely possible for a captive to become wholly integrated, or transculturalized, within the new community.[47] A one-way passage existed between culture groups in the United States: Indians adopted both whites and blacks, granting them full status in the community, yet whites who took in converted Indians or blacks did not similarly assimilate the newcomers; European Americans believed in the "superiority" of their civilization and lacked the desire to bring Indians or blacks into that society.[48]

Hammon could not become a transculturite in white culture, for the impermeability of Puritan society would allow him few if any privileges. His narrative does not really attest to his status as a black man; his tale, as captured black, tends only to confirm the white Protestant-dominated status quo that branded Native Americans (as well as Catholics and blacks) savage creatures. In fact, the nonracial quality of his account may explain why Hammon's narrative was published at all: colorless, it upholds a color-bounded society; a black man, himself probably a captive of European Americans, attests to the horrors of Indian captivity (and by extension, the benefits of *white* ownership). John Sekora asserts that it was the ability of Hammon's story to conform to white printers' agendas, specifically its similarity to a then-popular captivity narrative of a young white man, that enabled his story to emerge.[49] Eighteenth-century black men in their new, white worlds had often to describe themselves, not as black men, but as other kinds of men—religious seekers, nascent capitalists. For the Protestant convert James Albert Ukawsaw Gronniosaw, blackness *per se* marks him as one despised—yet he does not elaborate on this observation much further than this pathetic, curious statement made early in his narrative: "when I found out it [a Bible or prayer book] would not speak, this thought immediately presented itself to me, that every body and every thing despised me because I was black."[50] Venture Smith, like Gronniosaw and the more familiar Olaudah Equiano, an African of noble birth, similarly spends little time on issues of race: his quarrel with the world is his lack of financial achievement, and the rampant ingratitude of one or another relative or former servant.[51] For the minister John Marrant, his condition of otherness represents the essential alien state of a charismatic Christian in an unenthusiastic world rather than a paradigm for race relations in a polarized society.

In *A Narrative of the Lord's Wonderful Dealings with John Marrant, a Black* (1785), Marrant aligns himself with a Mary Rowlandson or a John Williams by interpreting his captivity in typological terms.[52] Little of the narrative discusses slavery, and that little appears only in the fourth edition approved by Marrant himself; editions other than those "Enlarged by Mr. Marrant" omit references to chattel slavery.[53] We must take care, furthermore, not to lump Marrant's narrative in with that of his fellow African-descended writers: Marrant was born a free black, and although he preached to black captives in the South it was as a free man, not as a fellow slave. Marrant's conversion narrative, for such it is, takes part in the discourse of evangelical Protestantism then so prevalent in the United States; it launches as well a branch of black spiritual autobiography. More intriguingly, a sermon Marrant preached in the following year shows a prototype of Afrocentrism.[54] In all versions of the *Narrative*, however, the conversion experience itself is paramount—the author's life before it; his difficulties with the unbelieving members of his family; his subsequent life among the Indians as an adopted tribe member and an informal bringer of Christian enlightenment; his evangelism to plantation slaves; and his official incarnation as Huntingdonian missionary. Like Phillis Wheatley, Marrant was a beneficiary of the Countess of Huntingdon, and he displayed even more zeal for Protestantism than the young poet.[55]

> I John Marrant, born June 15th, 1755, in New-York, in North-America wish these gracious dealings of the Lord with me to be published, in hopes they may be useful to others, to encourage the fearful, to confirm the wavering, and to refresh the hearts of true believers.　　*(76)*

Marrant intends to present his life as a service to fellow Christians and a model for those not yet called, much in the way that Wheatley, admonishing the boys at Harvard, says "an *Ethiop* tells you 'tis [sin] your greatest foe" (16). If Christ, aligned with the lowliest, can call sinners to account, so too can Africans alert white Americans to the pitfalls of a misspent life.

Marrant thus first portrays himself as a careless boy eschewing the toils of apprenticeship and caring only for the pursuit of music and dance: "I was now in my thirteenth year, devoted to pleasure, and drinking in iniquity like water; a slave to every vice suited to my nature and to my years" (77). The word "slave" is wielded in a moral sense, as synonym for one helplessly trapped by things of this world. The history of African slavery lurks as a palimpsest behind this rhetorical trope, although the connection becomes more obvious and more tragic in Marrant's fourth edition. As a boyish prank, he attempts to disrupt a revival meeting of George Whitefield. Instead Marrant "was struck to the ground [by Whitefield's sermon], and lay both speechless and senseless near half an hour" (78).[56] Brought home, he sinks into a depressed and restless mood, attempting to chase away the minister Whitefield sends. The religious man persists, and "the Lord was pleased to set my soul at perfect liberty, and being filled with joy I began to praise the Lord immediately" (79). Somewhat understandably, his family is alarmed and displeased by what they consider young Marrant's excessive devotion, but "the more they persecuted me, the stronger I grew in grace" (80). When Marrant decides to set out on his own pilgrimage into the "desart" [sic] and come face to face with Jesus Christ, wild beasts, and the unfriendly unsaved, his readers, familiar with the typological strategies of Protestant narrative, can easily understand the larger meaning Marrant intends by his individual tale. The story of John the Baptist, another notable wanderer in the wilderness, is but one of several biblical figures the author invokes.

Following his meeting with a lone hunter, with whom he spends some weeks trapping, skinning, and learning Cherokee, Marrant is taken to an Indian town. There he is seized as an undesirable alien and condemned to a lengthy and painful execution. Cast into a dungeon, Marrant, much like Rowlandson, interprets his oncoming death as a sign from God that he is indeed chosen: "the near prospect of death made me hope for a speedy deliverance from the body: And truly this dungeon became my chapel, for the Lord Jesus did not leave me in this great trouble, but was very present" (84). By praying in Cherokee (an idea Marrant attributes to Christ), the executioner is "savingly converted to God" and refuses to kill him. During Marrant's subsequent audience with the Indian leader, his enthusiasm leads the chief's daughter to examine and kiss his Bible; she too is taken with the glory of God. Intriguingly, and much like James Albert Ukawsaw Gronniosaw and Olaudah Equiano (the narrators of other black captivities), the chieftain's daughter remarks "with much sorrow, the book would not speak to her" (86)—an example of contact between literate and nonliterate, or Christian and non-Christian, societies. Henry Louis Gates Jr. has called "the figure of the voice in the text—of the talking book—as [one of several] crucial 'scenes of instruction' in the development of the slave on the road to freedom."[57] This trope can also be seen not so much as a white-black social dialogue, but as an example of "western" versus "nonwestern" contact: in the Marrant text, an educated black man brings the written word to "uncivilized" Indian nations. Adam Potkay has elaborated upon this recurring scene in early black writing, noting that in Equiano's and Gronniosaw's narratives "theological curiosity" and a "concern with origins" bring about this fascination with the book—for the book that will not talk to the Cherokee princess, Equiano, or Gronniosaw is one and the same: the English Bible.[58] Illustrating this point, Homi Bhabha writes that this same English Bible in India functions as a sign of imperial domination *and* colonial resistance:

> If these scenes, as I've narrated them, suggest the triumph of the writ of colonialist power, then it must be conceded that the wily letter of the law inscribes a much more ambivalent text of authority. . . . If the appearance of the English book [in Bhabha's example the English Bible] is read as a production of colonial hybridity, then it no longer simply commands authority. It gives rise to a series of *questions of authority.*[59]

In Marrant's interaction with the young Indian woman, then, the "African" can be viewed as both the agent of a white, Protestant, colonializing power and the colonial subject adapting and mimicking the sign of the colonizer. As Bhabha explains, "the signifier of colonial *mimicry* [becomes] the affect of hybridity—at once a mode of appropriation and resistance" (181).[60] With the timely conversion of the daughter, further proof of his God's powers, Marrant is released and adopted; he eventually travels to neighboring tribes to spread the Word.

Unlike Rowlandson, a white Puritan writing a hundred years earlier, Marrant does not see his captors as unsalvageable or inhuman, even though the projected method of his execution—to be stuck with small pieces of "turpentine-wood . . . stripped naked . . . and set on fire" (84–85)—can hardly be described as anything but cruel. Yet following his miraculous deliverance via the conversion of key Cherokee figures, Marrant writes "the Lord made all my enemies to become my great friends. . . . I had assumed the habit of the country . . . [and] learned to speak their tongue in the highest stile" (87).[61] He understands that violent engagements with white settlers prevent some Indian groups from seeking any kind of rapprochement: "When they [the Creek, the Choctaw, and the Chickasaw nations] recollect, that the white people drove them from the American shores, they are full of resentment. These nations have often united, and murdered all the white people . . . they could lay hold of. . . . I had not much reason to believe any of these three nations were savingly wrought upon"

(88). (Prudently, Marrant decides to return to the Cherokees.) Yet while Marrant attests to the "bloodthirstiness" of these peoples, he comprehends the historical and political context for their hostility.

Beginning with the metaphor of a sojourn in the desert, Marrant's story takes on additional typological meaning when he returns home in Indian garb but is not recognized by any adult members of his family.[62] By saying the "skins of wild beasts composed my garments . . . [with] a sash round my middle" (88), Marrant could expect his readers to hear an echo of Mark 1:3, where John the Baptist appears "clothed with camel's hair, and with a girdle of a skin about his loins." When the evangelist returns to his home town, only his youngest sister recognizes him. Save for this proverbial little child, no one sees the lost son in the wild-appearing stranger. Directly referring to the parable of the prodigal son, Marrant muses "Thus the dead was brought to life again; thus the lost was found" (90).[63] In Marrant's revision of the parable, however, it is the family who have dissipated themselves in secular living. Their uncharitable, godless ways spur the religious son's sojourn in the wilderness; the family's refusal to validate his conversion experience drives Marrant away. "Whosoever denieth the Son, the same hath not the Father: [*but*] *he that acknowledgeth the Son hath the Father also*" (1 John 2:23). The little sister, like the child often cited in the New Testament as a true believer, points the way to Marrant and the truth, and like many early Christians she suffers physical violence for her belief—in her case, for insisting that the wild man is her brother.[64] The missionary could well have added, "Suffer little children, and forbid them not, to come unto me, for of such is the kingdom of heaven" (Matthew 19:14). Like earlier Protestant captives, and as indicated by small but significant differences in editions of his narrative, Marrant sees his conversion and deliverance as events worthy of Christian notice. His life and escape take on a specific biblical meaning that is hard to escape—and the exemplary life meant to encourage and uplift is that of a black man.

In the various versions edited by the Reverend Aldridge but not authorized by Marrant, only the title page identifies the author as black; only the closing paragraph indicates his sentiments as a man of color.

> I have now only to intreat the earnest prayers of all my kind Christian friends, that . . . Indian tribes may stretch out their hands to God; that the black nations may be made white in the blood of the Lamb; that vast multitudes of hard tongues, and of a strange speech, may learn the language of Canaan, and sing the song of Moses, and of the Lamb. (95)

If one relied on passages like this, it would be easy to set down Marrant as a kind of black Puritan captive, a Christianizer whose contact with the "other" is not defined by color but by an imperial, western religion.[65] But as John Saillant, Sandra Burr, and Adam Potkay have all noticed, the Aldridge editions are less truthful than the one certified by Marrant. The various "Aldridge" editions reproduced regularly since the late eighteenth century leave one highly crucial passage out—three pages that change irrevocably the cast and intent of the black minister's narrative. Marrant, in fact, "in a voice apparently untouched by Aldridge's editing," brought out his own version in London within months of the original narrative's publication;[66] materials he restores or adds include the account of another southern ministry of Marrant's, to a group of plantation slaves in Cumbee, South Carolina, and expanded versions of incidents related in earlier editions (Potkay and Burr 72–73). Oddly for a narrative that detailed the black minister's work among Native American unbelievers, Aldridge's version of Marrant's life relates his eyewitness account of a young girl's conversion and early death, a story that would call to mind similar incidents in other early American religious accounts, while skipping Marrant's courageous, probably illegal attempt to bring the word of God to the ignorant. For in South Carolina the "heathen" do not attempt to chase Marrant away or to kill him; it is the white, Christian slave owners who attack him.[67]

On this plantation Marrant sets up a catechism class and religious school for the young slaves who, on hearing Marrant at worship, desire to know more of God themselves; adults, on hearing of the free black's ministry, swell the ranks of his class. The white mistress, hearing of these lessons, "determined to put a stop to it . . . she told [her husband] it was the ready way to have all his negroes ruin'd, and made him promise to . . . break up our meeting" (91). When the little band of pilgrims persists, they are seized after a meeting,

> tied . . . together with cords, till the next morning, when all they caught, men, women, and children were strip'd naked and tied, their feet to a stake, their hands to the arm of a tree, and so severely flogg'd that the blood ran from their backs and sides to the floor, to make them promise they would leave off praying. (91)

Although the wife wants Marrant flogged as well, providentially the husband refuses, fearing retribution if he punishes a free black. The slaves' persistence in their devotions is rewarded: shortly after Marrant leaves them "it pleased God to lay his hand upon their Mistress . . . and in a very few days after she was taken ill, she died in a very dreadful manner" (92). Why, when this instance of refusal to do the Lord's will is so plain and so relevant to the larger project of converting the lost, does Aldridge omit it from subsequent versions of the *Narrative*? Despite the antislavery leanings of many English divines (the Countess of Huntingdon, Marrant's and Wheatley's patroness, was one of many such well-known abolitionists), many otherwise sympathetic whites found the issue of whites who so despised the word of God a sore one—especially when the unbelievers were remonstrated with by a black. Phillis Wheatley had earlier warned the boys of Harvard against sin—"An *Ethiop* tells you 'tis your greatest foe" (16). Marrant, not simply warning of possible missteps but revealing white torture of black Christians, steps on thinner ice. The suppression of his ministry in the South and its recent revelation make for quite a different reading of his autobiography and of the way one version has come down to us and another, approved by the narrator himself, has not.

Thus for many years readers had to look to a different text to confirm Marrant's pride in his African origins and his hatred for white hypocrisy. Some years after his sojourn in the southeast, and not long after the appearance of his *Narrative*, Marrant would address an "African lodge" in Boston to outline his vision of a true, enlightened Christianity. "We are expressly told by the Apostle, that charity, or universal love and friendship, is the end of the [glorious] commandment [love thy neighbor as thyself]."[68] Whites whose actions contradict this commandment will displease the Creator:

> What can these God-provoking wretches think, who despise their fellow men, as tho' they were not of the same species with themselves, and would if in their power deprive them of the blessings and comforts of this life, which God in his bountiful goodness, hath freely given to all his creatures to improve and enjoy? *("A Sermon" 6–7)*[69]

Readers relying on earlier available versions of the book have pointed to the lack of references to chattel slavery in Marrant's narrative. Yet as his address to the Prince Hall Masons proves, this lack did not indicate an absence of racial consciousness.[70] Even more publicly than Wheatley, Marrant displayed a laudable pride in Africa and its American orphans. He furthermore recognized the commonality of all peoples' experiences and history, remarking that Africans were hardly the only humans to be enslaved.

Ancient history will produce some of the Africans who were truly good, wise, and learned men, and as eloquent as any other nation whatever, though at present many of them in slavery, which is not a just cause of our being despised; for if we search history, we shall not find a nation on earth but has at some period or other of their existence been in slavery, from the Jews down to the English Nation.   *(20)*

Marrant saw clearly the parallels between contemporary African Americans' plight and that of the ancient Israelites—and like his biblical predecessors, he demanded that "our Modern Egyptians"[71] let his people go.

A few words about one of Marrant's successors in the arena of itinerant African American ministry seem relevant here. Jarena Lee's *The Life and Religious Experience of Jarena Lee, A Colored Lady, Giving an Account of Her Call to Preach the Gospel; Revised and Corrected from the Original Manuscript, Written by Herself* appeared first in 1836; a later edition, published in 1849, added nearly seventy pages of additional material about her travels and itinerant ministry.[72] Like Marrant, Lee traveled widely to bring enlightenment to the unsaved; the journeys of these two ministers of the gospel illustrate Gilroy's notion of the literal movement in geographical space that undergirds the modern black consciousness.[73] Unlike Marrant, who eventually aimed his ministry specifically at those of African descent who planned to emigrate with him to the ancestral continent,[74] Lee confined herself to Anglophone North America, striving to work within the framework of the still-young African Methodist Episcopal (AME) Church.[75] The differences among Rowlandson's, Marrant's, and Lee's narratives should be noted, as Lee perhaps offers the most "pure" of the narratives generically, generally confining herself to matters of religion and conversion without referring to a personal captivity.

Beyond the introductions of William L. Andrews and Susan Houchins, Lee's two modern editors, Frances Smith Foster, Nellie Y. McKay, and Carla Peterson provide comprehensive discussions on Lee.[76] Foster places Lee's narrative in the great tradition of spiritual autobiography that began with Augustine and continued to the Anglophone American colonies: "In all essential features, *The Life and Religious Experience* and the beginning of *Religious Experience and Journal* conform to the basic patterns of American spiritual autobiography as derived from the New Testament example of Saul of Tarsus" (59). Yet Lee's narrative squarely falls into a tradition of early American black autobiography that is also, and significantly, inflected by gender. Both Foster and Jean McMahon Humez assert how profound was the experience of being a black woman preacher, for Lee, while not one of many, was not alone in her position as an African American female preacher of the Gospel. Speaking of Rebecca Cox Jackson, the black Shaker visionary, as well as other early black women preachers, Humez notes all had in common "the struggle, as women, with male opposition to their ministry within the black independent churches." (Humez believes Lee's work was known to Jackson.)[77] So while Lee may have been familiar with Marrant's narrative, she—more important—well knew the situation of being a black female evangelist in a godless world.[78] Lee "adopted a geographic self-marginalization whose power lay both in constant mobility and in the habitation of those liminal spaces opened up by the Second Great Awakening," as Carla Peterson has noted (75), although a similar comment could be made about Marrant. Nellie McKay, in her work on Lee and Jackson, discusses Lee's "overt feminist qualities: her rejection of the traditional woman's place as wife and mother, her determination to defy gender biases against women's spiritual leadership, and her physical ability to carry out the [itinerant] ministry she did" (148); she also draws out the commonalities between the works of African American women and African American men. Liminality and geographic wanderings alike mark Marrant's and Lee's evangelism, although Lee was further subject to the misogyny of male church leaders and members.

As had Marrant, Lee preached to white and black alike, although race and gender prejudices worked against her. In New Jersey, her oratory had an affect on at least one "obdurate" heart; a hardened slave-holder who'd thought "nothing of knocking down a slave with a fence stake" decides that perhaps black people do have souls—although Lee admits she never learns whether he is converted (19). In fact, Lee spoke much before "promiscuous" audiences—white and black, free and slave, male and female. Resistance came from quarters where she might honestly have expected support. Repeatedly, Lee notes the denigration of her talents and rejection of her offers to speak by African American men, as in her comments below:

> Rev. James Ward, a colored Presbyterian, assembled with us, although he was so prejudiced he would not let me in his pulpit to speak; but the Lord made a way where there was no way to be seen; there was no person to intercede until this sister tried to open the way; the men of color, with no spirit of christianity, remained idle in the enterprize. *(44)*

The struggles of Jarena Lee to become a fully recognized member, if not leader, of her denomination ironically parallel Marrant's efforts to be recognized, as the subordination of Marrant's own version of his life to a white-edited one attests. Lee's struggle for self-determination as a black woman preacher anticipates the postbellum writer Julia Foote's struggle within the same African Methodist Episcopal church,[79] even as her clashes over empowerment inscribe acts of resistance harking back to Marrant's.

The shifting alliances, parallels, and contradictions in the work of eighteenth- and nineteenth-century black Christian narrators, male and female, expand and amplify our notions of an intergroup dialogue over narrative into one marked by a congeries of discourses: among African Americans, between men and women, from white to black and back again.[80] African American writers in the decades following Wheatley continued the negotiation of dual, if not multiple, literary identities. If they wrote in forms heretofore deemed white, if their allegiances seemed more to institutions dominated by European Americans, we must remember that the authors themselves did not lose sight of their racial identity. If we cannot finally determine if or how Briton Hammon conceived of himself as "different" from his master, we do know that devout Protestants like Lee and Marrant had no difficulty conceiving of themselves as black and Christian. In the following discussion, we will see how Henry Bibb and William Wells Brown shed the evangelical position of their overtly devout predecessors and peers and moved toward a more secularized Christian stance, much as the authors of nineteenth-century "white" captivities moved away from typological, if not from ideological, interpretations of European American superiority. Yet even in this parallel movement, African Americans continued to extend the meanings of the forms they had enlisted in their rhetorical engagement with American literature.

3

ॐ

ENSLAVING THE SAVED

The Narratives of Henry Bibb and William Wells Brown

Once the genre of the captivity narrative had been extended for over a century, the divergence of intent between captivities penned by white Americans and those written by African Americans became even more apparent. By the antebellum period many in the latter group had shifted from producing "African"[1] tales of Christian trials and redemption at the hands of heathen captors, to writing narratives of oppression by "Christian" whites. Nineteenth-century black narratives were characterized by the deliberate inversion of the implicit structure and moral of those written in the century and a half before. Black Americans, whether enslaved by whites or Indians, were unlikely to espouse one aim of the Puritan captivity narrative—the advocacy of a "white" social and political hegemony. In black-scripted stories, the fiendish captors were the figurative descendants of the white Christian captives; the darker-skinned race were the luckless kidnapped, rather than the abductors. In fact, when Indian captors were recalled, their status as masters and heathens would be reconfigured from the colonial-era portraits offered by whites. Nineteenth-century African Americans fashioned the captivity and conversion genres into a form even more distinctive than that of writers like Lee or Marrant, mov-

67

ing away from an obviously typological or evangelical discourse to a more secular argument grounded in Christian ethics.[2]

Nineteenth-century African American writing illustrates how the distinctly American category of slave narratives was the logical next step in the development of the captivity genre. The "straightforward" captivity narrative, as such, did not disappear; it remained an important vehicle for white authors, although its intent changed as the century advanced. In the late colonial and early national periods, for example, captivities such as Rowlandson's could be reworked to promulgate Republican strategies, and well into the mid-nineteenth century captivities continued to attest to the savagery of Indians and the civilization of European Americans.[3] Still, the black held in bondage was also a captive, and must have seen the obvious utility of the genre as clearly as did any abolitionist editor or amanuensis. If, as Slotkin has noted, the Puritan captivity tale of the seventeenth and eighteenth centuries turns on a story of capture by Satanic creatures, a series of trials of faith, and the eventual redemption of the tried but true, then so too does the nineteenth-century slave narrative. While Slotkin was perhaps the first to remark "the most significant [new] use of the captivity mythology" (441) was its redirection in narratives of southern slavery, he did not discuss by author or title any of the African American-authored autobiographies, with the exception of the narrative of Josiah Henson—and that work is examined only in conjunction with Harriet Beecher Stowe's *Uncle Tom Cabin*.[4] For her part, Stowe openly acknowledged her debt to the narratives of former slaves: unsurprisingly for a life story said to be in part the inspiration for the fictional Uncle Tom's, Henson's 1849 narrative preceded the volume publication of *Uncle Tom's Cabin* by three years. Robert Stepto has even suggested that Henry Bibb's narrative had as much influence on Stowe as Henson's.[5] Thus it seems circumlocutory to discuss the slave narrative as inheriting and adapting the captivity tradition by focusing on a novel that draws on the slaves' stories. Slotkin's omission of African American authors is curious, for he insightfully notes "the captive's and the slave's . . . [becoming] true Christians under the stress of un-Christian circumstances" (441, 442). Like Harriet Beecher Stowe, former slaves were writers—and shapers of shared American mythologies as well. The structural and thematic affinities between captivity and slave narratives result from analogous ordeals being framed within similar narrative strategies.

Many critics have failed to link the two types of narratives—not noticing their similarities at all, much less exploring them at length. If we look, for example, at the manipulation of narrators' texts for ends more suitable to the editor, we see not only whites in charge of black texts—as with Child's reordering of the *Incidents in the Life of a Slave Girl* or the interpolations of Thomas Gray in Nat Turner's *Confessions*—but also male editors in charge of female stories. Cotton Mather's life of Hannah Dustan, collected in *Magnalia Christi Americani*, is intended to serve as a hagiographic model for Americans: "one of these women took up a resolution to imitate the action of Jael upon Sisera [and kill her captors]."[6] What designs Dustan herself had in giving over her story to the famous divine can only be conjectured. Mary Rowlandson's account was preceded by the imprimatur of an anonymous male editor who announced that "though this Gentlewomans modesty would not thrust it into the Press, yet her gratitude unto God, made her not hardly perswadable to let it pass . . . [so that] others benefit by it as well as her selfe"; her audience should not, therefore, cast aspersions on her womanliness.[7] Juvenile captives too, as in the case of the Oatman sisters in the mid-nineteenth century, would not appear without validation from a more powerful adult. Be the authenticator a white, a male, or an adult (and usually the editor represented all three), this genre of narrative was regularly issued with a higher authority's seal of approval. And as we have seen, the narratives of Marrant (at least the Aldridge versions) and Hammon did not significantly diverge from the previously established pattern of convert/captive relating his experiences in the hands of others *to* an other.

Announcing oneself as author was revolutionary; neither Hammon nor Marrant had proclaimed their stories as authored by the teller himself. So when Henry Bibb and William Wells Brown subtitled their narratives "Written by Himself," they were deliberately breaking southern law and literary custom alike, for a black man, much less a slave—who was juridically speaking not a man but a thing—was not supposed to be able to write. Jarena Lee, similarly subtitling her text "Written by Herself," represented a further impossibility—a black, *female* preacher-author. In becoming autobiographers, early African American writers adopted literacy, the powerful medium of their oppressors, to counter the ways in which language was used against them. This utilization of another culture's means without a corresponding espousal of that society's ends has been termed "antagonistic acculturation"; as sociologists Devereux and Loeb have determined, African Americans and other subordinate groups may adopt "the neighbor's means and techniques, the better to resist the adoption of his goals."[8] The thrust of the slave narratives, as well as of the earlier black narratives, was to affirm the essential humanity of the slave by showing his mastery of skills black captives were supposedly unable to comprehend. It was a strategy born of a world with few alternatives.

The words "Narrative [of the Life of]" came to indicate the *slave's* story, as dozens of former bondsmen and -women so entitled their autobiographies. For the most part formulaic accounts of the early life, sufferings, and eventual escape of an enslaved soul, these narratives, a literate strength in numbers, formed the bedrock of later African American literature. "I was born" becomes so familiar an opening that the acute reader is almost disturbed when she comes across a narrative that does not begin with this near-ritualistic invocation. These accounts invariably cover the slave's early childhood, often with the announcement that a white man (the master, in many cases) was his or her progenitor; gruesome accounts of whippings and tortures alternate with everyday scenes of slave life; the splitting apart of husbands and wives, parents and children, is commonplace. When read in great numbers, the narratives begin to blend into an *ur*-text of African American autobiography, a story of challenge, separation, and redemption, a genre that rings changes on the Puritan ordeals of the two previous centuries.

It has been noted that the similarity of the narratives stems from the genre's origin as abolitionist lectures: "What was done to you?" "How were you fed?" "Why were families separated?" "When did you first have an inkling of a better life elsewhere?"—such were the questions with which white abolitionists prompted black speakers:

> Proper interrogation [of the escaped slave] would identify, then guide, a true abolitionist. . . . Each speech was to include a detailed, forceful description of the conditions of the slave system, ordered according to the questions an indifferent or ignorant white audience would wish answered; an ardent appeal for slaves . . . and a repudiation of the slaveholders, clergymen, and politicians who supported the system.[9]

If "the white man owned . . . form," as Annette Niemtzow has written,[10] then why would the black man and woman participate in such a tightly controlled partnership? If the white abolitionist so carefully sifted out what would be effective and what would not, what did the African American provide other than raw facts? By briefly analyzing two narratives that take part in this seemingly unfair contract, and yet manage to subvert both the implicit designs of abolitionist editors and readers and the restraining form itself, we will see how a supposedly closed construct may be opened from within.

Black abolitionist Henry Bibb sets up his narrative in the standard manner:

> I was born May 1815, of a slave mother, in Shelby County, Kentucky, and was claimed as the property of David White Esq. He came into possession of my mother long before I was born. [In Shelby and the surrounding counties] I was brought up . . . [o]r, more correctly speaking . . . I was *flogged up*; for where I should have received moral, mental, and religious instruction, I received stripes without number.[11]

In a few terse lines Bibb provides the reader with an approximation of his date of birth, the facts of his and his mother's ownership, and the unceasing brutality—both the actual beatings and the psychological domination—to which he was forced to submit. That his first owner, David White, was an alien, un-Christian being can be inferred from his sacrilegious preventing of the young Bibb from gaining secular or religious instruction. Bibb finds out soon enough what is to be his role in the world—and what would be that of his white owner's daughter: "I was taken away from my mother, and hired out to labor for various persons . . . and all my wages were expended for the education of Harriet White, my playmate" (14). There was no recompense, there was no recourse.

> Complaints, when not answered with blows, would go unheeded: I have also been compelled in early life, to go at the bidding of a tyrant, through all kinds of weather, hot or cold, wet or dry, and without shoes frequently, until the month of December, with my bare feet on the cold frosty ground, cracked open and bleeding as I walked. *(15)*

We hear a clear echo of Mary Rowlandson's recounting of unsympathetic, heathenish masters—"I told them the skin was off my back [from carrying a pack], but I had no other comforting answer from them than this, than it would be no matter if my head were off too."[12] But we hear Douglass as well, and his evocation of Christlike suffering: "My feet have been so cracked with the frost, that the pen with which I am writing might be laid in the gashes."[13] As had John Marrant, Douglass, and other slaves versed in the Scriptures, Bibb could easily see in his mistreatment a biblical typology of the oppressed Christian. The imperative for these writers to chronicle the violence of whites against blacks cannot be overstated. As the earliest white captives were eager to relate the cruelties and abuse of their "heathen" captors, so did slaves focus their accounts on the brutality of the system that held them captive. To relate white attacks on helpless blacks was to reproduce the horror of similar depredations on white settlers. Thus Bibb would not shrink from including slave owner abuse of black children, especially as his family experienced it: "[My daughter's] little face was bruised black with the whole print of Mrs. Gatewood's [their owner's] hand. This print was plainly to be seen for eight days after it was done" (43). His goal, and that of other slave narrators, was to instill in the audience a deep-seated belief in the barbarity of slavery and the iniquity of its white proponents. The echo of the Puritan captivities is unmistakable. But to echo those earlier tales was not merely to replicate them: in the case of the white-authored narratives the subtext of the tale is to attest to the superiority of European American civilization and the necessity of eradicating or absorbing Native American society; narratives written by black authors insist that white Christians act as such—as civilized folk who read and follow the teachings of Jesus Christ. The primary aim of the earlier genre, to propound the will of the white settlers who would become a white majority, would be replaced by African American genre revisionists with the desire to re-form society in still another, egalitarian way.

One well-known episode in Bibb's narrative has often been cited as an example of the slave narrator escaping not only physical bondage but also the expectations of his audience. William L. Andrews identifies both Bibb and Brown as autobiographer-tricksters.[14] In his introduction to Bibb's story, abolitionist Lucius Matlack offers a letter from Silas Gatewood, Bibb's second owner, to demonstrate the fugitive's veracity; the truth of the narrative depends, as it were, on contested readings of a single event. In this document, the slave-holder attempts to justify his own actions while chastising Bibb for his:

> [Bibb] was guilty . . . of worse offences [than indolence. My father] watched his conduct more strictly, and found he was guilty of disposing of articles from the farm for his own use, and pocketing the money.
>
> He actually caught him one day stealing wheat—he had conveyed one sack full to a neighbor and whilst he was delivering the other my father caught him in the act.   *(iv)*

The editor, defending Bibb's actions, contends that duplicity "in a slave, is only a slight reflex of the stupendous fraud practiced by his master" (viii); Matlack points to Bibb's acknowledgment of the theft as evidence of his virtue ("I admit the fact"). Yet Bibb's impassioned reply, contained within the text itself, rejects any suggestion that his actions are, in any shape or form, at all duplicitous:

And who had a better right to eat of the fruits of my own hard earnings than myself? Many a long summer's day have I toiled with my
wife and other slaves, cultivating his father's fields, and gathering in
his harvest, under the scorching rays of the sun, without half enough
to eat, or clothes to wear, and at the same time his meat-house was
filled with bacon and bread-stuff; his dairy with butter and cheese. . . .
I did not regard it as stealing then, I do not regard it as such now. *I hold
that a slave has a moral right to eat drink and wear all that he needs,
and that it would be a sin on his part to suffer and starve in a country
where there is a plenty to eat and wear within his reach.* I consider
that I had a just right to what I took, because it was the labor of my
own hands.

(194–95; italics mine)

No scholar of Marx could have explained the alienation of labor better.
In fact, one might say that Marx was anticipated by slave narrators
who decried the starving of forced laborers while the masters dined
sumptuously.

When Bibb declares the immorality of *not* stealing, and the sinfulness
of allowing oneself to be deprived where there is plenty, the reader is
bound to reflect upon the contradictory admissions of Saint Augustine:
"For of what I stole I already had plenty . . . and I had no wish to enjoy the
things I coveted by stealing, but only to enjoy the theft itself and the
sin."[15] The Christianity of the saints cannot operate when one of its fun-
damental teachings—love thy neighbor as thyself—goes ignored. Unlike
Mary Rowlandson or John Williams, who see their trials at the hands of
Indian captors as divinely mandated, Bibb rejects the idea that his earthly
bondage results in any way from his own misdeeds: "I believe slaveholding to be a sin against God and man *under all circumstances*" (204; emphasis mine). Judging from this statement and his numerous rebellions, Bibb
may be said to be taking his text from Mather's *Magnalia Christi Americani*, in which devout Christians such as Hannah Dustan could and did
choose not to turn the other cheek.[16] Bibb demonstrates the similarity of
black and Puritan approaches to typology—both groups relied greatly on
Old Testament stories of vexed morality and divine retribution.

In narrative after narrative, the Christian slave bemoans—and
attacks—the professed religion of the slave-holding classes. Bibb rejects
their so-called Christianity, choosing instead to have faith in a God who
will sympathize with suffering rather than order it. Countless slave
autobiographers relate that the worst blows fall from the hands of their
fellow worshippers in the church. Bibb's experiences were no different

than most. Remembering his ordeal following a second escape attempt, Bibb writes:

> What made the matter look more disgraceful to me [was that] many of this [slavecatching] mob were members of the M.E. Church, and they were the persons who took away my church ticket, and then robbed me also of [my watch, pocket knife, cash] and a Bible. . . . yet my owner, Wm. Gatewood, was a regular member of the same church to which I belonged. *(87)*

As had Douglass, Bibb did not hesitate to underscore the essential incompatibility of affirming Christian principles and holding another in perpetual bondage.[17] European American narrators had no difficulty practicing Christianity while simultaneously asserting violent dominion over Native Americans; what appears an oxymoron today was legitimate to the Puritans. Examining the apparent contradiction of Christian precepts and physical violence in the early American colonies, Kibbey suggests that "the Puritan belief in the necessity and righteousness of deliberate physical harm was deeply indebted to the ideology of Protestant iconoclasm in Reformation Europe."[18] African Americans, neither orthodox Puritans nor voluntary settlers, understandably did not concur with an ideology that affirmed violent rule over others.

Henry Bibb, like Rowlandson and Marrant, served time as an Indian captive. After being sold to a "very wealthy half Indian"[19] by the gamblers who purchased him from his cruel Christian master (150), Bibb finds himself in circumstances that diverge significantly from Rowlandson's and Marrant's near-fatal brushes with their "heathen" captors. The reader sees the difference from the first exchange, when Bibb finds he will be a personal servant rather than a field hand; furthermore, the gamblers assure him that he'll have a better chance of getting away from an Indian than from a white man. The irony of Bibb's being helped by his penultimate owners, a group of gamblers and thieves, and not by the owner immediately previous to them, an allegedly devout Christian, is not lost on the reader: even assuming the paradox implicit in his being liberated by crooks from a deacon, Bibb repeatedly reminds his audience of this scandal—"He was represented to be a very pious soul, being the deacon of a Baptist church. . . . I afterwards found him to be one of the basest hypocrites I ever saw" (108, 110). In contrast, in the author's headnotes for chapter fourteen, Bibb announces "Slavery among the Indians less cruel" (152). Developing this assertion at length, the former fugitive details the reasons

why a Native American master was to be preferred: "he was the most rea-
sonable, and humane slaveholder that I have ever belonged to . . . the
Indians allow their slaves enough to eat and wear. They have no overseers
nor whip to drive them" (152). Summing up the situation, Bibb concludes
"all things considered, if I must be a slave, I had by far, rather be a slave to
an Indian, than to a white man, from the experience I have had with both"
(153).[20] Such experiences illustrate the cultural contact and exchange
noted by James Axtell and A. Irving Hallowell, which affirm the one-way
nature of white-Indian—or for that matter, white-black—relations.[21]
Although a Christian among Christians, Bibb remains among the real savages until he is enslaved by the putative "heathen."

Lest we limn Bibb's interlude among the Indians with a presentist,
"they're all people of color" brush, it bears keeping in mind that Bibb could
also gaze with "imperial" eyes, in Mary Louise Pratt's words.[22] After proclaiming his Indian master the best man who ever enslaved him, Bibb continues with this observation: "A majority of the Indians were uneducated,
and still followed up their old heathen traditional notions" (153). The
Christian Bibb does not choose to stay among the natives and convert
them, as had John Marrant. Instead, before the narration of his last, successful escape, he pauses for an ethnographic interlude worthy of any
white explorer:

> They made it a rule to have an Indian dance or frolic, about once a fort-
> night; and they would come together far and near to attend these
> dances. . . . In the centre they would have a large fire to dance around,
> and at each one of the small fires there would be a squaw to keep up the
> fire, which looked delightful off at a distance. . . . Their manner of danc-
> ing is taking hold of each others hands and forming a ring around the
> large fire in the centre and go stomping around it until they would get
> drunk or their heads would get to swimming, and then they would go
> off and drink, and another set come on. Such were some of the practices
> indulged in by these Indian slaveholders.   (153–54)

What's most curious in the above passages is Bibb's simultaneous raising of the Indian master above the hypocritical white and his lowering of
the master's entire group, now referred to as slave-holders, because of
their pagan, "drunken" revels. Bibb swings between the idea of the
Indian as an interesting foreigner—"their dress for the dance was most
generally a great bunch of bird feathers, coon tails, or something of the
kind stuck in their heads, and a great many shells tied about their legs to

rattle while dancing" (154)—and that of the Native American as a debased individual whose degradation somehow propels him into slave-holding, a post hoc ergo propter loc argument that supposes alcohol the cause of slavery. Even John Marrant, remarking on the "savagery" of various Indian nations, notes "when they recollect, that the white people drove them from the American shores, they are full of resentment" (88), an admission which acknowledges prevailing historical conditions. One could in fact compare this passage with Marrant's much-invoked talking book episode, referred to in the previous chapter. In each of these incidents of contact, African Americans re-enact the Protestant mission of their white-dominated country: both desire their Indian captors to be Christians, as they themselves are, although Bibb contents himself with a criticism of the Indians' customs and drinking; before lighting out for his territories, Marrant, an evangelist throughout his life, could count his weeks among the Cherokees as but another sojourn among the unenlightened. Pratt's comments about Mungo Park, the Scotsman who journeyed through the Niger region, prove surprisingly relevant here, if we substitute the name Bibb for Park: "In comparison with a great many other travelers, especially some of the Victorians who followed him, Park affirms plausible worlds of African [read Indian] agency and experience. His relational approach to culture raises genuine possibilities of critical self-questioning. At the same time, though they are relativized, or even parodied, European ideologies are never questioned directly" (84). Pratt might describe Bibb's responses to his Indian "keeper" in terms of "a 'contact' perspective [which] emphasizes how subjects are constituted in and by their relations to each other." Bibb's ironic descriptions of white Christian slave-holders call into question the superiority of European culture, if not in quite the same way that Park, and for that matter John Marrant, do.

In both the narrative of Bibb and that of his fellow activist Williams Wells Brown, however, the moral high ground of the victim did not necessarily prevent the writer from making errors of his own. Bibb, married as a young man, falls into the "trap" of loving something, or someone else, more than freedom—at least at first:

> To think that after I had determined to carry out the great idea which is so universally and practically acknowledged among all the civilized nations of the earth, that I would be free or die, I suffered myself to be turned aside by the fascinating charms of a female, who gradually won

my attention from an object so high as that of liberty; and an object which I held paramount to all others. *(33)*

The "fascinating charms" of mere femininity ensnare Bibb, pulling him away from his life-saving yet lofty goals:

> Malinda was a medium sized girl, graceful in her walk, of an extraordinary make, and active in business. Her skin was of a smooth texture, red cheeks, with dark and penetrating eyes. She moved in the highest circle of slaves, and free people of color. She was also one of the best singers I ever heard. . . . I considered Malinda to be equalled by few, and surpassed by none. *(33–34)*

That Malinda's name is so close to the reviled "Malinche" of Mexican contact literature is worth commenting upon. That historical figure too was denigrated for her intimacy with the white invader/enslaver; both women's names echo the Latin word for evil, *malignus*. Todorov writes that Malinche, betrayer of the Aztecs to the Spaniards, has been viewed as "an incarnation of the betrayal of indigenous values, of servile submission to European culture and power."[23] The parallel, coincidental or not, makes us wonder: was Bibb's wife's name really Malinda, or was the appellation bestowed on her by a disappointed and frustrated husband?[24] Well might Bibb ask, as would Harriet Jacobs, "Why does the slave ever love? Why allow the tendrils of the heart to twine around objects which may at any moment be wrenched away by the hand of violence?"[25] But Bibb's "mind was changed by the charms and influence of a female"; assuring himself that Malinda would support his two cardinal goals—"to try to comply with the requisitions of the gospel" and to gain freedom "before I died" (36)—they wed. Or at least they did so in their own and the slave community's eyes, for "there is no legal marriage among the slaves of the South" (38).

Despite the love he professes for wife and child—for he admits that even within slavery he found genuine, if clouded, happiness—Bibb resolves to make a bid for freedom: "I must forsake friends and neighbors, wife and child, or consent to live and die a slave" (47). In much the same way that Douglass would construct his highly individualized, remarkable, and empowered self by drawing upon white, American, nineteenth-century models of the self-reliant male, Bibb sees black family life and freedom as mutually exclusive states. Or so he initially poses the dilemma for his intended white, abolitionist-minded audience (Bibb, like Brown and

77

Douglass, was a speaker on the lecture circuit before publishing his story). As William L. Andrews insightfully puts it, "marriage [becomes] Bibb's metaphor of the inescapable presence of the past and of the claims of slavery on the psychic well-being of the freeman."[26] Andrews further notes that Bibb's solution to the emotional demands of a slave marriage is to end it—and then to put the blame on his still-enslaved wife (159).

Bibb's repeated escape attempts, first without and then with his little family, describe not only his desire to be free but also his competing desire to possess another, even if by the supposedly legitimate bonds of affection and matrimony. As both Deborah McDowell and Karen Sánchez-Eppler have pointed out, the assertion of husbandly rights by a slave replicates the problematics of ownership implicit in nineteenth-century American marriage; part of the "condemnation" offered by male-authored narratives like Douglass's and Bibb's, McDowell says, is located in the depiction of "slavery's legal denial of family to slaves, especially its denial to male slaves the rights and privileges of patriarchy, which include ownership of their wives and children."[27] Andrews rightly points out that Bibb's rejection of Malinda as an "adulteress" (for that is, in the end, the way Bibb absolves himself of the need for further forays into the South) is disingenuous and cruel: "Labeling Malinda's relationships with her master simply as adultery, without considering the 'wrongs, sufferings, and mortifications' that Harriet Jacobs's autobiography pleads on behalf of the sexually tyrannized slave woman, let Bibb close his case" (159). Yet in doing so Bibb shows slavery's foulness as, in part, stemming from its power to force his wife to "prefer" a white man to himself: "I learned, on inquiry, from good authority, that my wife was living in a state of adultery with her master, and had been for the last three years . . . that she had finally given me up. . . . [Our master] had sold her to this [current owner] for the above purposes at a high price, and she was better used than ordinary slaves" (188–89). When Bibb's mother confirms this, Bibb says he "gave her up into the hands of an all-wise Providence. As she was then living with another man, I could no longer regard her as my wife. After all the sacrifices, sufferings, and risks which I had run, striving to rescue her from the grasp of slavery; every prospect and hope was cut off . . . for she was living in a state of adultery, according to the law of God and man" (189). To add insult to injury, he adds, "it is quite probable that they have other children according to the law of nature, which would have a tendency to unite them stronger together" (190). Bibb, whose fair skin and status of slave-in-perpetuity well told him the reality of such tender bonds between white fathers and slave children, could have stooped no lower than to write this. His own guilt at having fathered a slave—he called having a child with Malinda his biggest regret in life (44)—thus converted into the patently absurd wish that Malinda's subsequent children, and Malinda herself, will "have some kind of attachment" to the white man who bought her for the express purpose of sexual bondage. Which is more cruel—to abandon Malinda physically and emotionally by that first voyage North, or to abandon her textually with disingenuous protestations of her adultery with a slave owner (and with self-congratulatory wishes for her happiness)?

Bibb's and Brown's successful use of the captivity genre—if not of prevailing standards of masculine behavior—seems to prove Richard Slotkin's remark that "Like the white Puritan captive . . . the slave is . . . a Christian in hell. If he succeeds in hell's terms, he becomes like the devils around him."[28] Slavery creates not only ruthless power mongers who sell children away from parents, but lovers and husbands who deliberately withhold their plans from their loved ones. Bibb, after all, does not even inform his wife the first time he runs to freedom: "Had Malinda known my intention at that time, it would not have been possible for me to have got away, and I might have to this day been a slave. . . . Strong attachments to friends and relatives . . . twined about my heart" (47). Yet he prefaces this sentimental confession with the information that "it required all the moral courage that I was master of to suppress my feelings while taking leave of my little family" (46). However lofty Bibb's rhetoric, his plans for a solo escape from slavery leave his loved ones in a slavery of abandonment.

William Wells Brown became internationally known with the publication of his *Narrative* (1847). Yet this autobiography, with prefaces by contemporary white authenticator-abolitionists Edmund Quinsy and J. C. Hathaway, enclosed within the "white envelope" that the late critic John Sekora has seen wrapping most antebellum slave narratives,[29] delivers a disturbing message along with the expected one of trials, triumph, and freedom.[30] Although Brown's story invokes the strategic ploys of earlier captivity and slave narratives, it not only commands the reader's sympathy but also confounds its predecessors' strategies. The expectations of Brown's liberal white audience are dashed by his displacement of readers' pity onto other black subjects, suggesting the inappropriateness of easy sympathy for the narrator. In this process of short-circuiting the reader's expected commiseration and support, Brown presents a complex, mischievous, and not altogether sterling character that breaks down, if not precludes, the sympathetic reader's expectations of an ex-slave narrator.

My interrogation of Brown's narrative follows William L. Andrews's "agenda for the criticism of Afro-American autobiography in the 1990s": not only would I like to understand Brown's curious life history—"What does it mean?"—but I want also to articulate its more disturbing strategies, or, simply put, ask "How does it work?"[31]

As had other antebellum narrators, such as Henry Bibb and Frederick Douglass, Brown does not repeatedly inveigh against the hypocrisy of slave-owning Christians, although the now-expected references to "evangelical blood-hounds and ... religious slave-holders" do surface.[32] Still, the message is clear. As opposed to his fictional treatment of this subject in *Clotel*, published a few years later, Brown does not include detailed analyses of the "deep, and dark, and foul" (in the words of Harriet Jacobs) outrages perpetrated on female slaves—though he does allude to such crimes, as when he writes that his sister was purchased by a white slavemaster for "his own use" (28). Brown's narrative, unlike others I have discussed, runs just under fifty pages in the second, enlarged edition (1848), so an elaboration of certain issues taken up by other slave autobiographers may be absent due to space limitations. Nevertheless, although the duplicity and cupidity of whites are carefully set out, Brown eschews a moralistic cast; Christianity, per se, is but one aspect of America, slave-holding or no. You need not be a Christian to be a slave-holder, nor an atheist to be an abolitionist. Such a compressed telling results in an apparently typical slave narrative that fairly races along to its virtually foregone conclusion: the worthy ex-fugitive from Missouri, now a lecturer for the Western New York Antislavery Society, pens his narrative in sight of the Bunker Hill monument (49, 46).

But if he does not fulminate on hypocritical Christians, Brown spares the reader no scene of violence or bereavement. His brief *Narrative* contains a veritable catalogue of tortured, abused, and murdered individuals. Scene after scene of men "tamed" by savage beatings and maiming, of women whipped for refusing men they do not love, of babies and children separated forever from their parents, assault the reader. In one three-and-a-half page span Brown details numerous hellish occasions:

> Mr. Colburn ... from one of the free states ... tied Aaron up in the wood-house, and gave him over fifty lashes on the bare back with a cow-hide ... [after] learning that he had been to his master with complaints, tied him up again, and gave him a more severe whipping. ... Mr. Colburn ... whipped [his slave girl Patsey] until several of the boarders came out and begged him to desist [she preferred a black man to her

owner]. . . . Col. Harney, a United States officer, whipped a slave woman
to death . . . Francis McIntosh, a free colored man from Pittsburg . . .
[was] burned at the stake. . . . In addition to [having to wear a ball and
chain at all times] John told me that his master whipped him regularly
three times a week . . . the last time I saw him he had nearly lost the
entire use of his limbs.   *(6–9)*

Brown himself washes the luckless Aaron's back with rum and later is the
victim of an enraged white man, who beats Brown's head with a cane; this,
Brown notes, caused "the blood to gush from my nose and ears in such a
manner that my clothes were completely saturated with blood" (9). These
scenes of physical tyranny appear to begin a concomitant hardening of
the narrator's heart; slavery, with its violent acts, embeds itself in Brown's
soul. As observed by Hortense Spillers, slavery's wounds inscribe themselves on man and text:[33] writer and story alike are deformed.

Richard Yarborough helpfully notes that

> most nineteenth century black writers were far more interested in
> breaking racial conflict down to it[s] simplest ethical components than
> they were in rendering the Afro-American experience with a degree of
> complexity that the average white reader could not easily digest.[34]

But in fashioning one of the best known of the narratives denouncing the
evils of slavery, William Wells Brown does reveal, if inadvertently, a
"degree of complexity." Yarborough identifies Brown's "casual" attitude
in "maintaining generic distinctions in his prose";[35] this nonchalance
may help to create his unsettling self-portrait of the ex-fugitive as modern antihero, not as "Heroic Slave." Brown's contemporaries were reluc-
tant to "fictionalize" the black experience, for

> the act of seriously committing him- or herself to the creation of a
> fictional first-person voice entails for an author a plumbing of his or
> her own psychic depths—a process that must have been exceedingly
> painful . . . [because of] keeping their more dangerous and unruly
> emotions under tight rein lest they lose the audience they were try-
> ing to reach.   *(112)*

What slippage we see between the generally understood goal of a slave
narrative—telling the truth in order to overturn a vicious, soul-killing,
and iniquitous system—and the equally understandable one of contain-

ing "dangerous and unruly emotions" could well undermine the author's objective. In the case of Brown's earlier *Narrative*, the tension between "What does it mean?" and "How does it work?" gets played out in two disturbing vignettes.

As an apprentice to the slave trader Walker, the young bondsman observes firsthand many instances of duplicity and depravity. Brown, as the trader's factotum, learns to blacken the graying hair of slaves and "set them to dancing [in front of prospective buyers] when their cheeks were wet with tears" (46). He witnesses in his travels the forced concubinage of black women and the selling into slavery of a freeborn poor white. Although his experiences afford him the clearest possible view of the sufferings of others, Brown rather unremorsefully recounts how he tricks fellow blacks, not once, but two times. Brown thus places himself firmly within the tradition of the picaro—if by that we mean the common definition of the picaresque as an account of roguish doings by a none-too-blameless self; these misadventures, in turn, comment upon the larger society's foibles. By casting himself in such a role, Brown locates his *Narrative* more in the tradition of Henry Fielding's *Tom Jones* than in that of Mary Rowlandson's *The Sovereignty and Goodness of God*, even though the slave narratives drew significantly on colonial stories of imprisonment at the hands of horrible and mystifying others. But while the Puritan Rowlandson's theft of a captive child's food establishes her desperation and near-loss of faith, Brown's tumbles down the slippery slope of sin are chronicled like boyish escapades—although they too can be construed as evidence of the "howling wilderness" into which the black captive has been cast. His seemingly inexplicable behavior can be seen as Brown's acculturation into the violent, amoral society of slave-holders; analogously, white captives and their would-be rescuers worried about the perils of "going native."

In the first episode, Brown describes how he duped another man into taking a beating meant for himself. Having displeased his slave-trading employer by awkward service, Brown is sent off to the local jail with a note; as was often the case, the bearer could not read the message within. The wily narrator engages a passing sailor to read the note, and so learns that his master plans to have him whipped. Thus enlightened, our hero determines to escape his unfair punishment.

> While I was meditating on the subject, I saw a colored man of about my size walk up, and the thought struck me in a moment to send him with my note. I walked up to him, and asked him who he belonged to. He said

he was a free man, and had been in the city but a short time. I told him I had a note to go into the jail . . . but was so busily engaged that I could not do it, although I had a dollar to pay for it. He asked me if I would not give him the job. . . . I watched to see that he went in, and as soon as I saw the door close behind him, I walked around the corner . . . intending to see how my friend looked when he came out.   *(22)*

In one of the more unusual tales of slave-beating, Brown waits to engage his "customer" upon his exit from the jail. The freeman, understandably incensed, "bitterly [accuses Brown of having] played a trick upon him"—a truthful accusation that Brown denies; he backs up his protest by disingenuously inquiring what had happened behind the closed doors of the lock-up. When the man shows him a return note confirming his punishment, Brown offers the victim fifty cents for it ("all the money I had"), takes the letter, and returns to his master with fake tears drying on his cheeks. Attempting to defuse the censure that would ensue from this revelation, Brown explains that "this incident shows how it is that slavery makes its victims lying and mean; for which vices it afterwards reproaches them, and uses them as arguments to prove that they deserve no better fate" (23).

Perhaps. Yet the detail and the relative lack of comment on his behavior *during* the incident (as opposed to the explanations of extenuating circumstances that follow), create severe doubt as to whether or not Brown sincerely repents of his deception. Certainly his whimsical and ironic appellations for the freeman—first "my friend," then "my customer"—swamp his expressions of remorse. A stated desire to make amends, briefly expressed at the end of the chapter, somewhat counters the reader's misgivings:

Had I entertained the same views of right and wrong which I now do, I am sure I should never have practised the deception upon that poor fellow which I did. . . . I heartily desire . . . to make him amends for his vicarious sufferings in my behalf.   *(23–24)*

Could Brown's duplicity then indicate one of those instances where "dangerous" emotions emerge and undermine the "truth-telling"?

In the second incident of Brown's confessions (for so I now call them) he leads a fellow slave's emotions astray in order to reach his ultimate goal of freedom. His last mistress, a Mrs. Price, decides to keep Brown happy—and housebound—by wedding him to another slave. Marriage, however, is not high on Brown's agenda: his contemporary Henry Bibb, as we have seen, attributed much of his misery to his marrying—or even loving—while enslaved, as many other slave narratives attested. His owner, however, is willing to depend on a love attachment to ensure Brown's continuing enslavement: it was and is well known that family and conjugal ties kept many slaves (if not Henry Bibb) from running away. When Mrs. Price presses Brown on this subject, he admits to liking one woman in particular: "She also discovered (or thought she had) that I was rather partial to a girl named Eliza . . . [although] I gave but little encouragement to this proposition" (38).

The Prices' subsequent purchase of Eliza as Brown's future wife places him "in a very critical position": "I had to keep on good terms with Eliza, for fear that Mrs. Price would find out that I did not intend to get married" (39). By intimating his love for Eliza, Brown convinces their mutual owners he has no escape plans; in fact, the fictitious romance clears the way for the family's boat trip to a free state: "I told [Mrs. Price] that Eliza was very dear to me indeed, and that nothing but death should part us. . . . This had the desired effect. The boat left New Orleans, and proceeded up the river" (40). At the first opportunity, Brown makes his successful move—without informing his "intended."

On board the night before his escape, Brown thinks of what has happened and what will. Although he tells us how the fates of the mother and siblings left behind in slavery gnaw at him, not once does he contemplate the effect that his absence might have on Eliza. We never learn whether she returns Brown's feigned affections; perhaps she is as dismayed as he at the impending match. If he has any remorse about staying "upon good terms with Eliza," we do not hear about it: like the nameless free black earlier described, Eliza is mentioned only in relation to her utility to him, as a curious incident in the unregenerate Brown's early life. Even more unpleasant, Brown pays no lip service to a desired future meeting and apology, as he does with the man he has whipped in his stead. The final mention of Eliza in the 1848 text comes when Brown expands on his new status as freeman and considers the reactions of those back in the South:

> I wanted to see my mother and sister, that I might tell them "I was free!" I wanted to see my fellow slaves in St. Louis, and let them know the chains were no longer upon my limbs. I wanted to see Captain Price, and let him learn from my own lips that I was no more a chattel, but a man! I was anxious, too, thus to inform Mrs. Price that she must get

another coachman. And I wanted to see Eliza more than I did either Mr.
or Mrs. Price! (45–46)

After this, Eliza's name appears no more. To his St. Louis comrades and
family Brown wishes to communicate jubilation; to the Prices, triumph
and self-satisfaction. Why is Eliza's name placed with the Prices, rather
than next to the mention of their fellow slaves, unless she is also to be
humbled by his escape? What may be the most disturbing aspect of
Brown's vaunting is its simultaneous silencing of Eliza: unlike the tricked
freeman or Brown's own mother and sister, all of whom have "speaking
roles," Eliza is reduced to a voiceless prop. She has no lines; what desires
she may have are filtered through the white owner's wants. Her only
crime may have been to care for Brown, or to not urge him to get his freedom, as his family had. She may have been a harpy or an angel—and
likely somewhere in between—but we will never know.

This final fling of the picaro nearly derails the sympathies of the contemporary reader, who was more often than not white, middle-class, and
female. Disturbing thoughts could interpose themselves between the
sympathies of such a reader and the meaning of the black-authored text.
If Brown intends to win this audience over, then why paint a self-portrait
of a man undeserving of his own people's trust? Why should the reader
believe his narrative? Does the revelation of unkind, if not cruel, aspects
of his character support or undermine his readers' allegiance? On crucial
issues, this narrative of Brown's seems to raise more questions than it
can answer.

Perhaps a look at the version of his autobiography that prefaces *Clotel*
(1853) will give us some clues. This curious revision, liberally quoting
from Brown's earlier writings and including pages of encomiums from
groups and individuals, at first appears to be the work of another, for the
author writes about himself in the third person. Robert Stepto says,

> [Brown's] posture as the editor and not the author of his tale disallows
> any true expression of intimacy with his personal past . . . he is willing
> to abandon the goals of true authorship and to assume instead the
> duties of an editor in order to gain some measure of control over the
> present, as opposed to illuminating the past. (Veil 29, 31)

For Stepto, Brown seeks less to write autobiography than to authenticate
his various projects as speaker, civil rights activist, and novelist. This latter narrative in fact "functions as a successful rhetorical device, authenti-

cating his access to the incidents, characters, scenes, and tales which col-
lectively make up *Clotel*" (30). With this odd self-removal Brown amends
his life in rather significant ways, taking the opportunity, as it were, to
live events over again—without the mistakes.

In the third-person narrative that prefaces *Clotel*, much material
from the earlier work is repeated. Brown even quotes verbatim long
stretches of the earlier text. Yet there are alterations worth noting. In
keeping with the melodrama of *Clotel*, the later narrative includes an
additional, pathetic incident: the story of the little blind slave boy whom
the slave-trader Walker sells for a single dollar ("Narrative of the Life
and Escape" 11–12). Yet in the 1848 edition of the *Narrative*, only the
poem "The Blind Slave Boy" by Mrs. Bailey appears, in an appendix to
the narrative; Brown does not indicate that the event took place while
Brown was hired out to the slave-trader.[36] This reassignment of a news
item in an afterword to personal memory should give the reader of both
life stories pause.

More surprises await his audience.[37] Strikingly, the two incidents discussed above—the beating of the free black and the duping of Eliza—are
absent. In Brown's recounting of the year hired to the slave-trader, his
months with the Prices, and his last owners, nothing substantive has been
substituted. The story moves along without a mention of either figure,
except for one glaring slip.[38] In retelling the story of his escape, and
specifically by including the passage cited earlier on the imagined
responses to his getaway, Brown forgets to excise a reference to Eliza, the
slave girl left behind. Her name floats alone, disembodied; a ghost in the
text, she becomes the ineradicable remnant of an event the more mature
Brown wished buried. The appearance of her name, to a first-time reader,
would mean little: without the sense given by the missing vignette,
"Eliza" could refer to either a lost sweetheart or a daughter of Brown's
last owners, the Prices. To one familiar with both narratives, though,
Brown's Freudian slip—a typographical return of the repressed—speaks
to the conflict within the antebellum African American author: Can he or
she raise with white audiences terms more complex than good/evil,
saved/unregenerate? Must the black self, in order to be freed—or even
heard—present only a blameless, error-free individual? Pathetic, melo-
dramatic, saintly: How constrained was Brown by these abolitionist-
approved, acceptable African American attributes, the verbal equivalents
of the emblems of the chained, kneeling, humble slave?

As an active lecturer in the antislavery movement, journalist, novelist,
and historian, Brown's subsequent activities may well outweigh the dev-

ilments committed under the influence of bad masters and a corrupt society. Nevertheless, we should meditate upon the meaning of Brown's first narrative. If the cunning and chicanery of Brown are more appropriate to a reformed picaro than a pious and worthy captive, more in keeping with eighteenth-century criminal confessions than abolitionist documents of moral rectitude despite adversity, then the inclusion of these "errors" within a genre that depends on "truth" is a highly risky maneuver. To deflect sympathy away from himself in this fashion, even if onto other African Americans, evokes pity and horror. But Brown's harsh truths and hardly laudable slave-self-characterization support his aim and that of the slave narrative—to tell the story and summon a corresponding outrage. Such acts assert his individual agency as well, in however flawed a manner. In this way Brown exhibits an African American "distrust of the reader": by revealing his awful past he can lead his white reader through the psychic text of slavery.[39]

His later narrative, written after he had won some measure of fame internationally, retreats from that initial position. By casting himself as an object rather than as the subject, Brown the lecturer and author distances himself from that younger, more ambiguous hero-self. He edits his past, much as Douglass did, omitting those escapades and emotions that might detract from his standing as an African American spokesman. The relatively unknown, youthful fugitive can admit to peccadilloes; the intellectual should not. In this way, although he gains a certain measure of control over the present and the tale of slavery, Brown's own complex past, and the truths of that history, are sacrificed.

Brown draws on the African tradition of the trickster, the apparently powerless individual who manages to come out on top regardless of the opponent's strength. That said, it should be an African American audience that would identify with his pranks and hail his eventual emancipation. With such escapades he signifies on the white-approved sign of the disempowered, victimized bondsman, for by penning an unexpurgated narrative Brown discards the hagiographic expectations of his white abolitionist audience. Bibb, less of an avowed trickster, joins Brown in a borderline misogyny by his faithless scorning of a still-captive wife. His self-serving interpretation of Malinda's plight echo Brown's barely suppressed delight at attracting, and then escaping, the admiration of another, female slave. Their ideal African American reader, then, might well be male rather than a more inclusive "we" who might find it hard to applaud disrespect of the black woman. Further to complicate our conceptions of an implicit alliance between the authors and their subjects along racial or "minority" lines,

Bibb's relations to his Indian master present additional ambiguities. While complimenting his last owner as being the best he has had, Bibb unhesitatingly brands him as heathen, drunken, and full of superstition: such were the white mainstream's stereotypical beliefs. Early African Americans may well, in Ralph Ellison's words, evade their readers' expectations "[sometimes] for the sheer joy of the joke; sometimes to challenge those who presume, across the psychological distance created by race manners, to know his identity."[40] Because fellow blacks and others struggling under the domination of white North Americans could be the objects of cruel jibes and prejudice, early African American authors could not claim an unimpeachable moral high ground.

Well before the Civil War, and especially after Britain abolished slavery in all its colonies in the 1830s, black Americans came to see their enslavement as finite. Heralding the fast-approaching conflict were numerous literary salvos that took up the cudgels of the dominant society to advance the cause of the minority. Conversion and captivity narratives from the white Protestant majority aided the early African American's rhetorical moves toward freedom and literary empowerment. Despite James Olney's affirmation that the genre itself captivated black narrators, that "they were captive to the abolitionist intentions,"[41] slave narratives, that literary moment in which African Americans finally did capture the captivity, extended the meaning of that Puritan form. Continuing a now-established black American tradition of operating within two realms, ex-slave narrators promoted their people's agenda within not entirely hospitable European-derived genres. The simultaneous mindsets did, as we have seen, induce some narrators into admissions neither white nor black readers would easily countenance. Appropriating the paradigm of the self-made American, newly reconceived as a representative African American, black writers continued their quest to write black selves into the mainstream of American literature.

4

⁊❧

"IT IS NATURAL TO BELIEVE IN GREAT MEN."[1]

Although it has been said that Frederick Douglass can be seen as Benjamin Franklin's "specific shade," for "in many ways, the black man in America is the white man's shadow,"[2] "alter ego" may be a better appellation—or even *Doppelgänger*, for Douglass's repeated inversions of the myth first articulated by Franklin represent more than imitation and simple reversal.[3] The life of Douglass, in history and in print, extends and amplifies the image of the ideal American set forth in Franklin's *Autobiography*—a person implicitly, if not explicitly, defined by whiteness, Protestant faith, and male gender. As Myra Jehlen remarks, "When Franklin offers his exceptional career as representative, he means that he believes everyone is potentially exceptional."[4] Yet Douglass and his African-descended compatriots would set out to prove in the nineteenth century that the white, Protestant male would not be the only Representative Man in American society; even more significant, the Representative American would not even necessarily be a *man*. The discussion that follows looks at what several autobiographies do and don't do with the paradigm of American selfhood set forth in Franklin's autobiography. In this chapter I will examine how Olaudah Equiano and Frederick Douglass engage with dominant beliefs about success; in the last chapter of this book I will consider how Elizabeth Keckley and Eliza Potter rework the American success genre.[5] Douglass grappled the most closely, if not the most consciously, with the burden of Franklin's model, and for this reason his narrative is discussed at greatest length here. (Equiano, a man who may best be described as an Anglo-African, wrote earliest; by some markers one could say that his story anticipated the *ur*-text of American self-made men.)

To understand the achievement of the *Narrative of the Life of Frederick Douglass, an American Slave*, we must review the life structure Douglass was, consciously or not, emulating and reversing. The lives of Franklin and Douglass are remarkable for their similarities; at times the congruences seem more abundant than the differences. A number of parallel events are worthy of comment: the rise from obscurity to renown; the bondage to a kinsman; the self-education process; the attitudes toward self vis-a-vis community. The striking likenesses become all the more notable for the relative lack of critical comment that has heretofore been made. In his scripted life, Douglass adopted and adapted the notion of a self-made man. Less apparent are the African American models on which Douglass could draw—like Olaudah Equiano, the earliest of Anglo-African success narrators, or Douglass's own family.[6]

Franklin's life can be viewed as parallel and progenitor to many slave narratives, and especially to Douglass's. The great emphasis on personal freedom, espousal of hard work and industriousness, and announcement of lowly origins are hallmarks of both works. If one biographer has seen the African American spokesman as a "black Ragged Dick," and another critic has seen Douglass as "a sort of Negro edition of Ben Franklin,"[7] it was the Philadelphia Founding Father who, by the self-conscious act of writing his life, began the all-American rags-to-riches genre. His self-styled movement from bondage to freedom, from powerlessness to power, provided a host of later autobiographers with a compelling ancestry, if not strictly a literal one. As James Olney so accurately notes, "Douglass's book fits both comfortably and uncomfortably within that general American autobiographical tradition begun by Franklin . . . [but it] begins another, alternative, tradition as it sets and points the course for [subsequent] black American writers."[8] If Franklin's *Autobiography* delineates the essential elements of the American dream—"the rise from rags to riches, the movement from impotence to importance, belief in individualism, belief in free will, and a philosophy of hope,"[9] then Benjamin Franklin's eventual wealth and fame, idiosyncratic intelligence, conviction in his decisions, and pragmatic Puritanism should lend themselves spectacularly to adaptation by African Americans.[10]

If we think of American literature as a series of intertextual dialogues within a chronological continuum, then the comparison of the autobiography of Frederick Douglass with that of his literary and historical ancestor, Benjamin Franklin, is logical. Each man was recognized as a prime mover of his age and should share much of the same historical spotlight. Yet when critic James M. Cox observed in 1971 that "an astonishingly large proportion . . . of so-called American classics" (253) are autobiographies, he failed to include any pamphlets, memoirs, or books by an American of African descent.[11] Douglass, and Cox's late contemporary Malcolm X, are absent from Cox's canon, for the critic apparently could not then avoid a cultural mindset that predicated separate but equal as policy in more than social organization. In recontextualizing Douglass and Franklin within a framework that allows for their similarities as well as their differences, the critic takes on a task perhaps as "bold and arduous" as Franklin's own pursuit of "moral Perfection."[12]

Franklin was hardly the only model of self-sufficiency available to the young abolitionist. In the 1790s Venture Smith and Olaudah Equiano, two native Africans kidnapped as children, published English-language narratives of their lives. Smith's narrative, a problematic text due to the intervention and editorial omissions of his editor (likely a white man), carries the disclaimer that the tale "is a relation of simple facts, in which nothing is added in substance to what he related himself." Because of its "co-authorship," I am not going to treat that particular autobiography in detail.[13] It is worth noting, however, that in the preface to Smith's *Narrative*, the anonymous editor compares the narrator to "a Franklin and a Washington, in a state of nature, or rather, in a state of slavery" (3). Better known both to their contemporaries and us, Equiano's narrative, a bestseller well into the nineteenth century and still widely anthologized and reprinted, prefigures both the Franklin memoirs and the Douglass narrative in setting forth a how-to of self-possession. Yet at the same time, Equiano's story can be placed within the tradition of spiritual narratives and captivity tales. *The Interesting Narrative* thus participates in several conventions simultaneously, yet remains fixed in none of them.

As I discussed earlier, the mode of captivity and conversion narratives was not new to writers of African descent, for *A Narrative of the Lord's Wonderful Dealings with John Marrant* preceded Equiano's autobiography by four years. The brief *A Narrative of the Most Particulars in the Life of James Albert Ukasaw Gronniosaw* appeared earlier still, in 1770.[14] Most of the attention paid to Equiano's story focuses on the truly remarkable events of his early life, his years as a Caribbean slave, and his self-emancipation through Franklinian efforts, points I will only touch on here. As already noted in chapters 2 and 3, Equiano, born in Benin (present-day Nigeria), drew readers with his dramatic and acute rendition of the horror of African slavery and enforced exile as it happened to one individual. Neither a mass of slaves at a West Indies auction, nor the supplicating and chained man emblazoned on Wedgewood crockery, Equiano, as an author, could personalize slavery through the act of writing his life. He and his fellow Anglo-Africans Ottabah Cuguano and Ignatius Sancho "fashion[ed] a new myth" about blacks; his "level of technical sophistication and moral authority . . . challenged his readers to consider new ways of seeing Africans."[15] Yet even though Equiano's autobiography is shaped somewhat by the dictates of abolitionist discourse—white colleagues were likely to urge him to divulge details of his early life in Africa, the horrific treatment of the captives during the Middle Passage, the way slaves were treated in colonial America, and so forth—his story remains his, individual, unique.[16] When he writes of his initial and horrible incarceration on a slave ship, "I was soon put down under the decks, and there received such a salutation in my nostrils as I had ever experienced in my life: so that, with the loathsomeness of the stench, and crying together, I became so sick and low that I was not able to eat, nor had I the least desire to taste anything. . . . I now wished for the last friend, death,"[17] the reader comes about as close to experiencing the visceral degradation that was slavery as possible. Rowlandson's repugnance at Narragansett foods and Brown's catalogue of slave-holders' viciousness combine here in a book that folds conversion, captivity, and picaresque together into a genuine New World document.

Faith upholds Equiano, a faith first envisioned as African and later, following his conversion experience, as Christian. In the first paragraph he renders himself as exceptional yet representative of his people: "did I consider myself an European, I might say my sufferings were great; but when I compare my lot with that of most of my countrymen, I regard myself as a *particular favorite of heaven*, and acknowledge the mercies of Providence in every occurrence of my life" (33). Fortune, if not God, operates to place Equiano in a favored space. Indeed, his first name "signifies vicissitude, or fortunate; also, one favored, and having a loud voice and well spoken" (42). Serendipitously named, Equiano finds his fortune overdetermined by supernatural forces; yet he also professes his faith in a Christian God. Until fairly recently, the "religious parts" of Equiano's narrative have been slighted by a number of readers who, in our secular age, prefer the picaresque or so-called "classic" slave narrative aspects of The *Interesting Narrative*.[18] The cuts made in abridgments of Equiano's *Narrative* confirm this observation. Again, let us heed the earlier warning about privileging certain sets of texts over others, whether for reasons of comfort or familiarity.[19] Without a solid grounding in the Christian Bible, specifically the King James Version favored by most Anglophone narrators in this era, we twentieth-century scholars are hampered in our reading. Comprehensive future work on Equiano and other evangelical Protestant narrators such as Jarena Lee and Julia Foote will have to take into account the ways the profoundly religious nature of these writers prevents modern readers from comprehending them as African Americans of their time. The scholarship of Sondra O'Neale and Phillip Richards on the poetry of Jupiter Hammon exemplify the directions such research should take.[20]

In order to adapt for his own needs the "white" literary medium of the conversion narrative, and to introduce a new variation on the captivity narrative "not designed to reinforce the predominant culture but to liberate the captive reader from it,"[21] Olaudah Equiano had to adopt the "means and techniques" of his white captors. In *Blues, Ideology, and Afro-American Literature*, Houston Baker Jr. focuses on the "adept mercantilism" of Equiano.[22] Yet while Baker's Marxian analysis of the conflation of money and personhood is provocative and germane, it is the adoption of a particular means—in this case, venture capitalism—rather than the end itself that signals something characteristic of early African American discourse. One can see Equiano's narrative, therefore, as a model for African American letters in general and for Douglass's *Narrative* in particular. Each author appropriates select aspects of the dominating white culture for his own ends.

Equiano, also known as Gustavus Vassa, first published his autobiography in 1789. The time he spent in America can be better measured in months than years. In fact, as most of his life was spent outside of the American colonies, he might not even be termed an African American.)[23] As a record of African life in the eighteenth century, Equiano's autobiography is nearly unique, and especially valuable for its affectionate, accurate, and nonpatronizing viewpoint of Benin culture.[24] More important for this study, however, is his adoption of the mercantilist and individualist attitudes current in Eurocentric countries, attitudes that foreshadow those revealed in Frederick Douglass's *Narrative*.[25] True to the form that was even then becoming part of American mythology, Equiano makes his way steadily up from his degraded position. After years of slavery, Equiano is sold to a Quaker who allows Equiano to work for his freedom—that is, his master allows him to purchase himself. Starting with a mere threepence, Equiano raises himself up, literally and figuratively, to a positively Franklinian level of self-possession. With a single-mindedness strikingly reminiscent, in both language and determination, of the Philadelphian plotting his road to the top, Equiano begins his path to comfort with even less coin than the newly arrived Franklin:

> One single half bit, which is equal to three pence in England, made up my whole stock. . . . At one of our trips to St. Eustatia . . . I bought a glass tumbler with my half bit, and when I came to Montserrat I sold it for a bit or six pence. . . . Finding my tumbler so profitable, with this one bit I bought two tumblers more; and when I came back I sold them for two bits, equal to a shilling sterling. . . . [In the space of a month or six weeks] my capital now amounted in all to a dollar, well husbanded. . . . I blessed the Lord that I was so rich. *(102–3)*

Honest, industrious, pious—possessing all the virtues St. John de Crevecoeur had already identified as American—Equiano moves in his freedom quest from fortunate boy to slave to African missionary, concluding with an outline of his plans to equalize African-European trade: not by traffic in souls, but by the imperialistic solution of exploiting native resources and exploring hitherto unknown markets. His espousal of what would later be called African colonization draws him into contradictory acts. One of the first black neocapitalists, Equiano pleads for "trading upon safe grounds. A commercial intercourse with Africa opens an inexhaustible source of wealth to the manufacturing interests of Great Britain . . . to which all the slave-trade is an objection" (193–94). Yet Equiano's own ambiguous relation to such trade should be recalled: as a free man he once signed on as assistant to a Doctor Irving, who later "purchase[d] some slaves to carry with us, and cultivate a plantation; and I chose them all my own countrymen"; when he later leaves the doctor's employ, "the slaves, when they heard of my leaving them, were very sorry, as I had always treated them with care and affection, and did everything I could to comfort the poor creatures" (171, 176). Although here he makes no reference to actions on their behalf, other than making them more "comfortable," Equiano does, in another episode, attempt to free a man kidnapped back into West Indian slavery (151–52). Surprisingly for us moderns, there seems to be in Equiano's mind little expressed conflict between a free black man's antislavery opinion and his past complicity with the slave trade: "Slavery was a dominant feature of the eighteenth century, and nearly impossible to escape."[26] This simultaneous holding of what we today consider incompatible views complicates our understanding of Equiano as a "black writer." New World capitalist or "free trade" supporter, Equiano was the first of the Africans to openly espouse white methods for black aims, believing that one system of trade could more humanely supplant another.[27] Nevertheless, as Equiano's modern editor, Robert Allison, states, "the slave trade changed African society in ways we are only now beginning to understand, and the colonial system that replaced it made it almost impossible for African societies to recover."[28] Equiano could not know what lay ahead, could not see that the imperial exploitation that replaced the slave trade would be nearly as devastating as chattel slavery itself.

Olaudah Equiano was not a lifelong victim of circumstances, as was Gronniosaw, or a former Indian captive nearly indistinguishable from his European-American fellow Protestants, as was Hammon. Like Franklin, Equiano became a success in his new home, if success can be measured by his best-selling autobiography, modicum of political influence, and marriage to an Englishwoman. Yet for black writers to make the once whites-only province of individualism and literacy truly their own, and African American, would mean the besting of the master at his own game and denouncing the game as well. Frederick Douglass would do so. This American, whose life could so resemble Benjamin Franklin's, provides African American literature with a paradigm of both generic appropriation and textual transcendence.

> Having emerg'd from the Poverty and Obscurity in which I was born and bred, to a State of Affluence and some Degree of Reputation in the World, and having gone so far thro' Life with a considerable Share of Felicity, the conducing Means I made use of, which, with the Blessing of God, so well succeeded, my Posterity may like to know, as they may find some of them suitable to their own Situations, and therefore fit to be imitated. *(Writings, 1307)*

At the opening of his *Autobiography* Franklin claims his "Poverty and Obscurity" as a kind of peculiarly qualifying birthright, a prerequisite to the world of "Affluence ... [and] Reputation." One can infer not only that wealth is to be sought after, but that poverty and obscurity of origins are desirable as well.[29] Franklin's quest for antecedents reveals land-owning but not high-born ancestors, successive generations of dyers, chandlers, and such. The genealogical notations of one of his uncles provide Franklin with "several Particulars" in regard to the family tree:

> From those notes I learnt that the Family had liv'd in the same Village, Ecton in Northamptonshire, for 300 Years, & how much longer he [my uncle] knew not. . . . —When I search'd the Register at Ecton, I found an Account of their Births, Marriages, and Burials, from the year 1555 only. *(1308–1309)*

Tradesfolk though they may be, Franklin's forebears go back two and a half centuries. When he addresses his memoirs to his son, he takes his place in the chain of male Franklins stretching back to Northamptonshire; discounting his maternal forebears, at least in the *Autobiography*, Franklin elects instead his father's clan as the important one.[30] Although a staunch republican, Franklin seeks to locate himself within a long line of descent; this is in itself significant, even though he may say the family is unremarkable. Pride of kin, if not of their actual achievements, retains its potency. In contrast, many a slave memoir calls attention to a missing patrilineage by the placement of the writer in a black, matrilineal genealogy along with the absence, or apathy, of a white father. That Franklin slights his matrilineage reflects the differently configured alignments of power in Anglo-American culture, where the condition of the child does not have to follow the mother's.

If Franklin is born into obscurity, his cloudy origins are only relative; he remains a white male in a society run by those phenotypically like him. Secure in birth records and patrimony, Franklin can address his memoirs to a son whose patrimony is also assured.[31] Douglass, on the other hand, is born into the limbo of American chattel slavery, where familial antecedents are likely to be either unacknowledged or absent. The ex-slave can therefore sum up his lineage in a few lines:

> My mother was named Harriet Bailey. She was the daughter of Isaac and Betsey Bailey, both colored, and quite dark. My mother was of a darker complexion than either my grandmother or grandfather. . . . My father was a white man. He was admitted to be such by all I ever heard speak of my parentage. The opinion was also whispered that my master was my father.[32]

Himself a father several times over by the year of the *Narrative*'s publication, Douglass could certainly have inscribed his autobiography to a son.[33] But he does not. Neither does he explicitly tell how a man of obscure antecedents can become a household word: in antebellum American society a Douglass could claim no meaningful ancestry and hence held meager authority. His own mother barely recalled, a grandmother from whom he was taken away as a child, his siblings fellow strangers—Douglass's genealogy is fractured, his individuality taken out of a familial context. Douglass's terse complaint, "white children could tell their ages. I could not tell why I ought to be deprived of the same privilege" underscores that the identity-less slave "know[s] as little of [his] age as horses know of theirs" (23). No deeper obscurity existed than slavery; to be both black and a slave was to be less than human. As Orlando Patterson remarks,

> [The slave] was truly a genealogical isolate.... He had a past, to be sure. But a past is not a heritage. Everything has a history, including sticks and stones. Slaves differed from other human beings in that they were not allowed freely to integrate the experience of their ancestors into their lives, to inform their understanding of social reality with the inherited meanings of their natural forebears, or to anchor the living present in any conscious community of memory.[34]

Rather than inscribe his memoirs to his free children, Douglass prefers to confront his readers immediately with his "natal alienation," reminding them of their implicit participation in such a system.[35] To break out of the "social death" of slavery, Douglass takes on the role of the self-made American man already known by the mid-nineteenth century.

Franklin depicts himself as without appropriate origins; so too, and with greater force, can Douglass. Frequently, part of a young man's journey from poor man to wealthy one involved his physical arrival in a new world. Such a transition figures significantly in both Franklin's and Douglass's memoirs. In his anecdote of immigration the Philadelphia printer wastes no time in pointing out the moral:

> I have been the more particular in this Description of my Journey, & shall be so of my first Entry into that City, that you may in your mind compare such unlikely Beginning with the Figure I have since made there. . . . I was dirty from my Journey; my Pockets were stuff'd out with Shirts & Stockings; I knew no Soul, nor where to look for Lodging. . . . [I went from the baker's] with a Roll under each Arm, & eating the

other. Thus I went up Market Street as far as fourth Street, passing by the Door of Mr Read, my future Wife's Father, when she standing at the Door saw me, & thought I made as I certainly did a most awkward ridiculous Appearance. *(1329)*

At first a bedraggled and penniless visitor, Franklin goes on to build up a successful business and win the hand of the very woman who once laughed at his outlandish appearance: the message could not be more clear. Even with all the mistakes, or errata, that Franklin strategically leaves in—or perhaps because of them—this portrait becomes the prototypical American success story, the life of the atypical yet somehow representative man.

In depicting himself as the providentially favored slave, Douglass also invokes a humble birth and the dirt of travel. As in the Franklin memoir, a woman serves as the guardian of New World manners and mores: "Mrs Lucretia had told me . . . the people in Baltimore were very cleanly, and would laugh at me if I looked dirty" (53). To arrive truly was to remove all of the filth identifying him as a country slave:

> I shall never forget the ecstasy with which I received the intelligence that my old master (Anthony) had determined to let me go to Balti-more. . . . I received this information about three days before my departure. They were three of the happiest days I ever enjoyed. I spent the most part of all these three days in the creek, washing off the plantation scurf. *(52)*

Baltimore has heretofore been held up to Douglass as the model of all things desirable: whatever object of beauty the boy could point out, his cousin Tom "had seen something at Baltimore far exceeding" (54). Such a mecca, contrasted with the charmlessness of his slave youth on Anthony's plantation, makes Douglass feel he knows the meaning of the saying "being hanged in England is preferable to dying a natural death in Ireland" (54). Although Annapolis, seen en route to Baltimore, impresses Douglass with its size, the latter city changes the young slave irrevocably. As Douglass soon finds out, the "city slave is almost a freeman, compared with a slave on the plantation . . . [enjoying] privileges altogether unknown to the slave on the plantation" (60). Able to hire his own time, associate with white playmates and fellow workers, and attend religious gatherings with his fellow blacks, Douglass makes the indispensable first steps to the self-made life. As he gratefully acknowledges, but for the mere circumstance of being removed from that plantation to Baltimore, I should have to-day, instead of being here seated by my own table, in the enjoyment of freedom and the happiness of home, writing this Narrative, been confined in the galling chains of slavery. Going to live at Baltimore laid the foundation, and opened the gateway, to all my subsequent prosperity.   *(56)*

At the age of eight, Benjamin Franklin had been marked for college, for Josiah Franklin had identified his youngest son as "the Tithe of his Sons to the Service of the Church" (1313). As Franklin recalls, "My early Readiness in learning to read (which must have been very early, as I do not remember when I could not read) . . . encourag'd [my father] in this Purpose of his" (1313). Grammar school and a "School for Writing and Arithmetic," however, are the highest levels of formal education he attains. Family finances necessitate the removal of the ten-year-old from school and his placement at a trade. From then on, the future printer, editor, and colonial leader is largely self-taught.

Franklin's first critic is his father, who comes across an exchange of letters between his son and a friend, John Collins. The two young men have been debating the "Propriety of educating the Female Sex in Learning":

> [My father] took occasion to talk to me about the Manner of my Writing, observ'd that tho' I had the Advantage of my Antagonist in correct Spelling and pointing (which I ow'd to the Printing House) I fell far short in elegance of Expression, in Method and in Perspicuity. . . . I saw the Justice of his Remarks, & thence grew more attentive to the *Manner* in Writing.   *(1319)*

Franklin paid attention to his father's advice, for he had already envied Collins's greater ease in speaking and broader vocabulary, believing the points won by his friend were gained on elegance, rather than on facts. If smoothness of presentation were lacking on his part, he would seek to gain that fluency—but love of language alone does not compel his efforts. Franklin properly links a command of the written word with power.

When Josiah Franklin points out, in response to his son's two published poems, that "Verse-makers were generally Beggars," Franklin is pleased that his father has saved him from being "most probably a very bad" poet (1318). His flair for versifying is channeled into rehearsals for his essays; to improve his vocabulary, he casts prose into verse, and then rewrites his exercises into essays. He begins with articles from the London paper *The Spectator*:

> The continual Occasion for Words of the same Import but of different Length . . . would have laid me under a constant Necessity of searching for Variety, and also have tended to fix that Variety in my Mind, and make me Master of it. Therefore I took some of the Tales and turn'd them into Verse: And after a time, when I had pretty well forgotten the Prose, turn'd them back again. *(1319–1320)*

A lack of formal schooling does not stop the young Franklin from winning friends and influencing people, for he merely works at his chosen craft in unorthodox ways. His first published essay, anonymously submitted, is mistakenly believed to have been written by "Men of some Character among us for Learning and Ingenuity" (1323); it appeared in 1722, while Franklin was still indentured to his brother.

Free time, at a premium for this colonial printer's apprentice, was skillfully rearranged in order that he might turn any spare minute to his advantage. To that end, and to save a penny and pursue his vegetarian diet, Franklin offers to board himself. His brother agrees, leaving the younger to eat "often . . . no more than a Bisket or a Slice of Bread, a Handful of Raisins or a Tart from the Pastry Cook's, and a Glass of Water" (1321). Raised by a Puritan father who taught his children not to pay attention to what was on their plates—only to consume it—Franklin makes the most of his newly freed-up time. By not going off with his brother for meals, he has the quiet shop to himself; the money he saves by stinting on his food allowance can be used to purchase books. The sacrifice, Franklin tells us, is all to the good: "I made the greater Progress from that greater Clearness of head and quicker Apprehension which usually attend Temperance in Eating and Drinking" (1321). This hunger for information, which Franklin invokes from his earliest conscious moments—"From a Child I was fond of Reading, and all the little Money that came into my Hands was ever laid out in Books" (1317)—young Frederick Douglass also exhibited.

Douglass cannot pursue reading at a tender age. Instead, he speaks of his early sorrow at another kind of ignorance:

> I have no accurate knowledge of my age, never having seen any authentic record containing it. . . . A want of information concerning my own [birthdate] was a source of unhappiness to me even during

childhood. . . . I was not allowed to make any inquiries of my master
concerning it. *(23)*

No days, no months, no years comprise a slave child's simplest facts; the
closest most can come to a birthdate is "planting-time, harvest-time,
cherry-time" (23). As Douglass discovers, the inquiring spirit of a Franklin
would be grounds for punishment in an African American. When Douglass
first begins his acquaintance with the written English language, he is about
eight years old; a serendipitous turn of fate has sent him to the home of his
owner's brother. There Douglass finds that a slave can be not only free of
fear but even comfortable in the presence of a white person. The "heavenly" disposition of Sophia Auld, his new master's wife, is further gilded
by her naïve belief that a young boy, whatever his color, should learn his
letters. "Very soon after I went to live with Mr. and Mrs. Auld, she very
kindly commenced to teach me the A, B, C. After I had learned this, she
assisted me in learning to spell words of three or four letters" (58).

At this point precisely, the real education of both Sophia Auld and
Frederick Douglass begins. Mr. Auld, upon discovering his wife's doings,
"at once forbade Mrs. Auld to instruct me further, telling her, among other
things, that it was unlawful, as well as unsafe, to teach a slave to read."
Hugh Auld well knows the fruits of that forbidden tree of knowledge:
"unmanageable . . . discontented and unhappy" servants (58). James
Franklin, dissatisfied with the increasing independence and "provoking"
nature of his younger brother, also finds that a little knowledge, in an inferior, is a dangerous thing.[36] A dismayed Douglass nevertheless appreciates
the "new and special revelation . . . with which my youthful understanding
had struggled": the continued enslavement of the black man to the white
derives in large part from the former's illiteracy. Auld's harsh prescription
impresses itself deeply on the perceptive boy, for the very vehemence of the
ban gives him direction. This prohibition of education spelled out the
means of Douglass's deliverance:

> Though conscious of the difficulty of learning without a teacher, I set
> out with high hope and a fixed purpose, at whatever cost of trouble, to
> learn how to read. The very decided manner with which he spoke, and
> strove to impress his wife with the evil consequences of giving me
> instruction, served to convince me that he was deeply sensible of the
> truths he was uttering. It gave me the best assurance that I might rely
> with the utmost confidence on the results which, he said, would flow
> from teaching me to read. *(59)*

Although master then of but a few written words, with this exchange the child leaps toward an adult's intellectual estate.

Like Franklin, Douglass has to steal odd moments from his daily tasks to build up his store of knowledge. "Nothing seemed to make her [Sophia Auld] more angry than to see me with a newspaper. She seemed to think that here lay the danger" (64). As his actions are closely watched, Douglass formulates a lesson plan dependent on his daily tasks. Local poor white children are his unwitting accomplices:

> When I was sent of errands, I always took my book with me, and by going one part of my errand quickly, I found time to get a lesson before my return. I used also to carry bread with me. . . . This bread I used to bestow upon the hungry little urchins, who, in return, would give me that more valuable bread of knowledge.　　　　　　*(65)*

Franklin also uses food as leverage for learning, preferring intellectual sustenance to filling his stomach. Douglass, a sufficiently nourished city slave, trades kitchen leftovers for fulfillment of an entirely different sort.

Writing, a matter of pragmatic style to Franklin, is initially to Douglass a literal means out. The former slave remembers his schoolroom as a "board fence, brick wall, and pavement; my pen and ink a lump of chalk." A careful study of the manner in which shipyard timbers are marked continues his ABCs (71, 70). The discarded workbook of his young master gives him the opportunity to practice penmanship:

> By this time, my little Master Thomas had gone to school, and learned to write, and had written over a number of copy-books. . . . When left thus [alone], I used to spend the time in writing in the spaces left in Master Thomas's copy-book, copying what he had written. . . . [A]fter a long, tedious effort for years, I finally succeeded in learning how to write.　　　　　　*(71)*

By early adolescence Douglass, like Franklin, finds works on which to model his own thoughts, if not the prose that will spring forth years later. Franklin lists Bunyan's *Pilgrim's Progress*, Plutarch's *Lives*, and volumes by Cotton Mather and Daniel Defoe as affecting his early development; John Locke's *Essay on Human Understanding*, Xenophon on Socrates, and a number of Enlightenment essays also fall into his hands (1317, 1321). Douglass can record few literary influences from his childhood. He does not mention the Bible, a great influence on his metaphoric style, perhaps because it seems too obvious for a nineteenth-century Christian to point out. Among many examples of the impact of the King James Bible on the *Narrative* are the previously mentioned "bread of knowledge" passage (65), which echoes the New Testament's "Man shall not live by bread alone" (Matthew 4:4), and Douglass's "They love the uppermost rooms at feasts, and the chief seats in the synagogues. . . . But woe unto you, scribes and Pharisees" (158), which paraphrases the Gospels: "Woe unto you, Pharisees! for ye love the uppermost seats in the synagogues" (Luke 11:43). The secular and popular *The Columbian Orator*, which Douglass acquires at about the age of twelve, collected a number of essays in defense of human liberty. The young bondsman is particularly affected by "a dialogue between a master and his [runaway] slave . . . the conversation resulted in the voluntary emancipation of the slave on the part of the master" (66). A speech for Catholic emancipation in Ireland shows him "a bold denunciation of slavery, and a powerful vindication of human rights" as well as the parallel of slave-master relations on a global scale (67). A paucity of actual rhetorical models remains the norm until he takes up life as a free man.[37]

Enlightenment ideals of liberty do a Maryland slave no good. Douglass soon finds gnawing at his soul "that very discontentment which Master Hugh had predicted would follow my learning to read." The horror of his captivity is impressed upon him all the harder by the awareness of another, free life. "In my moments of agony, I envied my fellow-slaves for their stupidity. . . . Anything, no matter what, to get rid of thinking!" (67) To the newly awakened, every word, every object, refers to independence—which tantalizes with its elusiveness. A few years later Douglass would see that the handwritten word could lead him to liberty; as the indentured Franklin had done, the slave would attempt to use his master's own words against him.

As teenagers aspiring toward "man's estate," Franklin and Douglass each use linguistic legerdemain to gain freedom. Having chafed for some time under the stern rule and iron rod of his brother, Franklin decides to use to his advantage his elder brother's troubles with the Boston colonial government. James, already censured by the authorities for publishing libelous materials, seeks to evade further punishment by allegedly placing the management of the *New England Courant* under his younger brother's direction; to do this, the elder Franklin "canceled" the first set of indenture papers, while drawing up another to keep in reserve.

A very flimsy Scheme it was, but however it was immediately executed, and the Paper went on accordingly under my Name for several

Months. At length a fresh Difference arising between my Brother and me, I took upon me to assert my Freedom, presuming that he would not venture to produce the new Indentures.   *(1325)*

As the younger man has guessed, James Franklin is not about to expose himself. Although the legitimacy of his brother's power has been successfully countermanded, the seventeen-year-old Franklin has little choice but to "light out for the territories": with father Franklin's support, James has blacklisted his brother in the area's printing establishments. Though free, the youngest son of Josiah Franklin faced the prospect of having a trade but no place to practice it—a similar situation faced decades later by thousands of freed blacks.

Over a hundred years later, another seventeen-year-old finds his enforced servitude insufferable as well. Douglass has emerged all the stronger from the worst physical degradation he would ever suffer, the nightmarish year bound over to slave-breaker Edward Covey. His new employer, William Freeland, a slave owner who feeds his workers well, allows them ample rest, and gives all as fair treatment as a slave can want, only inspires his newest hired hand further in his desire to be free: "The year [1834] passed off smoothly. . . . I went through it without receiving a single blow. I will give Mr. Freeland the credit of being the best master I ever had, *till I became my own master*" (115). To that end, Douglass contrives to make his escape under the protection of a false pass that he himself writes. Along with his own, he forges four others for his closest friends.

THIS is to certify that I, the undersigned, have given the bearer, my servant, full liberty to go to Baltimore, and spend the Easter holidays. Written with mine own hand, &c., 1835.

William Hamilton,
Near St. Michael's, in Talbot county, Maryland.
(119)

With the above "official" letter, Douglass assumes the guise of his owner's father-in-law, performing the hubristic acts first predicted by Hugh Auld nearly ten years before. In lettered whiteface, Douglass attempts to seize the withheld fire of independence. When his Promethean efforts are foiled by the betrayal of their plans, the little group's capture leads to a startlingly literal evasion: "Henry inquired of me what he should do with his pass. I told him to eat it with his biscuit, and own nothing; and we passed the word around, '*Own nothing;*' and '*Own nothing!*' said we all" (124).

When the literal act of eating one's words becomes this suggestive, the reporting of such an act takes on even greater moment, for the destruction of these white-owned, if not precisely white-authored, letters enables Douglass and his friends to attain their liberty again. More than Douglass's literal words are ingested: the false legality of white slaveholding is consumed as well.[38] As Franklin calls into question the legitimacy of his brother's reign, so does Douglass challenge the right of one man to hold another in thrall.

These legal superiors of the teenaged Franklin and Douglass are not strangers. Franklin's master is his brother James, whom the younger son must obey by the rules of both birth order and employer-owner. Their father, who has been worried that his youngest boy would run off to sea, presses Franklin to enter into service and learn the printing trade.

> I stood out some time, but at last was persuaded and signed the Indentures, when I was yet but 12 Years old. I was to serve as an Apprentice till I was 21 Years of Age, only I was to be allow'd Journeyman's Wages during the last Year. *(1317)*

Like many another indentured child, he has little choice as to the length of his service: it will expire when he reaches twenty-one. Until then, James Franklin will call all the shots, and the youngest brother can do little beyond bringing his grievances to their father's attention.[39] Although James Franklin is no Edward Covey, Franklin feels that he merits more allowances from a master who is also his sibling:

> Tho' a Brother, he considered himself as my Master, and me as his Apprentice; and accordingly expected the same Services from me as he would from another; while I thought he demeaned me too much in some he requir'd of me, who from a Brother expected more Indulgence. *(1324)*

Disturbed by his friends' admiration of the boy's work, the elder son expresses the belief that Benjamin will become "vain." Franklin, on his part, knows such fears will add to the strain already present. The tension erupts in physical intimidation. "My Brother was passionate and had often beaten me, which I took extreamly amiss" (1324). The blows lead Benjamin to his indenture subterfuge, a maneuver worthy of Brer Rabbit. Stepping into the role of an omniscient narrator, Franklin reflects upon the wisdom of such a ruse: "It was not fair in me to take this Advantage . . . [perhaps I was] too saucy and provoking." But he switches roles again to point to the republican moral of the incident: "I fancy his harsh and tyrannical Treatment of me, might be a means of impressing me with that Aversion to arbitrary Power that has stuck to me thro' my whole Life" (1325, 1324).[40]

Irresponsible power wielded by a blood relative would be a threat with which Douglass would become all too familiar. Part of the torture of slavery for Douglass lay in the natally alienated purgatory in which he and countless other black children were placed: "My father was a white man. . . . The opinion was also whispered that my master was my father" (24). The heart of the matter lay in the slave owner's "double relation of master and father" (26) to his black offspring, which the institution of slavery permitted or encouraged. As Werner Sollors recognizes, one of the great tragedies of American society is the denial of family on racial grounds.[41] Mulatto slave children like Douglass often suffered greatly for their status as living proof of paternal indiscretions: white wives, offended and incensed by these visible evidences of their husbands' infidelity, frequently took extra pains to "correct" the favored slaves' imagined wrongdoings; many whites would honor the children of such unions with such epithets as "yellow devil[s]" (123). The enmity of the wife, occasionally coupled with social opprobrium, often led to the curious "dictate of humanity" that would bring a man to sell his own children: "unless he does this, he must . . . whip them himself," for to do otherwise "only makes a bad matter worse, both for himself and the slave whom he would protect and defend" (26–27).

Captain Anthony, the probable father of Douglass, confirms this abhorrent picture by his frequent whippings of Douglass's Aunt Hester. His mother's attractive sister makes the mistake of preferring a black man, Ned Roberts, to Anthony. For her independence she is tied to a joist and whipped until "she was literally covered with blood" (28). A small child when he first witnesses one of these beatings, Douglass tells the reader that "[I] hid myself in a closet, and dared not venture out till long after the bloody transaction was over. I expected it would be my turn next" (30). Most readers will surmise that the cursing, sadistic brute probably fathered the young boy watching. The twentieth-century reader will find it hard to ignore the twinned dramas—an Oedipal scene ghastly overlaid with the sexual violence of chattel slavery.[42] The cruel irony of the situation is not lost on Douglass. Each use of the title "master" when referring to Anthony resounds with a peculiar chill.

> I was seldom whipped by my old master, and suffered little from any thing else but hunger and cold. I suffered much from hunger, but much

more from cold. . . . I was probably between seven and eight years old when I left Colonel Lloyd's plantation. I left it with joy. I shall never forget the ecstasy with which I received the intelligence that my old master (Anthony) had determined to let me go to Baltimore. *(51–52)*

No ties remain to link Douglass to his home. His mother has died; he has been taken away from his grandmother; his sisters and brother are strangers to him.[43] Douglass gladly "looked for home elsewhere, and was confident of finding none which I should relish less than the one which I was leaving." No hardships loom ahead that he has not already experienced, "Having already had more than a taste of them in the house of my old master" (53). The final, cruelest trial comes when Anthony dies suddenly, leaving no will. Whereas the white children look forward to receiving land and other goods, Douglass is "immediately sent for [from Baltimore], to be valued with the other property. . . . pigs and [slave] children . . . holding the same rank in the scale of being" (73–74). Any fond reminiscences of paternal guidance are well hidden.[44] In antebellum society, the lot of the slave-holder's illegitimate black child was not to inherit but to *be* inherited. When intersected by racial boundaries, natural affinities between parent and child were obliterated. Paternal care, or for that matter patrilineage, could not exist for Douglass.

Both Franklin and Douglass exhibit a peculiar, perhaps American, form of short-sightedness; some might call it egomania. They do not depict the struggles of equals joining against tyranny and oppression, despite the democratic ideals propounded in both books. Both men couch their striking accomplishments in an unaided first-person singular. Franklin frequently speaks of the various flourishing ventures he has undertaken or proposed. Relating the story of an early press he ran with a former co-worker, he notes "I perceive that I am apt to speak in the singular Number, though our Partnership [of Franklin and Meredith] continu'd. The Reason may be, that in fact the whole Management of the Business lay upon me" (1364). The forming of the Junto Club, the public library, the university— all are depicted by Franklin as accomplished with almost no outside assistance. When Douglass decides to make his first escape attempt, he "was not willing to cherish this determination alone. My fellow slaves were dear to me." Still, the former slave carefully places himself in the position of leader and guide, remembering "I therefore, though with great prudence, commenced early to ascertain their views and feelings in regard to their condition, and to imbue their minds with thoughts of freedom"

(116); his fellow bondsmen, however brave, are shown as more or less intelligent followers. In another parallel, Benjamin Franklin's steadfast helpmeet rates just a handful of lines in the *Autobiography*; similarly, Douglass's wife Anna, who helps to bankroll his second, successful escape attempt, appears just twice in the *Narrative*. By contemplating the treatment of interpersonal relationships in Franklin, we can see how Douglass both emulated and diverged from this model of successful striver.

Benjamin Franklin encountered Deborah Read within hours of his arrival in Philadelphia. Recalling his first stroll down the streets of Philadelphia while stuffing bread into his mouth, Franklin imagines that he "certainly did [make] a most awkward ridiculous Appearance" (1329) to his future wife. Within a short time he manages to make a more favorable impression on her, in part due to a new set of clothes and employment, but beyond the sketchy and infrequent details of their courtship and married life, Franklin does not care to expand. Fewer than ten references are made to Deborah in the entire autobiography, and those are hardly revelatory. In that era and well beyond, wives were generally viewed as extensions of their husbands; Franklin's was no exception.

The former Miss Read "prov'd a good & faithful Helpmate, assisted me [Franklin] much by attending the Shop, we throve together, and have ever mutually endeavour'd to make each other happy" (1371). Her diligence and thriftiness come in for commendation, for she "assisted me chearfully in my Business, folding and stitching Pamphlets, tending Shop, purchasing old Linen Rags for the Paper-makers, &c &c." (1381–1382). Very few of Deborah Franklin's personal qualities are revealed. The reader carefully combing through the *Autobiography* finds this the most intimate remark recorded about her; it is also the last made about her, though it comes only about halfway through the narrative:

> Being Call'd one Morning to Breakfast, I found it in a China Bowl with a Spoon of Silver. They had been bought for me without my Knowledge by my Wife, and had cost her the enormous Sum of three and twenty Shillings, for which she had no other Excuse or Apology to make, but that she thought *her* Husband deserv'd a Silver Spoon & China Bowl as well as any of his Neighbours. *(1382)*

Rather than make an observation on women's supposed desire for luxuries, or even his affection for this whimsy, Franklin ends the paragraph by counting these items the first in a collection that would be worth "Hundreds [of] Pounds." Delineation of his wife's character ends with this brief anecdote.

Douglass mentions his wife even less frequently. Freeborn Anna Murray, who receives no credit for her efforts on behalf of her intended in the 1845 *Narrative*, merits only a couple of references. The two married in September 1838, shortly after Douglass's escape from Baltimore.

> At this time, Anna, my intended wife, came on; for I wrote to her immediately after my arrival at New York, (notwithstanding my homeless, houseless, and helpless condition,). . . . In a few days after her arrival . . . [the Rev. J. W. C. Pennington] performed the marriage ceremony. *(145–46)*

Murray functions as little more than a human interest element in the story of Douglass's successful escape. Other than using the first-person plural to describe their passage from New York City to New Bedford, and celebrating the happiness of working "for myself and newly-married wife" (152), Douglass leaves Anna practically invisible. Like Franklin, Douglass remains a husbandly *isolato*. The help of Anna Murray Douglass in his second, successful escape attempt is not acknowledged, although his published remarks on his spouse can be read in the context of that era's cult of domesticity: her sphere is limited to the private, his encompasses the public. His silence about her aid can be seen as part of his reticence about his eventual voyage to freedom; publishing the first two autobiographies before the Emancipation, Douglass believed a certain amount of evasiveness was necessary. In later versions of his autobiography Anna Murray Douglass commands a larger space, but in the critically acclaimed and best-selling *Narrative* she is little more than a cipher. Despite her resourcefulness, perseverance, and attractiveness, we find her husband silent about her. As Valerie Smith notes, "most of the narratives by men represent the life in slavery and the escape as essentially solitary journeys . . . [suggesting] that they were attempting to prove their equality, their manhood, in terms acceptable to their white, middle-class readers."[45]

In the *Autobiography*, Benjamin Franklin's boyhood friend, John Collins, and his chum of Philadelphia and London, James Ralph, make quite an impression on both author and reader. As both men come to bad ends, there's an object lesson implicit in their misspent lives. Our earliest encounter with Collins introduces him as Franklin's debating partner; his youthful glibness foreshadows adult vice. Collins's further shortcomings are later hinted at when Franklin escapes from Boston, for his friend obtains pseudonymous passage for Franklin to New York "under the Notion of my being a young Acquaintance of his that had got a naughty Girl with Child, whose Friends would compel me to marry her" (1325–1326). When Collins, hearing of Franklin's success in Philadelphia, follows him there, his presence proves a burden: "during my Absence he [Collins] had acquir'd a Habit of Sotting with Brandy . . . & behav'd very oddly. He had gam'd too and lost his Money" (1336). A drunkard, gambler, and, finally, thoroughgoing reprobate, Collins moves on to Barbados, having borrowed all the money he could from Franklin. The meaning of Collins's life could hardly be more explicit.

The figure of James Ralph similarly serves as an admonition to those who wish to imitate a worthy model: Franklin could not write much more clearly of the way *not* to improve one's station in life. Ralph too leaves his home town with Franklin; they travel to England in search of work and adventure. Where Collins's unsavory dealings are merely hinted at by the recital of his escape ruse and his intemperate excesses, Ralph, with a wife and child, is revealed to be a genuine rake. Once in England, "thro' some Discontent with his Wifes Relations, [Ralph] purposed to leave her on their Hands, and never return again"; in fact, he "seem'd quite to forget his Wife" and she is quickly supplanted by another (1343, 1345). The perils of bad company become clear when Franklin, still under twenty one, begins to forget the promises he made to Miss Read. Indeed, the temporarily debauched printer falls so far as to make overtures to Ralph's new companion in his friend's absence. Franklin's licentious bumbling ends the friendship. He speaks further of it only to say that his mistake afforded him relief from ever-growing financial obligations (Ralph, like Collins, has the unfortunate habit of fiscal irresponsibility). Monetary matters, more than personal attachments, rule Franklin's loyalties.

In contrast, the friendships of Douglass's young manhood are remarkable for their emotional tenor. Until his year with Edward Covey and subsequent residence with Mr. Freeland, Douglass mentions no specific friends, only fellow slaves as a group. While with Covey, however, Douglass calls upon his fellow slave Sandy Jenkins for aid. The fellow offers "root magic":

> I found Sandy an old adviser. He told me, with great solemnity, I must go back to Covey; but [I must first harvest] a certain *root*, which, if I would take some of it with me, carrying it *always on my right side*, would render it impossible for Mr. Covey, or any other white man, to whip me. . . . To please him, I at length took the root. *(102)*

Depicted as an "ignorant" and superstitious sort, Jenkins appears to be the fatal flaw in Douglass's first escape scenario. The lone slave who backs out of the freedom bid, Jenkins is the man to whom Douglass turns the moment he senses they've been found out, saying "We are betrayed!" When Jenkins rather quickly answers that he has just had the same thought, a saddened Douglass realizes that his dreams of freedom have been dashed (121). Whether fearful of slave owner reprisals or desirous of whatever gain the betrayal would offer, the root man has evidently sold out his comrades.[46]

But Jenkins is not the only friend Douglass has. The two Harris brothers, Henry and John, are also involved in the escape plan. Described by Douglass as "quite intelligent" (112–13), they take reading lessons from Douglass and participate in his Sabbath school. In a group of "warm hearts and noble spirits" (116), the brothers impress Douglass with their manliness. When the arresting whites try to tie Henry up, the newly emboldened slave dares them to do their worst—"you can't kill me but once. Shoot, shoot,—and be damned! *I won't be tied!*" (123). Still, Mrs. Freeland insists that the Harrises would never have attempted to flee were it not for Douglass's baleful, mixed-blood's influence—and as Douglass has earlier spoken of instilling in his fellow escapees' minds a love of liberty, the reader might question the extent of Henry Harris's defiance. As Douglass has said of himself: "You have seen how a man was made a slave; you shall see how a slave was made a man" (97). For Douglass, the worst part of the affair is a permanent parting from his friends. The whites decide that Douglass is the ringleader: he alone will be punished.

> I regarded this separation as a final one. It caused me more pain than any thing else . . . I was ready for any thing rather than [this]. . . . It is due to the noble Henry to say, he seemed almost as reluctant at leaving the prison as at leaving home to come to the prison. *(126)*

Henry Harris and his brother remain behind in rural Maryland when the ringleader is remanded to the Aulds of Baltimore. Fond though they may be, Douglass's reminiscences of his friends in bondage carry a whiff of superiority. He alone is the superman able to will himself out, to help the deserving, to triumph against all odds. Although an agreeable and heroic picture, the *Narrative* cannot be said to be an entirely reliable one, as later versions of his life tell somewhat different tales.

In this earliest version of his life, Douglass depicts himself as a lone fighter, save for Sandy Jenkins's root in his pocket. All versions of Douglass's autobiography, however, recall the slave-breaker Covey asking for the assistance of another slave, Bill. *My Bondage and My Freedom,* published ten years after the *Narrative*, amplifies this co-worker's role in Douglass's pivotal battle with a white. There Douglass reports Bill's sarcastic rejoinders to Covey: "With a toss of his head, peculiar to Bill, he said, 'Indeed, Mr. Covey, I want to go to work. . . . My master [didn't hire me] to help you whip Frederick.' "[47] In this second version, another slave owned by Covey appears on the scene as well. Caroline, a physically powerful woman, also refuses to come to her master's aid; as Douglass remembers, "We were all in open rebellion, that morning." For her solidarity Caroline is beaten.[48] Both this and the virtually identical version in *The Life and Times of Frederick Douglass* (1892) contradict the *Narrative*'s image of Douglass as a man acting alone.[49] Perhaps an older Douglass, like the elderly Philadelphian, wished to correct the "errata" of his youth.[50]

Although it may seem unbrotherly of Douglass to downplay or not report the loyalty of his fellow slaves, the reasons for his doing so in the *Narrative* are strategic, at least in part. In the earliest version of his life, Douglass plays the role of isolato in order to win the approbation of his largely white audience, an audience weaned on such American heroes as Franklin and Andrew Jackson. For Douglass to win the laurels of self-made man meant that slaves as a whole would benefit, for Douglass's first autobiography has as much to do with slaves as a class as it does with the author as an individual bondsman. The stereotypical image of the whipped and bleeding slave would not always do to raise indignation. A passage from *The Life and Times* provides a gloss on his first incarnation: "Human nature is so constituted that it cannot honor a helpless man, although it can pity him; and even that it cannot do long, if the signs of power do not arise."[51] When he first joined the antislavery battle, the prescient Douglass realized that to simply tell his wrongs and sufferings, as his white colleagues urged him, was not enough. "It did not entirely satisfy me to *narrate* wrongs—I felt like *denouncing* them."[52] Not only interpretation was necessary, but self-mythologizing as well. To gain the undivided attention of his white audiences Douglass had to tap into the cultural myths already prevailing in mid-nineteenth-century America. A new image of a self-made man—a Franklinian Douglass—was the result.

> Properly speaking, there are in the world no such men as self-made men. That term implies an individual independence of the past and present which can never exist.[53]

In the last part of his life Frederick Douglass toured the country giving speeches and lectures on a variety of subjects, from the treatment of the

Negro to the legacy of the Civil War. One of his most popular speeches, "Self Made Men," revolved around the meaning and purposes of the individual who made himself from nothing.[54] In this speech, Douglass finds a standard in such historical figures as the white United States president Abraham Lincoln and the black mathematician Benjamin Banneker. Both men had the requisite humble beginnings, the "Obscurity" that Franklin would be among the first to invoke; both fit well under Douglass's rubric for such achievers:

> Self made men . . . are the men who owe little or nothing to birth, relationship, friendly surroundings; to wealth inherited or to early approved means of education; who are what they are, without the aid of any of the favoring conditions by which other men usually rise in the world and achieve great results.　　　　　　　　　　　　(6–7)

By employing this definition Douglass could place himself within a tradition of American representative men beginning with Benjamin Franklin. If any person could count himself as having owed "little or nothing to birth, relationship, [or] friendly surroundings," it would be the American slave.

In his *Narrative* Douglass succinctly portrays himself as such a self-created *man*, as Deborah McDowell has rightly perceived: "In [the 1845 *Narrative's*] focus on the public story of a public life, which signifies the achievement of adult male status in Western culture, autobiography reflects and constructs that culture's definition of maleness."[55] This literary maneuver presents precisely the image of the manly isolato acting "without the aid of any . . . favoring conditions." The support of his men friends is more generously credited than that of his wife, though such aid is described from the vantage point of a wiser older brother. Douglass's description of the great turning point in his life, his fight with Covey, exemplifies this isolationist, androcentric strategy.[56] Rightly regarded as the centerpiece of the *Narrative*, this epiphany on the connection between physical and psychological liberation must also be read as the text of one who wills and portrays himself as self-begotten:

> This battle with Mr. Covey was the turning-point in my career as a slave. It rekindled the few expiring embers of freedom, and revived within me a sense of my own manhood. It recalled the departed self-confidence, and inspired me again with a determination to be free. The gratification afforded by the triumph was a full compensation for whatever else might follow, even death itself. . . . My long-crushed spirit rose,

cowardice departed, bold defiance took its place; and I now resolved that, however long I might remain a slave in form, the day had passed forever when I could be a slave in fact.[57]

Depicted in the *Narrative* as a battle between two men, one white and free, one black and enslaved, the combat is in reality an attempt by the slave-breaker to physically intimidate one young slave; the effort is spoiled by the refusal of the other slaves to come to Covey's aid. To Douglass the author, however, it is important to show himself acting alone, both to bolster his image as self-reliant man and to improve the picture of slaves as a group.

What figures most significantly to the *Narrative*'s author about self-made men is not simply that they rise almost single-handedly, but that they do so "in open and derisive defiance of all the efforts of society and the tendency of circumstances to repress, retard, and keep them down."[58] As a black, Douglass is excluded from the category of human being; he is property. Under such a formulation, the invoked character of Benjamin Banneker is even more heroic than his white counterparts because he has overcome, in some respects, the obstacle of race prejudice. The dual purposes of the *Narrative*'s author—to depict Douglass as an heir to Franklin and other white American models, and to improve the reputation of African Americans among white Americans—conflate into ambiguity, presenting the twentieth-century reader with an interpretive puzzle. Can the reader extend the lessons of the *Narrative* to all of the enslaved, or should Douglass's story be read as that of a single, extraordinary man? Manifestly, Douglass means for us to think of him as an individual, even though he paints himself a synecdochic African American male.[59] We cannot assume white readers' ability to see him standing in for all bondsmen when most slaves' daily lives appeared to contrast with his so greatly.

Douglass's example of the self-made man extended the nascent tradition of American individualism by the very fact of his exclusion from it. Douglass was aware of his proscription, and depended upon his liberal audience's shame, as can be seen in his reliance on irony as a rhetorical device. This comment typifies his tone: "It was necessary to keep our religious masters at St. Michael's unacquainted with the fact, that, instead of spending the Sabbath in wrestling, boxing, and drinking whisky, we were trying to learn how to read the will of God."[60] Douglass's redefinition of what it means to be a pious citizen augments and extends the reader's understanding of American identity. If a temperate, hard-working, self-educated Christian—even one of "sable" complexion—could not be considered an American, the parameters of the term had to be delineated afresh. The effect of the *Narrative*, if not Douglass's explicit intent, was to break with the prevailing qualifications by including a black man in the category of "self made man."

A reading of the captivity narratives of the colonial period shows us that Americans have long viewed themselves as a New World *judaea capta*, a chosen people sent out into "a howling wilderness" in order to bring the light of Protestantism to a continent devoid of Christian teachings. Douglass and other black Christians, whether enslaved or free, similarly interpreted the trials of their people; there should be no surprise in finding a reference to Psalm 137—"By the rivers of Babylon there we sat down, yea, we wept when we remembered Zion"—in both black and white narratives. Common methods of typological explication and common experiences of deliverance from heathen oppressors dictated similarities of genre, if not of purpose. References to and echoes from mainstream works in the literature of black America herald the literary birth of another, quintessentially New World form.[61]

The nineteenth-century African American narrator's simultaneous self-placement within a continuum of New World trials and triumphs while viewing himself as a Christian seeking emancipation anticipated the double status W. E. B. Du Bois would seek to explain at the beginning of the twentieth century. Written less than a decade after Douglass's death in 1895, Du Bois's most oft-quoted lines provide insight into the *Narrative* and much African American writing:

> This American world . . . only lets [the Negro] see himself through the revelation of the other world. It is a peculiar sensation, this double-consciousness, this sense of always looking at one's self through the eyes of others, of measuring one's soul by the tape of a world that looks on in amused contempt and pity. One ever feels his two-ness,— an American, a Negro; two souls, two thoughts, two unreconciled strivings; two warring ideals in one dark body.[62]

Apposite amplification of Du Bois's conception of double-consciousness can be found in the work of symbolic anthropologist Victor Turner. The doubly conscious men and women of African descent reveal themselves to be those marginal actors Turner has termed "liminal entities . . . [possessing] no status, property . . . [or] position in a kinship system"; such individuals, he asserts, frequently come to stand for society's most human aspects.[63] Turner further notes that "liminality, marginality, and structural inferiority are conditions in which are frequently generated myths, symbols, rituals, philosophical systems, and works of art."[64] The very precariousness of nineteenth-century African Americans foretold their position as arbiters of moral direction and purveyors of literary commentary. Deprived of status and property, natally alienated and structurally inferior, Frederick Douglass's extraordinary success as self-made man can seem almost unsurprising.

If the self-conscious act of writing the *Narrative* makes Douglass the prototypical yet new American, then that confirms that a citizen of the United States—or any other modern state—should be conversant with and master of its written means of power. As Benedict Anderson shows, the rise of "print-capitalism," or vernacular literacy on a mass scale, "made it possible for rapidly growing numbers of people to think of themselves, and to relate themselves to others, in profoundly new ways."[65] Douglass's appropriation of the memoir of the self-made man illustrates the ability of the "socially dead" to seize upon literacy as a means of resurrection, if not of rebirth.[66] If "writing always increases the power at the disposal of a civilization, but who wields this power toward what ends is a cultural variable,"[67] then Douglass's literacy and subsequent scaling of the heights of nineteenth-century rhetorical excellence signal the coming of a new order—albeit a literary one rather than a social one. Whether Douglass specifically takes on the shade of Franklin becomes moot compared to his writing himself into a tradition then limited to white males. Franklin's memoirs, in circulation by the time of Douglass's manhood, could well have served as a template for the *Narrative*. More meaningfully for this analysis, correspondences between the two autobiographies should be drawn where they have been previously prevented by restrictive definitions of what makes American, and African American, literature. The "unreconciled strivings" of Douglass, attempting to be both the representative American man and an African American, produce much of the ambiguity and tension in his work. This ambivalence and strain prove that Douglass's struggles with the limitations of self-presentation were those of a genuinely Representative Man. Yet the autobiographical writings of Harriet Jacobs, Harriet Wilson, Elizabeth Keckley, and Eliza Potter demonstrate that the representative American was also a black woman.

5

ॐ

THE BLACKWOMAN IN THE ATTIC

Regardless of their feelings toward Stowe herself or toward her creation, early Afro-American writers inevitably wrote in her wake. This is not to suggest that most black authors consciously modeled their work upon *Uncle Tom's Cabin*. To do so would be to give the book, as great an impact as it had, more credit than it deserves. Rather, Stowe's best-seller embodied a whole constellation of preexisting, often conflicting ideas regarding race, powerfully dramatized them in a sentimental fashion, presented them with an unabashedly didactic reformist message, and finally, proceeded to sell like the dickens.

—Richard Yarborough

In ways Harriet Beecher Stowe could never have predicted, *Uncle Tom's Cabin* began one tradition of African American fiction, a tradition of signification upon those "preexisting, often conflicting ideas" about black Americans.[1] Although Stowe was a white woman writing for a white audience, she commenced a dialogue that would be concerned with the fictional definition—or self-definition—of the African American. Her 1852 novel, focusing on both white and black characters and coming at a time when interest in the slave was at an all-time high, was seen as the definitive statement on both the perils of slavery for whites and blacks and the nature of the enslaved. Her white contemporaries divided into pro- and antislavery camps, with the latter more or less convinced of the slave's humanity. Stowe's earliest black readers, on the other hand, while generally warm in their praise for her abolitionism, knew well that much was missing from the novel.

Discussing the role *Uncle Tom's Cabin* has played in shaping the course of African American fiction, Richard Yarborough has written that

Stowe's work played a major role of establishing the level of discourse for the majority of fictional treatments of the African American that were to follow—even for those produced by blacks themselves.... With its extraordinary synthesizing power, *Uncle Tom's Cabin* presented African American characters, however derivative and distorted, who leaped with incredible speed to the status of literary paradigms and even cultural archetypes with which subsequent writers—black and white—have had to reckon. *(46–47)*[2]

He notes that "most free northern blacks in the 1850s, however, saw *Uncle Tom's Cabin* as a godsend destined to mobilize white sentiment against slavery," even though many early African American writers objected to the stereotypes and attitudes expressed throughout the novel (68). Literate protests—carried on in editorials, personal letters, and novels—revealed that "early African American fiction writers inevitably wrote in [Stowe's] wake" (72). Despite the first, fictional responses to *Uncle Tom's Cabin*—William Wells Brown's *Clotel; or the President's Daughter* (1853), Frank J. Webb's *The Garies and their Friends* (1857), and Martin R. Delany's *Blake; or the Huts of America* (1859)[3]—novels were not the only genre of rejoinders.

Because Stowe made much of her argument via a story centered on the elements of family life, black or white, with special emphases on the trials of women and children, her most astute critics locked pens with her on just these grounds. *Our Nig*, called a "novelized autobiography" by any number of critics, was based on the life of its freeborn author, Harriet E. Wilson, and published in 1859.[4] Two years later Harriet Jacobs, born a slave in Edenton, North Carolina, published her autobiography, *Incidents in the Life of a Slave Girl*, under the pseudonym of Linda Brent.[5] Both Wilson's and Jacobs's autobiographies, in fictionalized, anonymous, or pseudonymous guise, drew upon the same conventions of the sentimental novel and an appeal to womanly instinct that Stowe had used. Yet like their coeval, Eliza Potter, both women drew authorial strength from anonymous or pseudonymous postures; such strategies of "fictionalization," as William L. Andrews has remarked, were ways of achieving rhetorical and intellectual freedom.[6] When Wilson and Jacobs appropriated the emotional tactics of Stowe and her fellow "scribbling women," the familiar scenes of seduction and abandonment, maternal love, and Christian home took on altered if not radical meaning. Of course, others besides black women manipulated the "feminine" stratagems of the day for the abolitionist cause: William Wells Brown and Jacobs's own editor, white abolitionist Lydia Maria Child, were but two among many.[7] As already noted, much of early African American fiction responded to the challenge posed by Stowe's novel: how could writers in the nineteenth century "write the unutterable"?[8] I expand that observation further by examining how two black women autobiographers respond not only to *Uncle Tom's Cabin* but also, though not as obviously, to Brown's *Clotel*.[9]

With the appearance of these three works, an African American rescripting of the domestic scenarios of *Uncle Tom's Cabin* was underway. These writers reiterated many of the issues Stowe had so resoundingly brought to the public, and there are many parallels between her strategies and those of her emulators and reinventors. The introductions and prefaces of *Our Nig* and *Incidents* show that Wilson and Jacobs assumed themselves to be different sorts of authors than Stowe: African American women were on the defensive in a way that a white woman, even one concerned about speaking in public, or even a black man such as Brown did not have to be. Therefore they would recast the model of the African American woman's home offered by Brown's *Clotel* as well. Their literary strategies, or offensives, are presented veiled or indirectly, in part because of the dangers of a black woman speaking "promiscuously"—not only to women but also to men, not only to blacks but also to whites. Although Wilson and Jacobs showed their allegiance to the reigning model of domesticity, they also rejected aspects of that vision, revising it to suit their own. In their figurative construction of homes or homelessness, all three authors impress upon their readers the significance of a black woman's physical space, in what Melvin Dixon has recognized as an identifiable strain in African American literature: "Against the constricting space for personal growth that was the plantation, singers and writers established alternative places of refuge, regeneration, and performance that would ensure deliverance from bondage."[10] Elaborating upon the dynamics of black female control over space, actual or absent, indoor or outdoor, to which Wilson and Jacobs point, I expand upon Jacobs's loophole metaphor and the examinations of domestic space developed by Valerie Smith, Harryette Mullen, Hortense Spillers, and Gilbert and Gubar.[11] Particularly relevant for me is the observation that black women's writing "differed in significant ways from that of black men in its ability to imagine cultural possibilities specifically engendered by women's *space* and woman's work."[12] Although they employ familiar literary, rhetorical, and ideological techniques, black women's autobiographical works begin the last part of the first stage of literature by all African Americans. Indeed, they do not succeed *despite* these preconditions but rather *because of* them: hemmed in by rhetorical limitations much as they were limited physically in their lives, black women authors at mid-century had to transcend the inherited texts of mainstream America.

Harriet Beecher Stowe's continual asides to her readers show that she assumes them to be of her own class and race, if not sex; her reliance on the ironical mode and her invocation of the holiest texts of white American culture—Fourth of July speeches, the Declaration of Independence—all stress her attention to a white audience and a white nation. Her questions interrogate the audience about what they would do if in the slave's place, confirming that black readers, if any, were not the targets of her appeal. If black Americans were to benefit from the lessons preached in Stowe's novel, it would be by their acquiescence to their transfer from the alleged paternalism of southern slavery to the patronizing dead-end jobs allowed in post-bondage society. To accept the world depicted in *Uncle Tom's Cabin* would be to accept a society in which "true" black Americans would be inferiors; talented and educated "mulattos" would be African-American misfits destined for exile. Then as now, this was not a world view that African Americans would receive without protest.

Unlike Brown, Jacobs, and Wilson, the educated, white, middle-class Stowe possesses inherent authority:

> The writer has often been inquired of, by correspondents from differ-ent parts of the country, whether this narrative is a true one; and to these inquiries she will give one general answer. . . . She has endeavored to show it [slavery] fairly, in its best and its worst phases.
>
> *(Uncle Tom's Cabin 2:310, 314)*[13]

A white woman speaking to her peers, Harriet Beecher Stowe does not begin her narrative with an admission of inadequacy or modesty, although such a confession was in keeping not only with classical rhetorical style but also with reigning ideas of female decorum. "In Victorian novels written by women, earnest direct address [the 'you' or 'dear reader' interpolations] evolved as an alternative to public speaking 'in person,' which was forbid-den to respectable females."[14] Yet curiously, although Stowe's narrative persona, prone to repeated direct addresses, is prominent from the first, her self comes across most insistently in the concluding pages rather than in the opening paragraphs, as one might expect. In her preface, not a single "you" intervenes; and while she apologizes indirectly for the sharpness of the pictures drawn, she does not apologize for the telling (*UTC* 1:vii).[15] I suggest further that her position as a middle-class *white* woman, the daughter, sister, and wife of Protestant ministers named Beecher, served as her bulwark against accusations of immodesty (although that position hardly exonerated her from such charges). What perhaps is most salient is not whether she writes as "male" or "female," but that she remains in the privileged racial category of "white." That option was not available to all who wrote in defense of African American society.

By prefixing both an author's preface and a "biography" of himself to *Clotel*, William Wells Brown self-authenticates his novel.[16] As noted in chapter 3, Brown rewrites his autobiography in the third person in order to present it as an authenticating document; he "is willing to forsake the goal of presenting personal history in literary form in order to promote his books and projects"—in this example, to introduce his first novel to a white audience.[17] This newly configured, sanitized biography of Brown parallels the autobiographies of Wilson and Jacobs in that it is apparently not told by the author himself, or told by him behind a screen. Such a tactic should not surprise readers already familiar with the trickster aspects of his first *Narrative*. But before he tells this cleaned-up life story, Brown includes an author's "Preface" signed W. Wells Brown, with his London address appended beneath. Already a published writer and notable figure in abolitionist circles, Brown here acknowledges his position of authority. The preface does not trade, as did Stowe's, on images of victimized "unhappy Africa" or ask for "sympathy and feeling for the African race" (*UTC* 1:vi). Brown instead takes the dispassionate stance of a historian, intoning that "more than two hundred years have elapsed since the first cargo of slaves was landed on the banks of the James River" and asserting that "were it not for persons in high places owning slaves, and thereby giving the system a reputation, and especially professed Christians, Slavery would long since have been abolished" (iii, iv). Rather than wringing his hands over an oppressed group or evil owners, Brown lays the blame squarely at the door of "higher" whites, northern and southern, who do nothing. Furthermore, this opening contains neither direct addresses to gentle (or otherwise) readers nor self-deprecating references to the author's lack of skill. Indeed, Brown firmly attests that if "British influence [is brought] to bear upon American slavery, the main object for which this work was written will have been accomplished" (v). In his preface at least, he avoids appeals to sentiment or maneuvers to bring morally uplifting tears to his audience's eyes.

For Wilson and Jacobs, such authority cannot be so immediately proclaimed. Like Stowe, black women writers of the age employed direct addresses to their audience, substantial irony, and the myths and symbols of the dominant culture to express authorial indignation. They wrote as outsider-advocates of righteousness in a world of ordinary civil injustice. Yet Jacobs and Wilson were not white women addressing their peers; they were black women writing for, appealing to, and castigating white readers for inaction and insensitivity. *Incidents* revises the rhetorical sympathy wielded so effectively by Stowe, as Dana Nelson has seen, for Jacobs "reformulates sympathy . . . [in order to] equalize the distribution of power."[18] Carla Peterson extends the discussion further, observing that "Both Wilson and Jacobs seem to have required a permission to narrate necessitated by their vulnerability as black women to the violence of race prejudice and slavery and signaled by their use of fictitious names and signatures" (152). Wilson, a former indentured servant, finds it necessary to begin with an excuse: "In offering to the public the following pages, the writer confesses her inability to minister to the refined and cultivated, the pleasure supplied by abler pens" (3). Using the familiar topos of modesty—"my humble position and frank confession of errors will, I hope, shield me from severe criticism"—Wilson locates her efforts among those of many others writing, of whatever race, and specifically points to the reasons she as an individual must offer "crude narrations" (3). Her mistress, "wholly imbued with *southern* principles," is responsible for the incomplete state of Wilson's education, and hence of the work before the reader. The unusual note struck in Wilson's preface is her direct "appeal to her colored brethren . . . for patronage"; she seeks approbation for her venture from her peers as well as from whites. Wilson hopes that rather than censuring her for reaching above her alleged station ("[do not] condemn this attempt of your sister to be erudite"), her fellow African Americans will "rally around me a faithful band of supporters and defenders" (3). They, like her white readers, are petitioned for sufferance; that they are referred to so specifically is noteworthy.[19]

Wilson intends the opening remarks to *Our Nig* as softening agents, as humble words meant to defuse the skepticism she, as a black woman writer, would almost certainly invite. To identify herself only as "Our Nig" was to shield herself from the disbelief of her white readers while simultaneously taking advantage of their convictions of black inferiority. Although her stated purpose in publishing the work is to provide a means of "maintaining [herself] and child without extinguishing this feeble life" (3), *Our Nig*'s preface reveals Wilson's motives to be more than economic.[20] Starting with her introduction, the author reveals the fallacy of Yankee benevolence through her ironic revelations of life in a "Two-Story White House, North." Although concerned with the approval of her readers, Wilson is more eager to reveal northern hypocrisy, as this nod to Stowe's cabin in the South indicates. Were she only interested in a monetary solution to her problems, an emotionally charged, sentimental story of a friendless widow and her sickly little boy would serve as well, if not better. Even Frederick Douglass, often noted for his "masculine" approach to slavery and freedom, does not hesitate to appeal to his readers' sensibilities, as the famous passage on his grandmother's "abandonment" by her former master proves:

> She had served my old master faithfully from youth to old age. She had been the source of all his wealth . . . she had attended him in childhood, served him through life, and at his death wiped from his icy brow the cold death-sweat, and closed his eyes forever. She was nevertheless left a slave—a slave for life—a slave in the hands of strangers . . . to cap the climax of their base ingratitude and fiendish barbarity, my grandmother, who was now very old, having outlived my old master and all his children, having seen the beginning and end of all of them, and her present owners finding she was of but little value, her frame already racked with the pains of old age, and complete helplessness fast stealing over her once active limbs, they took her to the woods . . . and made her welcome to the privilege of supporting herself there in perfect loneliness; thus virtually turning her out to die. *(Narrative, 76–77)*[21]

But Wilson does not straightforwardly adopt the sentimental mode. Like Douglass, she does not wish simply to narrate wrongs, she wishes to analyze them. Douglass, as a powerful male, can afford to look sentimental; Wilson must seek psychic and civil redress under the mocking pseudonym of "Nig."

Harriet Jacobs also seeks literary protection from an assumed identity, offering her story under the guise of "Linda Brent." Assuring her reader that "this narrative is no fiction" (1), Jacobs proclaims that she has not depicted slavery in its worst form. As does Wilson, Jacobs wishes "that I were more competent to the task I have undertaken" (1); she attributes her literary deficiencies to her upbringing under slavery. Economic necessity does not drive Jacobs to tell her story, for her children are grown at the time of its publication. In fact, her earnings from the book were in part used for her political activism (Peterson 150). A need for sympathy does not chiefly motivate her either. Instead, a "desire to rouse the women of the North to a realizing sense of the condition of two millions of women at the South" lends urgency to her task, for the truth of her own story—

and of the other "two millions"—has yet to be told (1). And although Jacobs would have expected some African American readers, she does not specifically address this group in her preface, shrewdly aiming her darts at those who can afford her book *and* profit from the lessons contained therein. Her abolitionism should have made her known to many in the literate black community, whereas Wilson, isolated in rural New England, counted fewer black "friends."[22] Jacobs, addressing an intended white audience, pays lip service to womanly modesty but speaks plainly enough to reveal the sexual exploitation of slavery in all of its ugliness. Even though she deals in euphemisms and omissions, the facts of the matter come across clearly: "Jacobs writes absences and gaps into the events which she chooses to present," as P. Gabrielle Foreman notes; her narrative is "undertold," truthful but hardly the whole story.[23]

Jacobs knew not all whites sought to hide the truth, for her editor, Lydia Maria Child, wanted to shatter the silence of "discreet subjects" herself. Placing her introduction after Jacobs's preface, Child does not at first break with the tradition of authenticating a slave's narrative, but attests that Jacobs "is personally known to me, and her conversation and manners inspire me with confidence" (3). She goes on to explain how a slave, though uneducated in the traditional sense, can write so fluently and insists that her own tasks were only those of an editor. Where Child distinguishes herself from Stowe and cements her solidarity with the aggrieved Jacobs is in her willingness to raise subjects believed unmentionable in polite discourse. "I am well aware," Child writes, "that many will accuse me of indecorum for presenting these pages to the public; for the experiences of this intelligent and much-injured woman belong to a class which some call delicate subjects, and others indelicate" (3–4). Child and Jacobs together force the reader into an apprehension of the entire nature of enslavement, although the nature of their cooperation has been debated vigorously. Although Bruce Mills, for one, believes "Child and Jacobs [alike] came to see that stressing domestic values would more powerfully promote Northern sympathy" (265), other critics have seen the limitations of Child's support. Sandra Gunning, for example, insists that "what Child sees as the point of danger for white women becomes a source of authority for Jacobs" (139).[24] Nevertheless, where Stowe examines the sexual circumstances of slavery via elliptical accounts of black female concubinage, Jacobs and Child ensure their readers understand exactly why the fugitive woman slave might well prefer death to a return.[25]

Stowe, Wilson, and Jacobs all knew the commonly agreed-upon elements of nineteenth-century literary discourse, particularly those allotted to the female author. The first instances we have of their differing approaches are contained within the addresses to the reader. Stowe, sure of her audience in a way that Jacobs and Wilson could never be, assumes a joking familiarity with her readers that the later, black writers could not; her amused and amusing use of the first-person plural indicates her surety. Having to win their audience's ear as well as their approbation, her African American women colleagues thought it necessary to apologize for their low status and alleged incapacities—whether they believed in these handicaps or not—before going on to the matters at hand. And Wilson and Jacobs, in the words of P. Gabrielle Foreman, "insist that they were able to imbue that sphere [of womanhood] with their own meaning, to turn 'motherhood,' as a noncapitalized object, into a 'Motherhood' as self-named subject."[26] "Black" motherhood needed to be rescued from its well-intentioned but misinformed advocates.

Uncle Tom's Cabin abounds with perfect mothers, "mother saviors."[27] From the Kentucky "abolitionist" Mrs. Shelby to the downy-cheeked and steadfast Rachel Halliday, Stowe's maternal models set the ideal for her audience. Mrs. Shelby, when thwarted in her attempt to save Eliza and Uncle Tom, conspires with the slaves Andy and Sam to safeguard the younger mother's escape: she emphatically warns the men not to ride the horses too fast, which her servants correctly understand as the signal to impede Eliza's capture to the fullest. Unable to aid Tom, the loyal factotum who refuses to take flight, Mrs. Shelby nevertheless expresses her irre-proachable sensibilities by going to Tom and Chloe's cabin and sobbing unrestrainedly with their family: "for a few moments they all wept in company. And in those tears they all shed together, the high and the lowly, melted away all the heart-burnings and anger of the oppressed" (1:145). A loyal Christian mother who has educated young Eliza to be the same, Mrs. Shelby possesses virtually no power in the male-controlled slavo-cracy. She can scheme with the slaves against her husband and she can cry sympathetically with them, but she cannot prevent their being sold. Only by properly raising her son George can Mrs. Shelby bring to fruition her dream of a free black peasantry. George's right thinking may thus be ascribed to a variant on "republican motherhood."[28] Having gained his majority, young Shelby frees the slaves in honor of the memory of his beloved, martyred Uncle Tom:

It was on his grave, my friends, that I resolved, before God, that I would never own another slave, while it was possible to free him; that nobody, through me, should ever run the risk of being parted from home and friends, and dying on a lonely plantation, as he died. . . . Think of your freedom, every time you see *Uncle Tom's Cabin*; and let it be a memorial to put you all in mind to follow in his steps, and be as honest and faithful and Christian as he was.   (2:309–10)

Good-intentioned as she might be, Mrs. Shelby can only act through her male descendant. And we must keep in mind that Stowe's solution to slavery is to replace it with a form of enlightened serfdom: the black families will stay on as laborers on the very plantation where they had been slaves; the chief difference lies in their being paid "wages for your work, such as we [Shelby and the workers] shall agree on. The advantage [of freedom] is, that in case of my getting in debt, or dying,—things that might happen,—you cannot now be taken up and sold." That Stowe had doubts about the ability of most former slaves to take care of themselves is revealed in Shelby's remark that it will take them "some time to learn" (1:309) about self-regulation.[29] In keeping with this view of Stowe as conservative and in opposition to most current estimations of Stowe, Lori Askeland goes so far as to assert that Stowe supports patriarchal authority rather than undermining it.[30]

The Quaker Rachel Halliday provides a more active type of concerned motherhood than the slave-holding Shelby. Within her orderly domain, a midwestern home populated by loving and obedient children, domestic tasks are accomplished by suggestion rather than by order:

"Mother" was up betimes, and surrounded by busy girls and boys . . . who all moved obediently to Rachel's gentle "Thee had better," or more gentle "Had n't thee better?" in the work of getting breakfast. . . . If there was any danger of friction or collision from the ill-regulated zeal of so many young operators, her gentle "Come! come!" or "I would n't now," was quite sufficient to allay the difficulty.   (1:204)

The entire household pitches in to do the work of the farm; with such a family, slavery is obviated. Accordingly, "The Quaker Settlement" is just the place for Eliza and Harry to fetch up—and for George Harris to rejoin them. Here would be "the first time that ever George had sat down on equal terms at any white man's table," a table where "the light of a living Gospel . . . preached by a thousand unconscious acts of love and good will" would demonstrate a relevant Christianity to the agnostic fugitive (1:205, 206). Quaker mother and father alike intend that no harm come to the fugitives, even if that means the imprisonment of Simeon Halliday. Should mother and children be left to run the farm, "Mother can do almost everything" (1:206). In this projection of a better, more wholesome United States, Stowe posits a country staffed and directed by thousands of women like Rachel Halliday. An exemplar of true womanhood would be one who not only "feels right," as Stowe says in her "Concluding Remarks," but does right as well. In real life, as Wilson and Jacobs well knew, such women would indeed be more precious than rubies.

Frado, Harriet E. Wilson's literary alter ego, has considerable difficulty finding such a mother, natural or otherwise. Writing against the scenario of the supportive white mother-substitutes helping Eliza time and again in *Uncle Tom's Cabin*—Mrs. Shelby, Mrs. Bird, Rachel Halliday—Wilson shows instead a constellation of white women who are either malignantly unmaternal, such as Frado's own mother or her employer-tormentor Mrs. Bellmont, or wholly ineffectual, like Jane or Abby Bellmont. The biological mother of Frado, a white woman psychically deformed by years of misfortune, can no longer function as a parent. Seduced and abandoned as a young woman, ostracized by the Singleton community following the birth and death of an illegitimate daughter, Mag Smith at last finds a defender in Jim, a black cooper. Compassion for the miserable woman spurs Jim's marriage proposal, and he counters her objections with the following argument:

> You's had trial of white folks, any how. They run off and left ye, and now none of 'em come near ye to see if you's dead or alive. I's black outside, I know, but I's got a white heart inside. Which would you rather have, a black heart in a white skin, or a white heart in a black one?
>
> (13)

Jim's death, however, hardens Mag's heart against the duties of mother-hood. When her new lover suggests that she give her children away, Smith's response is a disappointed snarl: "Who'll take the black devils?" (16). Claudia Tate asserts that the narrator "does not hold her mother personally responsible for her plight, understanding rather that Mag had no choice"; she believes "Frado reconstructs[s] her own caring mother" (Tate 36–37), interpreting the omniscient narrator's references to "Poor Mag" as evidence of the writer's affective bond with her mother. But empathy is not the same as love: understanding why someone performs certain acts does not mean you approve of, or even forgive, her. Despite differences between child-rearing practices now and those of the nineteenth century, a mother who describes her child as an inhabitant of hell, who gives her away because she's a "wild, frolicky thing . . . and . . . severe restraint would be healthful" (18, 20) cannot be seen as loving. When Mag worries about Frado's disappearance the night before she is to be given away, the reader remains unsure whether it's because the mother will miss her or because she fears her plans will go awry. In any event, once located, Frado is forthwith deposited at the Bellmont household while her mother departs with her lover and the younger child: "It was the last time she ever saw or heard of her mother" (23). Perhaps, as Wilson herself wrote, "It was not always thus. She *had* a loving, trusting heart" (5). Her desire for her lost mother—for a good mother of any sort—inevitably leads her to ambivalence, to memories of her mother calling her a "black devil" and of her own wracking sobs for a parent (46, 51). Perhaps because of these ambiguities, Wilson must "reconstruct her own caring mother" and "assume . . . the place of the mother for whom she had longed as a child" for her own son (Tate 37). The unceasing hardships of poverty and single motherhood lead to the cruel irony of Wilson herself being forced to place her child in a foster home. Therein lies her inability to condemn her mother utterly: how could she, when forced to reenact the abandonment of child by mother?

The six-year-old Frado is left in the hands of Mrs. Bellmont, a white mother of several children who rivals Simon Legree in brutality. Within days the small child weeps with weariness from being put to tasks beyond a young girl's ability. Her abuser retaliates with a rawhide whip, announcing Frado's tears "a symptom of discontent and complaining which must be 'nipped in the bud' " (30). Kept from school, save for a few years, Frado is worked ceaselessly. The smallest imagined infraction, such as the retrieval of the wrong size wood, calls for a savage beating: "Mrs. Bellmont, enraged, approached [Frado] and kicked her so forcibly as to throw her upon the floor. Before she could rise, another foiled the attempt, and then followed kick after kick in quick succession and power, till she reached the door" (44–45). To complain, to attempt to tell the truth, even to weep sympathetically over the illness of one of her only protectors brings Frado blows, kicks, gaggings, and other physical abuse. Small wonder, then, when the well-meaning but ineffectual Aunt Abby attempts to reform Frado's uncharitable thoughts toward Mrs. Bellmont's virago daughter Mary, the little servant muses: "S'posen she goes to hell, she'll be as black as I am. Would n't mistress be mad to see her a nigger!" (107) Not until she leaves the Bellmont household does Frado find white women who are prepared to help her, but she finds as many who are ready to hinder her efforts at self-determination. At the end of her story Wilson notes her mistreatment "by professed abolitionists, who did n't want slaves at the South, nor niggers in their own houses, North" (129).

To have asked the young Wilson to honor an ideal of motherly love, or even feminine solidarity, would have been ludicrous. *Our Nig* launches a counterattack on the ideology of the "mother savior" limned in *Uncle Tom's Cabin*. Elizabeth Ammons believes there is "no nurturant maternal world" in Wilson's novel, that the author "jeers at the myth of the mother-savior and the idea that there exists some powerful, subversive, subterranean community of sisterly love among women" (182–83). Although Ammons reads Wilson's bleak depiction of female violence as an argument against a woman-centered society, one does wonder how much white female identity has to do with Frado's predicament: Wilson may in fact make a case for the impossibility of sustaining *any* human relationships in racially bipolar America. The women in *Our Nig* who do not actively mistreat Frado either cannot protect her or appear too late to do much good: Aunt Abby, Mr. Bellmont's sister, gives Frado food and cheering talks whenever she can; the older invalid sister, Jane, does little but murmur indignantly; Mrs. Moore and the women who succor Frado along her path to financial independence appear after her health has been permanently impaired. The male, and presumably powerful, members of the Bellmont family are the obvious shirkers here: neither the father nor either of the two sons present intercedes on Frado's behalf; what interest they have has been construed, very possibly, as sexual.[31] Although it may seem commonsensical, had Harriet Wilson's fictional alter ego been able to claim even one black family member or friend, free or slave, the story would have been very different: contrast Frado's racial isolation with the web of African American social relations recalled by Jacobs. Although the father is described to the reader as "a kind-hearted African," after his death Frado has no African American parent or friend in the world. Even more significant, without the invaluable counsel of an older, experienced black woman—the grandmother figure often encountered in African American literature—the newly free Frado makes an unwise match with the first black man she meets. Without the normal kin and social network of the African American, even in slavery, the antebellum black orphan is more friendless than the worst-off heroine of the era's "women's fiction."

Consider, then, the earlier portrait of black motherly counsel limned by William Wells Brown in *Clotel*. Clotel is the offspring of Thomas Jefferson and his housekeeper, Currer; when Jefferson is "called to Washington" his former concubine, the slave of another, is left behind with her two daughters. She resolves to bring them "up as ladies, as she termed it, and therefore imposed little or no work upon them." Unlike the fictional Cassy and Emmeline, whom sexual service repels, or the real-life Jacobs, with her fighting spirit, Clotel's mother desires that her daughters be noticed by whites; Currer hopes these men will take the girls as concubines so her offspring will "be emancipated and free" (61). Clotel, who does indeed enter into a "marriage" with her white owner, demonstrates an attitude more in keeping with the black female-authored portraits of such arrangements: when she becomes the mother of a daughter, she "reflected upon the unavoidable and dangerous position which the tyranny of society had awarded [Mary and] her soul was filled with anguish" (81). Clotel's worries echo Jacobs's thoughts on the birth of her daughter: "my heart was heavier than it had ever been before. Slavery is terrible for men; but it is far more terrible for women" (*Incidents* 77). Even if Brown wishes to demonstrate to his readers that slavery degrades women, turning some of them into liars or thieves, as his own autobiography declares, why introduce to white readers one who seems oblivious to the sexualized infamy of bondage? Antebellum whites certainly needed no "evidence" of the licentiousness of African American women. Brown may begin the novel with a condemnation of the immorality of slavery, noting that "the marriage relation . . . is unknown and unrecognised in the slave laws of the United States," but he then continues, "when you take into consideration the fact, that amongst the slave population no safeguard is thrown around virtue, and no inducement held out to slave women to be chaste, you will not be surprised . . . [that] *most* of the slave women have no higher aspiration than that of becoming the finely-dressed mistress of some white man" (59; emphasis mine).[32] By subsequently introducing the story of Currer and Clotel, Brown leaves the reader to contemplate what makes Currer less concerned with her daughters' purity than the daughters themselves. White readers, noting that Currer is described as mulatto while Clotel is said by all to be virtually Caucasian, could arrive at the conclusion that it is Clotel's "whiteness"—and thus closeness to European American "morality"—that makes her more concerned with her daughter Mary's eventual status.[33] With defenders like these, Jacobs, Mary Prince, and countless other women ex-slaves might well say, who needs enemies? Nonetheless, Ann duCille would have us recall that Brown's "larger, dialogic context" was that "of nineteenth century sentimental fiction in which white women writers envisioned white heroines who challenge patriarchal authority and oppressive political systems"—and that some of his heroines do just that.[34] As in his self-portrait, discussed in the previous chapter, Brown's tactics here evade easy categorization.

In contrast to the scarcity of good mothering, black or white, in Wilson and Brown, Jacobs's *Incidents in the Life of a Slave Girl* portrays a young slave's life made bearable by the love and support of her grandmother.[35] Unlike Frado, left completely without family after the death of her father and the abandonment of her mother, Jacobs can recall a happy life with both parents: "[We] lived together in a comfortable home; and, though we were all slaves, I was so fondly shielded that I never dreamed I was a piece of merchandise" (5). When Jacobs is six her mother passes away; her father dies before she reaches her teens. In a further blow, Jacobs's sympathetic owner passes away without giving the young slave her freedom, which her friends had surmised would be done. Willed to a five-year-old niece, Jacobs falls under the power of the lascivious Dr. Flint, the child's father. Her persecutions range from abuse by his jealous wife to sexual harassment and physical intimidation by the doctor. Yet unlike the luckless Frado, the young Jacobs has a freed grandmother living in the same small town. Providing her granddaughter with spiritual guidance, moral support, and greatly needed additions to the meager fare and scanty clothing that Dr. Flint allows, Aunt Marthy offers a literally lifesaving counterweight.

As Jacobs recalls, her grandmother "always met us with a smile, and listened with patience to all our sorrows. She spoke so hopefully, that unconsciously the clouds gave place to sunshine" (17). The hard-working Aunt Marthy is known and liked by white Edenton as well, even though the ex-slave once chased at gunpoint a white man who had insulted one of her daughters. In general, though, the older woman counsels patience rather than resistance or flight: "Most earnestly did she strive to make us feel that it was the will of God: that He had seen fit to place us under such circumstances; and though it seemed hard, we ought to pray for content-ment" (17). Safety seems to lie in forbearance and trust in a heavenly reward, although earthly troubles are to be assuaged whenever possible. Her never-ending devotion to her family earns Aunt Marthy the closing lines in Jacobs's narrative:

> It has been painful to me, in many ways, to recall the dreary years I passed in bondage. I would gladly forget them if I could. Yet the retro-spection is not altogether without solace; for with those gloomy recol-lections come tender memories of my good old grandmother, like light fleecy clouds floating over a dark and troubled sea. *(201)*

Although at the end of the narrative Jacobs still regrets that she has not "realized" her life's ambition, to live with her children under a single roof, she nevertheless can compare her current lack to past memories of loving parents, a faithful grandmother, and a *home*.

In Stowe's novel, humble black homes, implied by the subtitle "Life among the Lowly," take second billing to the place where most action occurs—the plantations, lovely or decaying, of whites. Even in a story attempting to illustrate the lives of slaves, their homes rate but the briefest of descriptions: the implicit injustice of Tom's precarious residence is reflected in Jacobs's explicit lack: "I do not sit with my children in a home of my own . . . however humble" (*Incidents* 201). Uncle Tom and wife Chloe's little house may merit a chapter of its own—"An Evening in Uncle Tom's Cabin" (chapter 4)—but more notable is Tom's absence from that home: for virtually the entire narrative he lives elsewhere, and not by choice. As suggested by Stowe's tour guide-like remarks—"Let us enter the dwelling" (1:38)—the white visitor to Tom and Chloe's home will see, among other items, "a bed, covered neatly with a snowy spread; and by the side of it . . . a piece of carpeting, of some considerable size"; over the fireplace are hung "some very brilliant scriptural prints, and a portrait of General Washington" (1:40). Their home is fit for any working person, white or black; it calls to mind nothing so much as the tidy homes admired in New Bedford by the newly escaped slave Frederick Douglass.[36] The very exterior of the slave couple's cabin is charming and, to the white reader in search of the foul pits of slavery, somewhat unexpected:

> In front it had a neat garden-patch, where, every summer, strawberries, raspberries, and a variety of fruits and vegetables, flourished under careful tending. The whole front of it was covered by a large scarlet bignonia [sic] and a native multiflora rose . . . in summer, various brilliant annuals, such as marigolds, petunias, four-o'clocks, found an indulgent corner to unfold their splendors. *(1:33)*

As picturesque as this log dwelling might be, the fact remains that the cabin is "Uncle Tom's Cabin" only by the leave of the paternalistic Shelbys. Tom and Chloe cannot own it, being themselves property. As Houston Baker Jr. remarks, human property could only escape that status by ownership (of other "things," of self); Gillian Brown observes that Stowe's recognition of Tom and Chloe goes only so far as to place them in the category of loved, "properly owned property."[37] That a black American in possession of herself might also be in need of a home is a truth not universally acknowledged.

Perhaps somewhat oddly, as far as readers in the twentieth century are concerned, William Wells Brown responded favorably to Stowe's depiction of the "peculiar institution" and its "pleasant homes."[38] In the same year *Clotel* was published the abolitionist-turned-novelist praised Stowe's novel, saying "Uncle Tom's Cabin has come down upon the dark abodes of slavery like a morning's sunlight . . . awakening sympathy in hearts that never before felt for the slave."[39] Even though *Uncle Tom's Cabin* had been hugely successful as a serial the preceding year, we can surmise that the complimentary Brown wrote his first novel as an addition, if not a corrective, to Stowe's best-seller. More intriguing, Stowe's point of view was shared by another writer whose work Brown appropriated nearly wholesale, making the question of influence more complicated. The early sections of *Clotel* incorporate large chunks of Lydia Maria Child's short story "The Octoroons." While Brown does credit his source, he does it somewhat offhandedly, acknowledging in the "Conclusion" that, "To Mrs. Child, of New York, I am indebted for part of a short story" (222). In both novel and story, much mention is made of melting Negro eyes, sighs, and ill-fated love across the color line; genteelly raised light-skinned young women take poison or go insane rather than submit to sexual bondage. There are differences in the treatments of pale-skinned black women by Stowe, Child, and Brown, however: Ann duCille notes that "rather than dying of broken hearts . . . [Brown's mulattas] use imagination, ingenuity, and courage to outwit their oppressors"; and Carolyn Karcher has earlier noticed Brown's "discomfort with the 'tragic mulatto' theme."[40] Here I examine the way Brown constructs the homes of these "bright, light, and damned near white" heroines, rather than his creation of the characters themselves.

In *Clotel*, Brown's heroines live in homes not of their own selection. The lovely cottage the eponymous heroine inhabits is but a symbol of her degradation: as Shakespeare has written, "lilies that fester smell far worse than weeds." In "The Quadroon's Home," the author sketches out the rise and fall of Clotel's modest love and hopes with a description of the external locale of those dreams:

> About three miles from Richmond is a pleasant plain, with here and there a beautiful cottage surrounded by trees so as scarcely to be seen. Among them was one far retired from the public roads, and almost hidden among the trees. It was a perfect model of rural beauty. The piazzas that surrounded it were covered with clematis and passion flower. The pride of China mixed its oriental looking foliage with the majestic magnolia, and the air was redolent with the fragrance of flowers, peeping out

of every nook and nodding upon you with a most unexpected welcome. The tasteful hand of art had not learned to imitate the lavish beauty and harmonious disorder of nature, but they lived together in loving amity. . . . The gateway rose in a gothic arch, with graceful tracery in iron work, surmounted by a cross, round which fluttered and played the mountain fringe, that lightest and most fragile of vines. *(68)*

This gorgeous setting exhibits the orientalism of the Negro "other" that Hortense Spillers has identified in Stowe's description of St. Clare mansion: "the markings of landscape all signify the 'exotic,' the strange, the foreign."[41] Brown's adoption of the language of Child, whose work may be said to acquiesce to white superiority, leaves little metaphorical room to maneuver. Commenting on the ways gender informs Brown's revisions— that in fact his "tragic mulatta" figures as a female example of slave resistance—M. Giulia Fabi underscores Brown's inability to escape prevailing conventions: "lost between the genteel female passer and the predominately male representatives of the slave community is the female slave who cannot pass . . . testif[ying] to the [the] inadequacy of the paradigms of true (white) womanhood" (647). Carla Peterson might add that his narrative of a concubine's home "privatizes" the subjection of the heroine (155). A light skin or seclusion, however, does not always predict entrapment. The ways in which African American women characters are hidden, secrete themselves, or take to the outdoors says much about the ability of real-life heroines to manage exterior and interior space.

When Wilson chooses to relate the story of bondage "in A Two-Story White House, North" (1), she, like Brown, consciously or unconsciously counter-writes the home implied in *Uncle Tom's Cabin*. The black daughter in *Our Nig* would not have been able to recognize Tom's abode as the home of a Negro man, or even of a poor white. Her "white trash" mother's previous establishment was charmless, "a hovel she [Mag Smith] had often passed in better days, and which she knew to be untenanted" (8); the days of the Smith family were frequently marked by hunger, not delicious bake-smells. Smith lands a "more comfortable dwelling" following her marriage to Jim, the father of her mulatto children, yet when he dies of consumption, she returns with her two children to the abandoned shack.[42] When Frado finally moves to larger quarters, the description seems at first to resemble that of Tom's cabin, at least in terms of plantings and homey situation:

[It was] a large, old fashioned, two-story white house, environed by fruitful acres, and embellished by shrubbery and shade trees. Years ago a youthful couple consecrated it as home; and after many little feet had worn paths to favorite fruit trees, and over its green hills, and mingled at last with brother man in the race which belongs neither to the swift or strong, the sire became grey-haired and decrepid, and went to his last repose. . . . The old homestead thus passed into the hands of a son.   *(21)*

Quite deliberately invoking the image of a cherished family home, Wilson juxtaposes this initial pretty picture with the actual dwelling in which Frado is beaten regularly, has wooden gags stuffed into her mouth to prevent outcries, and given scanty meals to be eaten while standing. In contrast, in Stowe, a house of horrors trumpets its evil, as can be told by the first prospect of the Louisiana plantation on which Tom meets his end:

What was once a smooth-shaven lawn before the house, dotted here and there with ornamental shrubs, was now covered with frowsy tangled grass, with horse-posts set up, here and there, in it, where the turf was stamped away, and the ground littered with broken pails, cobs of corn, and other slovenly remains.

Wilson, portraying the "black back regions" of the Bellmont home, offers her readers the view below stairs, the heretofore-invisible life of the black forced laborer.[43] Stowe's Chloe, the stereotypical genius black cook, "beams with satisfaction and contentment . . . [with] that tinge of self-consciousness which becomes the first cook of the neighborhood" (1:39); despite the bondage of the deepest South, the creative talents of a Dinah can "scandalize . . . the Northern cousin Ophelia," or even "alarm" her.[44] Whatever artisan's pleasures the Bellmont house may once have had for its servants,[45] Frado does not enjoy them: her behind-the-scenes labor includes "a large amount of dish-washing for small hands," "all the washing, ironing, baking, and the common *et cetera* of household duties, though but fourteen" and the impairment of her health "by lifting the sick [James Bellmont] . . . and by drudgery in the kitchen" (*ON* 29, 63, 81). The closest built structure that offers Frado the security of a home is the barn, for no white Bellmont will follow her there, except to offer food or sympathy. Save for a brief period during her relatively comfortable early childhood, when the girl's father was alive and able to provide for her mother, her sibling, and herself, Frado never inhabits a real home. As Harryette Mullen has remarked, "the compartmentalization of the [Bellmont] house confines the colored servant 'in her place' " (254). Even if fed, clothed, and sheltered, Frado is homeless.

Homeless in the same sense as Frado—that is, as a black female servant subject to daily abuse—Jacobs still can paint a warm picture of her grandmother's home, if not of the one she lived in before "running away."[46] That perspective of homelessness, as Sidonie Smith has pointed out, "underscores the grim reality of Jacobs'/Brent's status as exile in her own country" (98). The difference between "Aunt Marthy's" home and that of the fictional Tom is that the charms of the former, a freed black's domicile, have been hard won by its inhabitant. Jacobs's homelessness, even as a child, is not absolute. Nevertheless, the lack of a permanent, actual home remains, even after her escape: Sandra Gunning sees in Jacobs's "refus[al] to validate the freedom [and home] offered to her in the North" a stinging critique of her so-called liberty.[47] Throughout *Incidents*, the homey attractions of the grandmother's house serve as background to the story. Hungry adolescent Jacobs—fictionalized as the girl Linda Brent—describes her now-freed grandmother feeding her when her cruel owners will not: "there was a grand big oven there [at Aunt Marthy's] . . . and we [Linda and her brother] knew there was always a choice bit in store for us" (17). The grandmother's home rises more than one story, and she owns another house on the same lot.[48] Possessions seemingly beyond the reach of blacks further improve Aunt Marthy's life: during a house-to-house search following the Nat Turner uprising, astonished poor whites find "silver change . . . a large trunk of bedding and table cloths . . . silver spoons which ornamented an old fashioned buffet . . . many jars of preserves . . . white quilts [and] rooms with flowers" (64–66; 63). Even when sorrowfully recalling her confession of sexual activity and her outraged guardian's response, Jacobs provides the details of what was, for a southern black, a charmed life: she can evoke the sound of her grandmother's "little gate, which I used to open with such an eager hand" and recall her "mother's wedding ring and her silver thimble," which the elder woman tears from her fingers (57). The inclusion of such mementos of her family's "good taste" counters the authority of the garish reproductions of General Washington enshrined by Aunt Chloe.

Stowe's novel describes homes and antihomes. Uncle Tom's cabin, decked out with those wildly colored pictures, an orderly and bustling kitchen, and a "parlor" bed as well as an area where the family really sleeps, is the very model of a comfortable workingman's home (1:39–40). A pacific and cultivated outdoors accentuates its serenity, with a "neat garden-patch . . . where, every summer, strawberries, raspberries, and a variety of fruits and vegetables, flourished under careful tending" (1:38). Even though his subsequent sale and new master bring him far from his cabin in Kentucky, Tom's new home in New Orleans appears less alien because of luxurious furnishings set off by tropical vegetation:

> Two large orange-trees, now fragrant with blossoms, threw a delicious shade; and, ranged in a circle round the turf, were marble vases of arabesque sculpture, containing the choicest flowering plants of the tropics. . . . Tom got down from the carriage, and looked about with an air of calm, still enjoyment.　　　　　　　　　　　　　*(1:236–37)*

In Stowe's and her protagonist's opinion, Tom's new home is properly set off by a carefully tended garden; bad things will not happen in an orderly paradise.

Brutality takes place in the lonely, left-to-ruin environment of the "Dark Places," the swampland plantation where Tom will meet his end.

> [The way to it] was a wild, forsaken road, now winding through dreary pine barrens, where the wind whispered mournfully, and now over log causeways, through long cypress swamps, the doleful trees rising out of the slimy, spongy ground.　　　　　　　　　　　　　*(2:179, 176)*

On Simon Legree's lonely plantation, as one overworked slave exclaims, "de Lord an't here" (2:186). The very trees and grasses have a malevolent aspect; the atmosphere exudes a noxious miasma. Rather than a cultivated plot of flowers to refresh the soul and vegetables to nourish the body, Legree's plantation is a plant—a place of production. Tom's new dwelling place falls far below his most pessimistic expectations, for the slave quarters

> were mere rude shells, destitute of any species of furniture, except a heap of straw, foul with dirt, spread confusedly over the floor, which was merely the bare ground, trodden hard by the tramping of innumerable feet.　　　　　　　　　　　　　*(1:182)*

No food is raised here, only the cotton that pricks at the fingers of the weary slaves and burdens their already aching backs. Beyond the cotton fields and the decaying house lies "the labyrinth of the swamp . . . deep and dark" (2:263), a place trackless, foul, and dangerous, where only the most desperate slaves will flee. A fugitive's last resort, the quagmires around Legree's plantation will swallow those who can bear up no longer: the only other alternative is death, slow or quick, at the hands of Legree and his minions.

Like Stowe, Harriet Jacobs sees the isolated, wilder parts around her town as places of danger rather than freedom. When harassed by her tormentors, "Linda Brent" can go to her grandmother's home or the house of a friend. Jacobs fears the "small house [built by Dr. Flint] for me, in a *secluded* place four miles away from the town" (53; emphasis mine). There could transpire the scenes of her worst degradation, for her master intends that she be moved there out of the sight and sound of any who can intervene—her grandmother, the doctor's outraged wife, or any sympathetic whites.[49] Plantation life—the scourge of Uncle Tom—is the ultimate threat held over Jacobs's head, yet she would prefer it to an isolated cottage. When her children are threatened with the same fate, however, Jacobs makes her move. Should the children be placed in the same household as their mother, "[it] would fetter me to the spot . . . [for the plantation] was a good place to break us all in to abject submission to our lot as slaves" (93–94). Backbreaking work is acceptable for herself, but not for her son and daughter. Following her initial flight, she stumbles into wild, snake-infested territory:

> I flew out of the house, and concealed myself in a thicket of bushes. . . .
> Suddenly, a reptile of some kind seized my leg. In my fright, I struck a blow which loosened its hold, but I could not tell whether I had killed it; it was so dark, I could not see what it was; I only knew it was something cold and slimy.   *(98)*

This encounter with untamed nature leaves Jacobs with an infected leg that nearly kills her. During a second time in the woods, a refuge sought again to avoid discovery, she finds herself surrounded by all manner of animal peril:

> We were covered with hundreds of mosquitos. In an hour's time they had so poisoned my flesh that I was a pitiful sight to behold. As the light increased, I saw snake after snake crawling round us . . . these were larger than any I had ever seen. To this day I shudder when I remember that morning.   *(112–13)*

Yet the fear of her white persecutors is greater than that of the dangers lurking in the swamps and undergrowth. Death from snakebite is preferable to her fate as an attractive slave mother: "large, venomous snakes were less dreadful to my imagination than the white men in that community called civilized" (113).

Annette Kolodny notes that whereas men sought to tame and conquer the frontier, nineteenth-century frontier women sought to make a frightening wilderness like the homes they already knew. "In place of intimate woodland embraces, women hailed open rolling expanses broken, here and there, by a clump of trees. In place of pristine forests, women described a cozy log cabin."[50] When applied to Jacobs's and Stowe's narratives, Kolodny's theory only partly explains the aversion to "wild," that is, "unimproved," territory. Harriet Wilson diverges from this pattern in her reliance on the outdoors as a sanctuary from the attacks of her white employer. Countless slaves, male and female, saw wild areas as free zones. Temporarily or permanently, the wilderness offers a literal out from the arbitrary dictates of white control.[51] Former bondsfolk who did not leave written records have recalled in oral histories men and women who escaped to the outdoors: "Aunt Kitty, Uncle Ben and Isaac Jones had all told me of the woman who hid with her children in the woods. Uncle Ben . . . placed her time of hiding at two years, but the others believed it to be four or five."[52] Nathan Irvin Huggins avers "that despite the danger, isolation, and the wildness imposed on fugitive life, maroon colonies [communities of escaped slaves] persisted through much of Southern history."[53] The wilderness was a place of refuge for the abused black worker, slave or free. For the black woman, the outdoors could offer a precious extra modicum of security.[54]

The luckless Frado finds happiness in the woods precisely because there are no human beings, much less whites. In Frado's claustrophobic world of endless housework, the only other humans present are European American. And although a majority of the Bellmonts appear sympathetic, they are unable or unwilling to protect her. At one point, the younger daughter attempts to victimize Frado by lying about an after-school mishap:

> Turning to her husband, [Mrs. Bellmont] asked,
>   "Will you sit still, there, and hear that black nigger call Mary a liar?"
>   "How do we know but she has told the truth? I shall not punish her," he replied, and left the house, as he usually did when a tempest threatened to envelop him. No sooner was he out of sight than Mrs. B. and Mary commenced beating [Frado] inhumanly.   *(34)*

Then as at other points in her life, Frado can hope for nothing better than a postponement of punishment. The eldest son, at first absent and then ailing, attempts to teach her Christian patience; he reprimands his mother but does not actively intercede on Frado's behalf. Following a conversation with Mr. Bellmont in which he tells Frado "when she was *sure* she did not deserve a whipping, to avoid it if she could," the girl finally stands up to Mrs. Bellmont: "Stop! . . . strike me, and I'll never work a mite more for you" (104–5). The senior Bellmont's qualified encouragement to "avoid" whippings is the most protection Frado gets. Small wonder that as a child she chooses to run to the swamp or the barn: inanimate things afford more protection than the meaningless sympathy of the well-intentioned. A guilt-ridden do-gooder can only offer a qualified protection for the indentured servant.

In keeping with runaways' idea of the wild as sanctuary, and in contradiction to the fears of the fictional Eliza Harris or the actual Harriet Jacobs, Frado loves the outdoors. When little more than a toddler she spends the night out in "a thick cluster of shrubbery" after a long walk takes her and a friend far from their homes; she also attempts to banish her little friend's fears (19–20). Frado frequently flees the confines of that "White [owned] House" to express irrepressible emotions—to sob without witnesses or simply to run freely. Even after years of arduous labor her good spirits cannot be extinguished. Pent-up emotions are reserved for the outside. Among her tasks is shepherding, and one day, irritated by a ram who always knocks her down at feeding time, Frado decides to teach him a lesson. Perched at the edge of a stream, the girl holds aloft a dish: "Should she by any mishap lose her footing, she must roll into the stream, and without aid, must drown." When the ram dashes headlong toward the girl she skips aside, sending the impetuous beast for a ducking; Mr. Bellmont's workmen, looking on, laugh uproariously (54–55). But experiences outside the Bellmont home do not always recharge her soul. The barn, the usual habitation of creatures rather than girls, is the scene of Frado's tearful confessions to her dog, Fido. One summer day the elder Bellmont son overhears her:

> "Oh! oh!" I heard, "why was I made? why can't I die? Oh what have I to live for? No one cares for me only to get my work. . . ." She was crouched down by the hay with her faithful friend Fido, and as she ceased speaking, buried her face in her hands, and cried bitterly. (75)

On an earlier occasion, subsequent to Frado's flight from the house to avoid an undeserved beating, the two sons find her "far, far into the fields, over walls and through fences, into a piece of swampy land" (50)—a location recalling to readers the Great Dismal Swamp, the renowned sanctuary of many a fugitive slave.

Even for those who preferred to dwell within four walls rather than in the great outdoors, there were degrees of contentment and confinement within dwellings of the sophisticated:

> 'Tis pleasant, through the loopholes of retreat,
> To peep at such a world,—to see the stir
> Of the great Babel, and not feel the crowd.[55]

The above lines, taken from William Cowper's "The Task" (1784), form the epigraph of chapter 21 of *Incidents* ("The Loophole of Retreat") and provide an apt gloss on the predicament of Harriet Jacobs. Jacobs's editor, Lydia Maria Child, had cited Cowper twice before in *An Appeal in Favor of That Class of Americans Called Africans* (1833), and used his verse again in *The Freedman's Book* (1866).[56] Although it might well have been the editor rather than the autobiographer who selected this verse, its appropriateness is incontrovertible. In the "Loophole" chapter, Jacobs stops running from Dr. Flint and chooses instead to battle him from an unseen position. Though physically confined, Jacobs can needle, manipulate, and otherwise harass her former tormentor. Much has rightfully been made of her use, both literary and actual, of her aerial dungeon—a dungeon that was reproduced in the North, as Mullen (249) and others have seen. Valerie Smith writes that Jacobs manipulates "linguistic spaces" to gain literary points as much as she uses the various spaces of her confinement—"unwed motherhood . . . the concealment in one friend's home, another friend's closet, and her grandmother's garret"—to gain what liberation she can.[57] Jacobs is but one woman among many who write of the uses to which an enslaved woman can put physical, domestic space—"the not-quite spaces of an American domesticity."[58]

In *The Madwoman in the Attic*, Sandra M. Gilbert and Susan Gubar have extensively examined a number of tropes in the imaginative work of the nineteenth-century woman writer. Significant among these is the image of the woman struggling to escape the literal and figurative confines of the day, whether they be tight lacings or social conventions. Referring specifically to white women, Gilbert and Gubar assert that

> literally, women like Dickinson, Bronte, and Rossetti were imprisoned in their homes, their father's houses; indeed, almost all nineteenth-century women were in some sense imprisoned in men's houses. . . . It is

not surprising, then, that spatial imagery of enclosure and escape, elaborated with what frequently becomes obsessive intensity, characterizes much of their writing. *(83)*

The crucial difference of nineteenth-century black women's creative works comes from the harshness of their authors' imprisonment: even if technically free, African American women found their horizons set far lower than those of their Caucasian contemporaries. In slavery, black women's bondage was, of course, literal: their confinement, actual not metaphorical, results in a quite understandable "obsessive intensity." Whether literal or figurative, confinement might be usefully described as a category that can be classed as either voluntary or involuntary. Joanne Braxton refers specifically to Jacobs's autobiographical persona Linda Brent as a "virtual madwoman in the attic" (26), and Mullen says Jacobs's "various confining positions within the sub- and super interiors of the white household become loopholes in the patriarchal institutions of property, slavery, and marriage . . . allowing her to question and revise the figure of the woman whose interiority is derived from her confinement in domestic space" (249).

Harriet Beecher Stowe notes in *Uncle Tom's Cabin* the many interiors to which a woman can be consigned. Although Stowe's character Eliza is the female slave who comes quickest to the memory of most readers, Cassy eerily prefigures Jacobs. Like Harriet Jacobs, Cassy finds the will and cunning to mastermind an escape attempt that hinges on a self-incarceration. Proud and educated, the once-beautiful Cassy has become deranged by years spent on a lonely, unkempt plantation. The imprisonment alone cannot account for her deterioration; successive terms of concubinage to white slave-holders have added their own scars. As Harriet Jacobs writes:

> If God has bestowed beauty upon her [the black bondswoman], it will prove her greatest curse. That which commands admiration in the white woman only hastens the degradation of the female slave.[59]

When Simon Legree plans to replace Cassy as his sexual victim with the fifteen-year-old Emmeline, the older woman is roused to action. With the backing of Tom, she formulates a plan that parallels Jacobs's mode of hidden revenge. In order to carry out her scheme successfully, Cassy first must turn to her advantage Legree's superstitious nature. The myths already in circulation at the Red River plantation serve her well:

The garret of the house that Legree occupied, like most other garrets, was a great, desolate space, dusty, hung with cobwebs, and littered with cast-off lumber. . . . it was a weird and ghostly place; but, ghostly as it was, it wanted not in legends among the superstitious negroes, to increase its terrors. Some few years before, a negro woman, who had incurred Legree's displeasure, was confined there for several weeks. What passed there, we do not say.   (2:253–54)

From the time that slave's dead body was taken away, the remaining slaves have whispered that "wailings and groans of despair" emanate from that attic (2:254). Cassy, playing on Legree's fears, pretends that movements and noise coming from above her bedroom keep her awake nights; to further her claims, she places a bottle neck in a garret crevice so that the wind will create a moan or shriek. As the days and nights proceed Legree becomes more and more fearful, while Cassy increases the suspense with insinuating remarks and leading questions: "*What's the matter with that garret*, Simon, do you suppose?" (2:260). When Legree will no more go up to the attic than shoot himself, Cassy pretends to escape with Emmeline. As the entire plantation takes off in pursuit, the two women double back from their supposed destination of the swamp, and head for a sojourn in the garret.

Like Jacobs, Cassy arranges her hideout so as to keep an eye on her tormentor. Although Jacobs has to bore a hole through the side of the wall, Cassy's garret comes equipped with a small dusty window. Jacobs cannot even stand up in her crawl space, but Cassy provides herself and her young charge with furniture, bedding, and supplies of all kinds. Even more important, where Jacobs has to guard her every movement for fear of discovery, Cassy scornfully announces that "we may make any noise we please, and it will only add to the effect" of the garret's being haunted (2:266). Following the murder of Tom, Cassy drapes herself in a white sheet and goes to the guilty party's bedside; she wakes Legree with a cold-as-the-grave touch and the words "Come! come! come!" Playing upon his suppressed guilt—for the savage beating of Tom, for the rejection of his dying mother—the avenging Cassy sends the tyrannical slave-holder into a fatal drinking binge. Cassy has reversed her situation by manipulating the space controlled by Legree. Once she is able to reshape the plantation—by retreating to the haunted garret, shrinking her field of action—Cassy can take the offensive.

Stowe could well have drawn on Jacobs's self-incarceration as the basis for Cassy's tale of escape through confinement. Jacobs, who was at first urged by abolitionist Amy Post to write her story with Stowe's assistance, was in hiding from August 1835 to June 1842, well before *Uncle Tom's Cabin* appeared. Post became a personal friend of Jacobs in 1849, and judging from the trust between them, evident in the letters the two women exchanged, it seems unlikely that Post would have revealed the particulars of Jacobs's story without her express permission.[60] Yet the similarities between the two stories strike one as almost uncanny. Could Jacobs's story—one of strange and solitary attic exile—have been in oral circulation among abolitionists before Stowe wrote her novel? Once Stowe learned the actual details of the former slave's life, she suggested that Jacobs's story be subsumed within the forthcoming *A Key to Uncle Tom's Cabin*. An indignant Jacobs withdrew from any implied agreement.[61] Certainly the story, in its barest outlines, would lend itself well to telling. That a woman barely out of her teens should match cunning with a slave-holder decades her senior, and manage to place herself out of his reach yet keep him for years within sight and sound, is marvelous. Jacobs most emphatically did not wish her life to be another gloss on the now-formulaic story of the family-sundering peculiar institution; it was her own, individual "Perilous Passage."

Harriet Jacobs flees to one friend and then another between the time she leaves the Flint plantation and enters into the "loophole." In fact, she spends time in more than one such cramped hideaway. At her second place of concealment, Jacobs finds both luxurious and subterranean accommodations. Most of her time is spent in a small, rarely used locked room over her protector's own bedroom, where she notes with gratification that from atop "a pile of feather beds . . . I could lie perfectly concealed, and command a view of the street through which Dr. Flint passed to his office. Anxious as I was, I felt a gleam of satisfaction when I saw him" (100). When her discovery by Dr. Flint seems imminent, the cook Betty moves Jacobs to a spot under the kitchen floorboards: "In my shallow bed I had but just room enough to bring my hands to my face to keep the dust out of my eyes; for Betty walked over me twenty times in one hour, passing from the dresser to the fireplace" (103). Although Jacobs's stay below the floorboards numbers but a few hours, following her return to the upstairs hiding place she mourns: "It seemed as if I were born to bring sorrow on all who befriended me" (104). When Flint's search for Jacobs begins afresh, her friend Peter leads her to a new home in her old one, where the "air was stifling; the darkness total" (114).

Jacobs spends a biblical seven years in a crawl space over her grandmother's storage room. Such solitary confinement appears the only way she can escape Dr. Flint's clutches. With the town so small and the ways of exit so closely watched, escape attempts seem bound to fail. In summer she almost stifles with the heat in an area so small she cannot even stand up; in winter, without a stove, she suffers from frostbite and exposure. She hangs on, watching her children through a hole she bores in the side of the house, biding her time.

> The laws allowed *him* [Dr. Flint] to be out in the free air, while I, guiltless of crime, was pent up here, as the only means of avoiding the cruelties the laws allowed him to inflict upon me! I don't know what kept life within me. Again and again, I thought I should die before long; but I saw the leaves of another autumn whirl through the air, and felt the touch of another winter. *(121)*

Jacobs repairs to the garret as much to gain power over Dr. Flint as to elude him. As she had from the storage room at the sympathetic slave-holder's house, Jacobs can watch—and to an extent manipulate—her owner's attempts to recapture her, harass her grandmother, and threaten her children. In an ironic reversal of Bentham's panopticon, the jailed can view her jailer with impunity.[62] She writes letters, which her friend Peter has mailed from various northern cities, decoying the doctor away from Edenton and "lighten[ing] his pocket" (104). When her white lover is about to move to Washington to take up a congressional post, Jacobs manages to meet and speak with him under the ruse that she has heard of his departure and comes to plead their children's case. As does her fictional counterpart Cassy, Jacobs arranges a safe place in her own home—and from that sequestered spot begins to direct her own destiny.

Of all three heroines, fictional and real, only Frado cannot manipulate interior physical space to her advantage. In his introduction to the modern edition of *Our Nig*, Henry Louis Gates Jr. attests "Frado at last finds a voice with which to define her space" when she finally raises her voice to Mrs. Bellmont, refusing to be struck. "A physical space of one's own signifies the presence of a more subtle, if equally real, 'metaphysical' space, within which one's thoughts are one's own. This space Frado finds by speaking" (liii). Yet what "space" Frado allegedly holds here signifies little, metaphysical or otherwise: she does not control it, even though like Frederick Douglass she may at last be able to announce that "however long I might remain a slave in form, the day had passed forever when I could be a slave in fact."[63] Wilson's story illustrates that one cannot free oneself without the ability to mark out one's own space, for the "minimal sense of physical places in this story," writes Karla F. C. Holloway, attests to the author's disadvantaged state.[64] Though she dwells in an attic room, it is not *hers*. Cassy and Jacobs each manage to take over a space, however small, and from there control a certain amount of the action.[65]

From the moment Frado arrives at the "Two-Story, White House, North," Mrs. Bellmont ensures that all domestic space is hers to name and thereby command, identifying the young girl's "L chamber" as only "good enough for a nigger" (26). Thus negatively marked, the chamber can be no sanctuary from Mrs. Bellmont's verbal or physical assaults. Even though a sympathetic Jack Bellmont leads Frado to her new quarters, it remains a surplus room to which she is relegated:

> It was not yet quite dark, so they ascended the stairs without any light, passing through nicely furnished rooms, which were a source of great amazement to the child. He opened the door which connected with her room by a dark, unfinished passage-way. "Don't bump your head," said Jack, and stepped before to open the door leading into her apartment,— an unfinished chamber over the kitchen, the roof slanting nearly to the floor, so that the bed could stand only in the middle of the room. A small half window furnished light and air.   (27)

When Jack remarks to his mother that Frado will probably soon grow too big for such a room, Mrs. Bellmont callously replies "When she *does*, she'll outgrow the house" (28). The only place for Frado is the one Mrs. Bellmont has selected; should that not suffice, no replacement is forthcoming. Even should Frado withdraw to the L-room, her mere presence in the house could invite further aggression on the part of her mistress.

Frado knows she must seek a place outside of the Bellmont homestead if she is to have any selfhood whatsoever. Even after her status changes with the attainment of her majority, her former habitation remains Mrs. Bellmont's. When illness forces her to return to the very place where her health was broken to beg for assistance, even this L-chamber is denied her. Relegated to an outbuilding "where cold and rain found unobstructed access" (119), the ailing Frado is finally brought back indoors by Aunt Abby. But the unmarried sister of Mr. Bellmont is herself on sufferance. Grudgingly bestowed by her sister-in-law, Aunt Abby's chambers serve as the slimmest of buffers against further mistreatment. The aunt seems almost as disenfranchised as the young black servant through her inability to have her own home. Frado's subsequent attempt to create her own home, to find in an alleged ex-slave a husband and provider, proves disastrous; they end in a rented room "obtained of a poor woman" (128). Subsequently he deserts Frado and their infant son. Further and further into the perilous life of a lonely free black she sinks, until she and her child land in the county home. The book we read, her bid to rescue her son from his foster placement, gives tragic evidence of her ultimate homelessness.

The women, real and fictional, of *Uncle Tom's Cabin*, *Clotel*, *Our Nig*, and *Incidents in the Life of a Slave Girl* tell us that without her own dwelling, the nineteenth-century black woman was incapable of self-emancipation. As Jacobs sadly writes at the close of her narrative,

> The dream of my life is not yet realized. I do not sit with my children in a home of my own. I still long for a hearthstone of my own, however humble. I wish it for my children's sake far more than for my own. *(201)*

Jacobs's thrice-repeated possessive phrase "my own" emphasizes her desperate need for a home, not just a room, of her own. To control one's domestic space meant not only to grasp the intellectual freedom that Virginia Woolf so coveted, but to claim the even more desirable, practical, and elusive state of physical autonomy. Despite one critic's statement that Wilson and Jacobs "provide their *own* homes for themselves and their children," at the time of their books' publication they do not.[66] Jacobs poignantly ends *Incidents* with the wish for "a home of [her] own," a galling reminder of her relative impotence, despite the fact that she has freed herself, daughter, and son from the furnace of slavery. Northern freedom appears something of a Pyrrhic victory for Jacobs.[67] Harriet Wilson's essentially fruitless "experiment" fails to win her dearest aim, for her young son dies six months later.[68] Houses in and of themselves do not provide security—the wilderness can do as much for a black woman. A living space does not vouchsafe freedom: "the house remains a sheltered 'feminine' space, that is, a *hus* [protective shelter] for true spiritual growth, which by virtue of its enclosure in the 'masculine' domain of materialism and commercialism, always remains in danger of being invaded and corrupted by it."[69] Stowe and Brown end with the cozy, *foreign* homes of their virtuous heroines; Jacobs, writing at the dawn of the Civil War, had to work and wait for her opportunity. Wilson's autobiography confirms most resoundingly the fragility of a black woman's hopes for psychic and physical shelter in the nineteenth century. The barn and the swamp remained the best, if contingent, places for the indentured servant; motherhood and the attempt to save her child would force her back again into a cold "White House, North."

Writers like Harriet Beecher Stowe and Lydia Maria Child tended to identify the image of the white woman with the image of the slave because both "personhood[s] can be annihilated . . . and owned, absorbed, and unnamed"; Sánchez-Eppler rightfully asserts, however, that the quandary lies in "preventing moments of identification from becoming acts of appropriation."[70] Despite Stowe's sympathy for exploited and oppressed black women, she still viewed their stories—Jacobs's quite literally—as fragments to be subsumed within her own text(s). William Wells Brown, appropriating the sentimental fiction of both Stowe and Child when he published *Clotel*, delivered a black-authored abolitionist novel at odds with itself.[71] The work of Brown and Stowe demonstrated, to their black women readers at least, that the interiors of American slavery and racism had to be rescripted by those most acquainted with its rooms.

Jacobs and Wilson each tackled the difficulties of merging "mainstream" forms with "minority" issues, although they assuredly did not think of the problem in those terms. They spoke, even if it seemed their words were snatched from public hearing as soon as uttered: "judgment was to be passed on . . . slavery, not on deviations from conventions of true womanhood," as Hazel Carby shows.[72] Similarly, notions of slave or "free" black status should be rethought. Jacobs, casting her pseudonymous life story within the dual framework of the slave narrative and the sentimental novel, rejected the pedestal offered to her white compatriots. She knew such a lofty and revered position would be denied any black woman: firmly she says, "Still, in looking back, calmly, on the events of my life, I feel that the slave woman ought not to be judged by the same standard as others" (56). As she would in her battles for the literal space in which to control her own and her children's destinies, Jacobs tried to assume the upper hand when casting her own story—"written by herself"—within the common territory of "women's fiction." But the charming homes of Clotel and Eliza, fictional representations of the black woman in slavery, were not to be hers. Fiction went only so far; real life a shorter distance.

Our Nig underscores the shared heritage of all African Americans, northern or southern. Because Frado spends her entire life within Caucasian New England, she is as duped as the whites are by a black man posing as an ex-slave. She can sympathize with his feigned oppression, yet her inability to read him as an insider costs her what little ground, and what hopes for a home, she has. Despite her remove from the black community, Wilson indicates her desire to be included within that circle by appealing to its members to stand behind her publishing venture.[73] By requesting forbearance from both her white readers and her black "brethren," Wilson acknowledges her bicultural status:

> Unable to control the terms of her own cultural identity or to trust others similarly defined, Wilson speaks both to and against those—black or white, male or female—who see her as a cultural type. . . . Wilson signified on her own culturally determined identity in her use of "Our Nig" as the title of both the book and its author.[74]

By deliberately and directly addressing both the "colored brethren" and "our good anti-slavery friends at home" (3), Wilson concedes both her inadequate preparation for speaking to a national constituency and her distinction from her racial peers. Like Douglass, she is an exceptional representative. Neither a "true" black, nor an ex-slave, nor a white New Englander, Wilson and her liminal identity have for years kept *Our Nig* on the outskirts of both African American and mainstream American literature, much as she herself was kept in the barns, swamps, and outdoor places of New Hampshire.

The frustrating, and sometimes frustrated, struggles of Wilson and Jacobs to rewrite the popular script offered by white supporters such as Stowe, as well as that perhaps unintentionally provided by William Wells Brown, demonstrate the traps inherent in using the master's tools to dismantle the master's house. But the more-than-casual reader should acknowledge how difficult was that path to "a free story." Harriet E. Wilson was long lost at the crossroads of multicultural America, but the author of *Incidents* has also suffered from the belief that ineluctable, identifiable qualities should appear in every text written by an American of African descent. Perhaps from the perspective of the late twentieth century, mid-nineteenth-century black writers did not succeed in creating an identifiable African American literature. Yet to demand that prescience of them is to reveal our own ahistorical agenda. Stowe, Wilson, and Jacobs all contributed to the debate and discussion on the place of women, black and white, during the mid-nineteenth century. Stowe became a public figure following the serialization and release of *Uncle Tom's Cabin*. Harriet Jacobs gained a certain amount of celebrity, if not notoriety, with the publication of *Incidents*.[75] Wilson fared the worst, for her novel appeared and disappeared in short order; until recently *Our Nig* was not even believed to have been written by an African American.[76] Even if its "forced" experiments sometimes fell short of the desires of author and reader alike, a distinct African American literature *was* nascent by 1870. Still another mid-century strategy, African American literature without African Americans, would round out these experiments.

6

⁊❧

DRESSING UP AND DRESSING DOWN
Elizabeth Keckley's *Behind the Scenes at the White House*
and Eliza Potter's *A Hairdresser's Experience in High Life*

> Why, then, should not the hair-dresser write, as well as the physician and
> clergyman? She will tell her story in simpler language; but it will be none the
> less truthful, none the less strange.
>
> —*Eliza Potter*
> A Hair-dresser's Experience in High Life

A few years ago, Deborah McDowell asked if Douglass's *Narrative* is "any
more . . . a paradigm" for African American autobiography than Harriet
Jacobs's *Incidents*; she refers to the tradition of black literary criticism that
privileges male-authored depictions of African American identity over
those written by females.[1] Yet the rapid growth of black women's studies
has catapulted Jacobs to a visibility that seemed impossible twenty years
ago and unlikely even five years ago. Scholarship has burgeoned to the
point where literary critics can now state of past critical efforts: "The
dominant trend in literary scholarship has been to privilege the slave narrative as *the* African-American literary form of the antebellum period,
focusing in particular on Frederick Douglass's . . . and Harriet Jacobs's
[autobiographies]."[2] Revision of the canon of nineteenth-century African
American texts has gone beyond including male and female slave narrators alike, to encompassing a multiplicity of genres. *Incidents* should be
counted no more paradigmatic of nineteenth-century black letters than
Douglass's *Narrative*, for the slave narrative and sentimental writing do
not begin to define the extent of African American genres before the
twentieth century. Like others, I seek to re-envision and enrich con-

temporary critical discourse on the crucial and still-underread period of antebellum African American literature.

Though my previous chapters have explored the ways in which black American authors masked their intentions within familiar genres, I may still configure autobiographical "success stories" or generic appropriation in predictable ways, from a Franklinian model of hard-working man become Great Man to a Richardsonian one where "virtue rewarded" is almost inevitably constructed as female.[3] Those definitions depend on a model of separate, gendered spheres well known in the nineteenth century, yet that model lives on in our collective subconscious. Douglass's self-depiction as an American success story—his "profound endorsement of the . . . plot, the myth of the self-made man"—was welcomed and seconded by thousands of abolitionist-minded whites; his story underscores the prescriptions for masculine achievement familiar to his contemporaries.[4] Jacobs, belatedly heralded for her courageous stance against sexual aggression, "outraged motherhood," and yoking together of the sentimental and slave narrative modes, formulates another paradigm of black literary success.[5] For Elizabeth Keckley and the anonymously self-published Eliza Potter, renown came more slowly. Initially, their efforts were met with either the self-satisfied approbation of a midwestern in-crowd or the hypocritical howls of "foul play" from whites eager to hear the worst of Mrs. Lincoln. Twentieth-century critical apprehension of their works remains in an early stage. Although Keckley's name and book have never remained far from historians' notice, neither author has received her due.[6] Perhaps this results in part from each author's decision to write a black autobiography without African Americans—a point to which I will return.

Paul Lawrence Dunbar uses "mask" as a synonym for the performance of an identity fit for white consumption—or, as Webster's Third New International would put it, to mean a "disguise [for] one's true character or intentions." I would like to add a metaphor with more specifically "feminine" connotations, one resonant of black texts in the America diaspora: the veil. In any discussion of African American literature, Du Bois's renowned image of the veil—the nearly palpable screen drawn down between white and black Americans, the cloud that, paradoxically, lends a second sight to those of African descent—cannot be avoided. The double-consciousness of the American of African descent is almost inescapable. Herein, however, the feminine "inscriptions" of veil serve as the primary guides to a specifically gendered style of masking. We might consider the image of a doubled veil, one that brings to mind further female inscriptions of fashion, disguise, and mourning. A veil disguises, protects, and adorns, calls a paradoxical attention to the female face by concealing it.[7] By its nature a veil obscures, and "withholds from public knowledge"; it evokes the cloistered life and the fast lanes of high fashion, modesty and daring, deep grief and frivolity. Lydia Maria Child's presentation of "the veil withdrawn" (4) in Harriet Jacobs's autobiography intended to alert white readers to the sexualized nature of slavery; her condemnation of white women's blindness to abuse in their homes and country can be extrapolated to an inability to see the class and race bias within a hierarchical, increasingly stratified American society. Joanne Braxton, speaking to the experience of being a black woman academic writing about African American women's autobiographies, refers both to the Du Boisian notion of the veil behind which African Americans live and to the female experience of being removed from the male mainstream:

> As black American women, we are born into a mystic sisterhood, and
> we live our lives within a magic circle, a realm of shared language, ref-
> erence, and allusion within the veil of our blackness and our female-
> ness. We have been as invisible to the dominant culture as rain; we have
> been knowers, but we have not been known. This paradox is central to
> what I suggest we call the Afra-American experience. . . . For the black
> woman, there is a veil within a veil.   *(1, 3)*

Peterson's comments on Stowe and Wilson enlarge this notion further: in creating "fictionalized versions of both self and Other from multiple perspectives . . . [black women strove] to escape the scrutiny of the dominant culture and achieve perspectives of omniscience denied them."[8] Simply put, to become "knowers," for black women, almost demanded rhetorical—if not actual—reclusiveness.

Keckley's and Potter's rhetorically veiled selves exemplify a dynamic of black female autobiography that deploys a fashionable and fashioned sense of the white world in order to reveal its failings. This literary veil protects the black female narrator from any scrutiny save one suitable for a black woman conscious of her tenuous status within middle-class American society. If, as P. Gabrielle Foreman has said, in a riff on Karen Halttunen, a white, female audience of mid-nineteenth-century America could not "admit to the[ir] comprehension of the sexually determined black 'back regions' of her [Harriet Jacobs's] textual performance," then it follows that certain black women authors cognizant of the apparent "delicacy" of their European-American readers would take advantage of that alleged delicacy to withhold nearly everything about themselves while speaking at length on white faults and peccadilloes.[9] "Dressing Up and Dressing Down" thus refers not only to the fashionable women for whom Keckley and Potter perform services but also to the implied and explicit critiques these two artisans produce along with their dresses and hairstyles. By "dressing up" we mean the putting on of garments for a special, if not formal, occasion; by "dressing down" we mean a scolding, if not a social leveling. To be dressed down is to be publicly divested of *social* garments—figuratively defrocked, unveiled, exposed.

Between the public revelation, however screened, of the black woman's multifold degradation in slavery (as in Jacobs) and the public pronouncements that scarcely tell anything private of a black woman (as with our two travelers in middle-class lands) arises an apparent dichotomy of approaches. These conflicting strategies speak to what historian Elsa Barkley Brown has seen as the paradoxical narrative of African American female history:

> It is not just that African-American women did different, seemingly contradictory, things at different times, which they did, but that they did different, seemingly contradictory things simultaneously. It is the simultaneity of their seemingly contradictory actions and beings for which we must account in our historical analyses. . . . The simultaneous promotion of two seemingly contradictory sets of values (some of which may be quite conscious, some of which may be unconscious but understood as necessary) is essential to the survival of individual African-Americans and of the African-American community as a whole.[10]

Keckley and Potter write autobiographies that contradict and complement each other's memoirs, and that also counter the reigning genre of slave narrative and the "by the bootstraps" self-helped story already in circulation by the late 1850s.[11] Such accounts constitute an intriguing doubleveiling: as black women authors, they withdraw the veil from the frivolous and self-centered nature of their white women employers at the same time they draw the veil over their own lives. Potter, for example, never mentions her own two children; Keckley's only child, a Union soldier who died in battle, receives the briefest of references. Both women found marriage unfulfilling, leaving their husbands and relations to pursue their careers—yet those same careers partly consisted of their commentary on the marital situations of the white women for whom they worked. For these black women, indirection prevailed when it came to autobiography. Historian Darlene Clark Hine has seen similar displacements in the everyday sphere: "Black women, as a rule, developed and adhered to a cult of secrecy, a culture of dissemblance, to protect the sanctity of inner aspects of their lives. . . . Only with secrecy, thus achieving a self-imposed invisibility, could ordinary Black women accrue the psychic space . . . needed to hold their own."[12]

Richard Yarborough remarks on the "avoidance of the first-person point of view in most Afro-American fiction before World War II":

> the act of seriously committing him- or herself to the creation of a fictional first-person voice entails for an author a plumbing of his or her own psychic depths—a process that must have been exceedingly painful for black artists who had to expend a considerable amount of energy in simply keeping their more dangerous and unruly emotions under tight rein lest they lose the audience they were trying to reach.[13]

Although speaking of men and women alike, Yarborough's assessment of the reluctance of black writers to reveal their innermost desires, beliefs, or emotions rings particularly, painfully true for the two female memoirists and autobiographers I discuss here, as well as for Wilson and Jacobs. Robert Stepto's identification of an African American "discourse of distrust," that it is not the storytellers who are unreliable, but their white readers, is also relevant to our understanding of Keckley and Potter.[14] The autobiographical terrain was too risky, so "scriptmines" and other rhetorical avoidance mechanisms were needed for black women to voice their concerns.[15] Even when cloaking her world view in anonymity, pseudonymity, or fiction, the African American woman writer at mid-nineteenth century walked a thin line between righting wrongs and revealing places on her soul and body too scarred for public view. Legally a nonperson, the antebellum black female had no rights that a white was bound to protect, no physical presence except what a white chose to acknowledge: her invisibility, like her veil, was doubled, imposed from within and without. The postbellum African American woman, with only the fiction of civil rights laws to protect her, was her virtual twin in literal and figurative negation.

Karen Halttunen's analysis of nineteenth-century American social hierarchies, class anxiety, fashion, and deportment gives us another perspective from which to view black female authorial strategies of dissemblance. Such tactics permit or even encourage commentary on the vagaries and vicissitudes of the white female society Halttunen described—even as they allow the black female self to remain hidden:

In what was believed to be a fluid social world where no one occupied a fixed social position, the question "Who am I?" loomed large; and in an urban social world where many of the people who met face-to-face each day were strangers, the question "Who are you really?" assumed even greater significance. In an open, urban society, the powerful images of the confidence man and the painted woman expressed the deep concern of status-conscious social climbers that they themselves and those around them were "passing" for something they were not.   *(Halttunen 1982, xv)*

The key word for African Americans would be "passing," although Halttunen transfers that strategy of "upwardly mobile" racial liminality to white society. As Eliza Potter knew, the lines between "white," "black," "society," and "lower" classes often blurred. Drawing on her personal observations, Potter could remark, "Some of these [socially mobile Cincinnatians] pass for white, and some, again, are so independent they will be thought nothing but what they are" (155). To be white was not simply to be without African ancestry; it was also not to be perceived as a member of the servant class (a fear about misperception that exists to this day). Yet the eyes of the servant, because they belong to the socially low, can see without being seen. Such a distinction might, following Orlando Patterson's formulation of the American black slave as one "socially dead," lend new and inverted meaning to the old saying "dead men—and black women—tell no tales."

As Janie Starks's grandmother says in Zora Neale Hurston's *Their Eyes Were Watching God*, "De nigger woman is de mule uh de world."[16] Others, including Hurston, have gone on to imply that as black women constitute the lowest rung of the American social ladder, they can function with relative invisibility and impunity, twin liberties that black women authors sometimes assumed as rhetorical strategies. Although Barkley Brown has convincingly argued that a belief in black women's relative invisibility has led to a lack of comprehension of the ways they have, sometimes violently, been oppressed, the fact that Keckley, Potter, and others like them were employees within an intimate female world gave them a peculiar entree into, and a kind of power over, white women's lives. For as Brown herself has seen, in the late nineteenth century "increasingly black women relied on constructing not only a respectable womanhood, but, in large measure, an *invisible* womanhood."[17] Although Barkley Brown speaks here specifically of the desire to "construct a desexualized persona" following centuries of white public perceptions of an African American female hypersexuality, I propose that the desire and need to cloak their personal lives from the gaze of whites would necessarily impel writers to remove most, if not all, evidence of the private sphere. Black women, given access to the boudoirs and dressing rooms of white women, were treated like furniture with arms and legs; they could subsequently reveal others' lives without revealing their own. The intense friendships Smith-Rosenberg has seen between white American women might have their parallels between white and black women—the Keckley-Lincoln friendship is a prime example— but racial fractures and the everlasting imbalance of power between whites and blacks virtually doomed any genuinely interracial "Female World of Love and Ritual."[18]

The publications of Eliza Potter and Elizabeth Keckley bracket the Civil War years. Potter's *A Hair-dresser's Experience in High Life* (1859), self-published anonymously, appeared before Lincoln's pivotal first election and the commencement of hostilities between North and South. Keckley's *Behind the Scenes; or, Thirty Years a Slave, and Four Years in the White House* (1868) appeared during the Reconstruction period, at a time when optimism for the cause of civil rights could still be justified, if less optimistically than in 1865. The war, barely a shadow on the horizon in Potter's book, envelopes and determines the shape of Keckley's, for Potter was born a free woman in New York and Keckley a slave in Virginia. Nevertheless, congruences in their respective works identify the authors as sharing the cultural matrix of black femaleness in the mid-nineteenth-century United States. To be a free woman, as opposed to a female slave, did not imply a status marked by liberty of action. A black female slave entrepreneur could make the difference between bond and free small indeed. Potter, one of the first of a long line of American black female hair-dresser-entrepreneurs,[19] and Keckley, an acknowledged "modiste" in her own time, do not base their narratives on thrilling escapes from slavery, nearly miraculous attainments of literacy, heroic sacrifices for their children, or sexual captivities that make lifelong bondage look like two kinds of hell. (Keckley's first three chapters certainly do comprise a slave's narrative, but the "incidents" of her life seem somewhat restrained in the telling, pointing to a desire for privacy as well as, perhaps, to the wish for reunion Andrews has seen in postbellum black autobiography.)[20] Instead, their life stories, if indeed we can call them that,[21] depend on two fulcrums: the revelation of secrets that black women were known yet not acknowledged to have—the unveiling of the white "back regions" of middle-class society—and the black female entrepreneurship that could lead as easily to fame and fortune as to infamy and ill will.[22]

In today's parlance, Potter and Keckley can be called small-time entrepreneurs securing stable economic niches through the few occupations
allowed them. As hairdresser and dressmaker, the two would hardly have
been placed in the same category as Douglass or William Wells Brown,
charismatic male speakers who began their careers on the abolitionist lecture circuit; later on, as journalists and writers with international reputations, both attained a prominence and respect unavailable to black
women. Although Potter's civil disobedience and Keckley's advocacy for
contrabands should not be belittled when compared to their male contemporaries' more publicly known activities, neither woman worked as a
professional orator for freedom.[23] Nevertheless, Keckley and Potter were
self-employed, and employed or trained others (Potter refers to having
students in both England and the United States, and in her showroom
Keckley gave work to more than twelve seamstresses). What Houston
Baker Jr. has said of Olaudah Equiano also applies to his mid-nineteenth-
century successors: "only the acquisition of property will enable him to
alter his designated status *as property*";[24] it is by economic skills that
Potter gains geographic freedom and Keckley wins her legal one.[25] Much
as earlier slave narrators who preceded them had inscribed "written by
himself" or "herself" across their title pages, these two women would, as
it were on the flyleaf of their own lives, inscribe "employed by herself."
They thus took their places among those nineteenth-century African
Americans who, slave or free, wrested control of their lives from whites.

Eliza Potter self-published her tart tell-all *A Hair-dresser's Experience in
High Life*. Appearing without an author, identifying the narrator solely by
the nickname "Iangy" and her clientele as a dizzying array of Mrs. D—s
and Miss A—s, the book seems to have been written as much to satisfy
Cincinnati society's appetite for gossip as to air the opinions of its quite
opinionated author. Potter, apparently born free, was raised in the state of
New York. As a child she was put in service, possibly as an indentured servant, and subsequently married. Succumbing to her desire to see "*the
Western world*" (11), though, she extricated herself from wedlock without
much of a backward look. Her travels through Europe as nursemaid to the
well-off and the well-born, and her successful business as a ladies' hair-
dresser, gave her an entree into circles that most of her readers, like the
later audience of *Behind the Scenes*, would never know. Her transatlantic
migrations, furthermore, both attested to her geographic liberty and
ensured that freedom by her acquisition of wide social experience and sal-
able skills. Yet were it not for a nineteenth-century librarian's desire to

classify the author racially, *High Life* might well have remained "a secret book," for the chronicler of white high life in Europe and the United States was an outsider.[26] That she was an African American woman, writing a memoir at mid-nineteenth century, who dared comment upon fashion-conscious Caucasian Americans, makes her book comparable to that of Keckley, nearly a decade later—though with some telling differences.[27]

Potter's justification for writing a narrative was not that she had been a handmaiden and witness to specific members of the upper classes. As she did not identify any of her patrons by name, whether countess or wealthy matron, interest in her book would not accrue from its being an account of celebrities. And her story, "a sketch of my experience in those walks of life where fate has led me" (11), is not merely a relation of experience. Like Frederick Douglass, Potter wants to give the philosophy as well as the facts; she also realizes, like her predecessor, that even her avowed friends may not wish her to do so.[28] For that reason, choosing not to reveal herself as a "colored" female hairdresser can be seen as evidence of authorial strategy rather than dissemblance, for certainly there is some evidence in the text, particularly at the beginning, revealing her to be a Negro. Potter knows her story, artless or trivial as it may appear, has a larger meaning:

It may perhaps be considered presumptive for one in my humble sphere of life to think of writing a book. . . . The physician writes his diary, and doubtless his means of discovering the hidden mysteries of life are great. The clergyman, whose calling inspires the deepest confidence, and into whose ear the tales of sorrow are unreservedly breathed, sends forth his diary to an eager world, and other innumerable chroniclers of fireside life have existed; but the hairdresser will yield rivalship to none in this regard. If domestic bitterness and joy, and all the heart-emotions that exist, cannot be discovered by her, she defies all the rest of the world to find them out.   (iv)

If casual perusers of her book think that the high and mighty have no sorrows and thus no stories to compel a reader, she continues: "No one need go into alleys to hunt up wretchedness; they can find it in perfection among the rich and fashionable of every land and nation" (iv). Her lovely figure of paradox—a perfection of wretchedness—speaks directly to her mission and missive. A black woman need not write of chattel slavery or sexual abuse to descend into the alleys: the disorder that allows a society to turn a blind eye to racial bondage ensures degradation and despair in other quarters. The hidden stories of abuse and folly that Potter relates are not confined to African Americans; indeed, although she includes many tales of slaves, it is the whites who appear foolish. Like those in the other listening professions, she has been told where the bodies, figurative and literal, are buried: white professional males are not the only ones to whom secrets are committed.

Eliza Potter chose to veil her identity. This tactical anonymity was relative, of course: like Harriet Wilson's, her name appeared on the reverse of the title page as the holder of copyright. Sharon G. Dean notes that many of Potter's midwestern readers knew just who she was, and may have been pleased to have been included in her mural of Cincinnati society (xlvi–xlvii); such inclusion attested to their social standing. Potter could stand behind the veil of conduct befitting a black female servant and pontificate on what she saw. And what "Iangy" (Potter's professional nickname) saw she found little difficulty disparaging, or praising, as she saw fit. Much of what the "hair-dresser in high life" did see drew her disapprobation. Potter felt little compunction disputing agreed-upon facts, castigating an individual's personal appearance or behavior, or passing judgment on who was genuinely of the *ton* and who was not. Potter makes herself more invisible than does Keckley, and this invisibility protects her from the public censure that the dressmaker would later garner. As a veiled narrator, Potter is partly but not entirely screened from view; like the women she writes of, who conduct assignations from closed carriages, she can appear publicly without being seen. More precisely, the "double invisibility" of her status as a "black woman . . . [and] employee" enables her to comment freely on others (Dean l). Yet we also see evidence of that "culture of dissemblance" forged through the fire of the antebellum African American woman's status as an allegedly oversexualized, enslaved laborer. We should not be surprised that Potter reveals virtually nothing about her private life.

As a black woman, Potter finds the status of invisibility adhering to her automatically, as she allows early on when describing her voyage on a Toronto-bound steamer: "I was alone in the world—self-exiled from home and friends, to be sure—but it was not until we were out some distance on the rolling waters of the lake, that I realized my isolated condition. I sat upon the deck, surrounded by people; but being a stranger among strangers, I had no claim on the notice of anyone" (12). If her readers do not then understand her "condition"—and she may here be punning on "previous condition," the nineteenth-century American legal term for former enslavement—Potter makes a corollary point later, when a group of whites including the Governor-General of Canada befriends her: "Well-bred people perfectly understand the art of making all comfortable around them, no matter what their color or condition may be." The true elite acknowledge her, even if they sometimes patronize her; an imperfect appearance can be better than perfect invisibility. Other black women knew the virtues of seeing without being seen, of acting without being acted upon. Harriet Jacobs, who would publish her autobiography just two years after Potter's book, first escaped from slavery by the risky maneuver of hiding herself in her grandmother's attic. She titles the chapter in which she first attains this paradoxical freedom "The Loophole of Retreat," after the abolitionist William Cowper's poem musing on the satisfaction of seeing without being seen.[29] Jacobs finds lonely amusement in her hideaway by watching her thwarted owner search in vain for her. Potter, free from the intrusions and abuse of a slave master, will also use whites' inability to see her in order to comment on their foibles.

Throughout *A Hair-dresser's Experience in High Life* Potter presents herself as an observer unobserved. In a mid-nineteenth-century world of watering holes and summer resorts of the rich and would-be rich, Potter ranges widely, from the dressing rooms to the ballrooms. Her "bird's eye" view encompasses sickness and health, Europeans and Americans, widows and young marrieds, servants and served. That many of her clients are themselves watchers underscores the truth of her visual weighing-in: as Karen Halttunen remarks, in the mid-nineteenth century, there was "a crisis of social identity faced by these men and women who were on the move both socially and geographically"; increasing numbers of Americans sought confirming signs of social place, gentility, and rightness in "a sentimental ideal of social conduct" (xv, xvi). So when Potter writes, "One evening, during the crowded season [in Saratoga Springs, NY], when there were about fifteen hundred people at the hotel, I concluded to look around and see how such a vast crowd would amuse themselves" (81), she announces to her readers that she will participate, if only as a watcher. She looks into "the parlor where two or three hundred people were collected . . . on the promenade . . . to the grounds . . . the cottages . . . the club-room . . . the bar-room . . . the private dining-rooms"; she sees "signs of the deepest emotion—of hope and despair, of sorrow and joy" (81–83). Moira Ferguson, speaking of Phillis Wheatley, would have us consider carefully this reversal of gazer and gazed-upon: "By claiming public subjectivity, African writers reversed colonialist depictions of 'others' who might be gazed upon at will. . . . [Wheatley] appropriates [whites'] view of her by gazing back and commenting on what she sees."[30]

Similarly turning back the gaze, Potter inverts expectations by depicting those used to imagining others.[31]

Later, as an established businesswoman in Cincinnati, she makes the following observations:

> One winter morning I noticed every countenance and dress I met with on my walk—first was a man with his black beard whitening with the frost, muttering to himself; he looked as though he or some of his friends had been unfortunate. Then came another with such a smile on his face, looking as pleasant as though he had some hot buckwheat cakes and nice rolls for breakfast, and had been spoken kindly to by both wife and children. . . . I [later] went to the house of the gentleman who looked so sad, and told his wife I had met her lord that morning, and he looked as if his coffee was muddy, his bread had been burnt, or his cakes not very high for breakfast that morning. "You are right, Iangy," she said, "both were bad and he left in a very bad humor." *(224)*

Another occasion finds her discovering, by literally walking into him, "a man laying in the street, either dead or drunk" (228). Unsure what to do, Potter waits for "some gentlemen coming toward me" to decide the case. But they ignore both drunk white man and sentient black woman, marginal characters at best in their "high life." A second group of white men coming along "noticed him, and seeing me looking at him" ascertain he is merely in an alcoholic stupor and prepare to leave—but they obviously feel put on the spot by her silent questioning. Only when it appears they will leave him lying there does Potter speak: "Gentleman, if he is drunk he is a man; let him be taken to the station house and cared for, and be punished when he is sober" (229). With these and other anecdotes, Potter establishes herself as one who knows, the unseen viewer who kens the minds of whites who pass her by without a thought. Apparently secure in their whiteness and middle-class status, Potter's subjects allow her to operate in their own back regions; casting her as invisible, they mistakenly believe their own actions are equally obscured. They could learn from the lessons of Bentham's panopticon, where an unseen watcher keeps all in view and subject to external judgment.[32] Potter understands the place to which white society would consign her, and how she can be present without being seen. She is therefore quick to seize the advantages inherent in whites' mistaken ideas about blacks, women, and those who inhabit that dually marginal space.

Potter explicitly refers to the increasing level of social anxiety early in her discussion of Saratoga, the renowned nineteenth-century American resort: "so many new people are springing up upon the Saratoga platform now-a-days, that the old select circles are beginning to retire from the scene to more rural and quiet retreats" (60). At the spa, "*lynx-eyed fashion*" discerns fake jewelry and sniffs out impostors and poseurs (54), yet it is this same fashion that "is carried to an extreme which is positively vulgar, and *I*, the poor hair-dresser, can see it as well as the poor devils of husbands who have it all to pay for" (61). Money may buy the genuine jewels that purchase entree into the right circles, but mere cash can't win everything: "Oh! if tesselated hearths and satin tapestries could speak, what tales of agony they might tell!" (iv). Potter's "lynx"-like vision will reveal the chronicle of gilded, guilty living. That Potter goes "out, at an early age, to earn my living, in the service of people of *ton*" (11) was not unusual for a free-born black.[33] That she then viewed this necessity as a virtue, or more specifically, saw this job-bred talent for discerning "*ton*" as a professional skill, recalls the peculiar remark Keckley makes regarding the brutal punishment she received as an inept four-year-old baby-sitter: slavery can be "bless[ed] . . . for one thing—youth's important lesson of self-reliance" (*Behind the Scenes*, 19–20). "When life gives you lemons, make lemonade" could be the motto of both of these black women entrepreneurs. Potter's discernment of the falsely titled, of "confidence men and painted women," becomes yet another professional strength of the hairdresser, who by the very nature of her chosen career becomes the confessor of her clients. Yet the confidante role has its dangers: "Ladies are in the habit of saying a great many things, not only to the hair-dressers, but to others, which would be a great deal better unsaid. [But] When these things come to be talked about they forget saying them to any one but the hair-dresser" (201–2). Rather than cast aspersions on those of their own race and class, white employers will first scapegoat the employee—a lesson Keckley would learn too well, too late. Potter has her say from behind the veil, offering up a social critique while obscuring her own life.[34]

Numerous times in the course of her memoir, Potter remarks upon the ways that the whites she comes into contact with are taken advantage of and bilked.

> I know a young lady . . . beautiful and accomplished, who lived principally at the most fashionable hotels, where she made the acquaintance of an Englishman, who was reputed immensely wealthy, and who fell in love

with, and married her. . . . The gentleman [later] obtained possession of his wife's jewelry, and, with all the money he could collect, left for parts unknown. . . . It frequently happens that those who marry foreigners for their titles or wealth, find themselves thus deceived. I can not but laugh sometimes to see how some of our upper tens get picked up. *(232–33)*

Early on, Potter identifies herself as one who can spy out the well-born or well-mannered. Her "experiences in high life" come replete with observations such as: "I saw at once she was a *parvenu* woman" (31); "where there were so many congregated they could not all be ladies" (85); "She said, 'Yes; I come here to drink water, recruit, and get a husband' " (152); the Canadians she meets early in her career believe that all deserve courtesy, and show up the *"parvenu* ladies and gentlemen" whom the *"humblest servant"* can identify (13). Potter's satisfaction is complete when she warns one of her clients that an Englishwoman she admires is really an impostor: "I know enough of them [English nobility] to know one in any part of the world I may meet them; I can even tell a servant that has been in their employ." She promises her patron "five years' hair-dressing" if she is wrong, and "expect[s] a valuable present" if right; is the reader surprised when Iangy comes around later to have her savvy acknowledged (216–18)? The talents for discerning falsehood and knowing where supporters can be found, of being able to know one's employers while shielding oneself—gifts born of a demeaned racial status and low social condition—become Potter's ticket to the middle class. Holding one's tongue becomes less a sign of sensibility than evidence of business sense. " I was much oftener the receptacle of secrets than I desired to be. I often wished that they [the ladies of Saratoga, NY] had better sense; though, after all, I did not care much *what they did,* so they paid me my wages" (68). Her fortune depended in good measure on keeping her mouth shut: Dean has ascertained that at forty, Eliza Potter had real estate valued at $2,000 and personal property valued at $400 (xlv).

In a "western" society (of which, in the 1850s, Ohio was still very much a part), where fortunes rose and fell rapidly and those with a little cash could readily parlay it into increased social standing, Potter's influence on the right folk was bankable. To be from "the West" was often—and sometimes still is—linked with being a social climber or *nouveau riche.* The hairdresser reports with relish various occasions of white women asking her to intercede for them, to engineer an entree into a social setting above their present one. One woman says, "some of them [the upper class of Cincinnati] I know you know very well, and through your influence I expect they will come; do not tell me you can not persuade them" (243). Potter asserts that many hostesses "at the issuing of invitations [will ask] 'Iangy, do you know any one I have forgotten?' "; she then describes how she "got an invitation for a young lady of this city, to the party of one of our grandest places" (271). Obviously, this position as behind-the-scenes mediator pleases Potter, for she can, by proxy, be admitted herself. Although Potter, whose clients were wealthy rather than politically promi-nent, saw little of the kind of political "back region" maneuvering Keckley came to know, she could consider herself an actor in a way that the modiste perhaps did not. Potter feels confident enough about her acumen to describe four classes of Cincinnati society, a skill prized now that "It is much easier to get into the higher circles ... than when I first became a hair-dresser" (196).[35] Potter's clients' concern with being seen as *parvenus* or western hicks would be shared by Keckley's Mrs. Lincoln, whose profligate spending on dress and accessories was due in part to her fears at being looked down upon by Washington "society."[36] While Keckley reveals the class and regional anxieties of the Kentucky-born and Illinois-wed Lincoln, Potter excels at limning the breakneck social climbing going on across an entire spectrum of mid-nineteenth-century Americans, years before Mark Twain and C. D. Warner made such behavior infamous in their novel *The Gilded Age* (1873).

"Many Americans were attempting to pass for more than what they really were, in the sense that they were trying to rise in society, to assume a new and better social identity" (Halttunen 117–18). And "more than what they really were" for African Americans could mean white rather than black. Over two centuries of systematic interracial rape and concubi-nage had produced thousands of light-, if not white-, skinned Americans of African descent; countless slaves took advantage of their phenotypical sim-ilarities to their owners and made tracks for the North.[37] We should not be surprised, then, that Eliza Potter displays such a sharp eye and caustic wit for the efforts of white folks to get ahead; she has seen such efforts by her own people. She contrasts maneuvers by whites and blacks, leaving no question about whose side she takes: in one passage quoted above, Potter relates the story of a white American who gets swindled when she marries a titled Englishman who turns out to be a phony; she ends "laugh[ing] to see how some of our upper tens get picked up [deceived]." Immediately fol-lowing this anecdote, Potter tells another story:

Some few years ago a gentleman came to this city, who passed himself off as the son of an Indian chief; he was gallanted here and there, and par-

ties were given him by some of our first families. This chief turned out
to be a fugitive slave; he actually both roomed and slept with some of our
gentlemen, and did not feel as if he had lowered himself at all. This went
on for a few weeks . . . and [then] he was captured by his master. *(233)*

Unlike the upwardly mobile young woman, the nameless fugitive is wittily
complimented, and the gullible whites are ribbed, by Potter's sly observation that *he* did not feel in the least demeaned by bunking with white men.
She closes the story by writing of their subsequent meeting in Canada: "He
was as smart a man as I had the pleasure of conversing with in Toronto"
(233). In matters of passing, whites are foolish, while blacks are ingenious
or "independent."[38]

Potter makes it clear throughout her volume that she is one of the independent ones. On numerous occasions, she describes herself, or is described,
with just that word: "perfectly independent of anyone" (30); "she thought
me a bold, independent woman" (164); "you seem to be very independent
here lately" (227). She also calls herself "high spirited" (243) and has no
qualms about repeating a white client's assertion that "Iangy . . . is so cross
and proud" (277), for that criticism is the very petard on which she'll hoist
the woman—and before her friends, too. Although Potter could well be
thought of as consigned to the category of "uppity nigger," or "sassy" black
woman, she seems happy to claim that characterization.[39] Her entire memoir serves as illustration of Potter's verbal feistiness, with incidents such as
the one just mentioned and the following incident, which we can call the
episode of the silk dresses.

In relating her successful battle with an Albany railroad company,
Potter demonstrates, as always, her reversal of white expectations. En
route to Saratoga for a summer season's work, Potter's railway train
catches on fire. Although she and the other passengers escape without
serious injury, "many were in great distress, and were crying—they had
lost their all. . . . I myself was not among the fortunate ones, as I had some
things no money could pay me for" (98). She, along with other travelers,
applies to the home office for restitution. There one man "decided to give
me two hundred dollars, which [another] thought was a great deal too
much for me to handle, and thought one hundred enough" (99–100).
Without directly referring to her status as a woman alone, much less as a
free black woman, Potter delineates the patronizing airs of white male
businessmen. The money, however, is not enough to reimburse her; one
who travels with high society must dress the part. On her return to press
for full payment she finds that

they seemed all perfectly astonished at the list of my clothes. Mr. F. was aghast at the idea of my paying thirty-five dollars for a moire antique dress, and said his wife never had a dress cost so much. I laughed, and told him I had a dress which cost me fifty dollars, and a mantle to suit which cost me fifty more; and if his highness pleased, I had a suit that cost me one hundred and fifty dollars. . . . To be behind the door and see their wide-open eyes and hear their catched-up breath when they came to any articles more expensive than others; and when Mr. F. came, on the list, to a velvet basquine trimmed with deep fringe, he seemed to think it was an impossibility; but there were so many persons both in Albany and New York that knew the extent of my wardrobe, that he could no longer doubt. . . . [they believed it] an impossibility for a working woman to have such a wardrobe.   *(100–1)*

Men who doubt that "a working woman"—much less an African American one—could have such clothing could easily come to the conclusion that she should indeed *not* possess such items. The men of the Albany railroad company continue to stall, resorting to delaying tactics to shake Potter off. But she persists: "Every morning I went down to the office after breakfast, staid there till dinner time; went to dinner, returned, and staid there till night; and I assure you my tongue never stopped, nor was I tired commenting on all that came under my notice" (101). When she finally decides to apply to the president of the firm and learns he is away in New York, she goes there; when she learns he has just left, she stays for a vacation, and proceeds to tell her reader of her escapades. Returning refreshed for the battle, she at last corners the lion in his den, finds him "a perfect gentleman," and that though "he did not give me what I thought was sufficient to repay my losses, yet he gave me more than the others were willing" (110). Possessed of sang-froid and determination, this "working woman" is no one's fool. The unmarried, self-supporting woman who traveled with ten silk dresses in her suitcases knows her worth, whether others agreed with her or not.

Whereas other free black women had to remain employed at their earliest professions—as domestics, laundresses, or nursemaids—the young Potter, working in France, launches a professional offensive:

I became so weary of my monotonous duties [of tending young children], that I concluded to quit my place and learn the art of flower-making. In this I succeeded pretty well, though I soon grew tired of it, and thought I should like dress-making; but, after a short trial, find-

ing that did not suit me, I took a notion to learn cooking, but soon
gave that also up. Nothing but hair-dressing pleased my fancy for any
length of time. (27)

That Potter found her early work as nursemaid unsatisfying and determined to quit it might have struck even the tiny number of resolutely middle-class blacks of the time as quixotic, if not self-destructive. Potter listens
to no one—at least as she tells it—and like the cat in the fable, walks by
herself (save, of course, for the two children who are never mentioned). The
same sense of self-confidence leads Potter to her innumerable pronouncements on society foibles, fashion, and marital troubles; the book overflows
with her detailed descriptions of fancy dress sorties and lovers' spats.

But Potter's proffering of "high life" to her readers masks fierce antislavery beliefs, although she refutes the sobriquet of abolitionist as a label
best applied to what we would today call "armchair activists." From the
opening pages, when Potter discusses the difference in attitude between
Americans and Canadians, throughout the rest of her memoirs, depictions of racist actions and antislavery sentiment counter the effervescent
portrait of "high life." Although one reader, writing thirty years ago,
believed Potter gave "to the slavery issue . . . only minor attention," the
opinionated hairdresser pulls no punches in her condemnation of slave-
holding.[40] In fact, Potter is incarcerated for several months as an aider and
abettor of a fugitive slave; she learns, while working in Kentucky as a
nursemaid, of a young man's threatened sale—and advises him to flee. "I
frankly told him all I knew of Canada. I informed him how he could reach
there . . . and yet . . . a doubt rose in my mind, as to whether I had been
his friend, or his enemy, in thus directing his steps to a new world and a
new home" (17). For her Christian charity, Potter is rewarded by arrest
and imprisonment as an accessory to the crime. Convicted in an Ohio
court, Potter is remanded to Kentucky and incarcerated for three months
in a Louisville jail. Only through sheer luck, it seems, is she not lynched
or falsely sold into slavery herself.

Beyond her own act of defiance, Potter recounts numerous "incidents
in the life of" slavery: the beating of a slave woman in Memphis (42–43),
the vow of a Kentucky beauty that she will manumit a mother and
child—a promise the woman reneges upon but is repaid for when her current maid runs away to freedom (142–43). The chapter "Natchez–New
Orleans" abounds with tales of horror, from the chained, beaten slave who
fights back and kills his master to colored, and cruel, slave owners.
Although Potter says at one point that a slave treated kindly won't leave

his master (88), she contradicts this assertion frequently: she quotes the Kentucky beauty as saying "let servants be treated as well as they can be, they want to be free" (142); she espouses what can only be described as equal opportunity slave-holding ("the whites should also own each other" [191]); she includes an anecdote about white women who inveigh against slave traders but themselves hold people in bondage (170). Her statement against "abolitionists" to an inquiring white woman appears to countermand such illustrations:

> The lady commenced the conversation with me by saying, "I am an abolitionist." "I am very sorry indeed to hear that," I replied. She started, and looked at me in perfect amazement; when I said, "I don't like abolitionists, nor any that bear the name, as I have seen so much injustice and wrong, and actually speculation done in that name, that I hate to hear it; but I like every person—slave-holders, free-holders, or any other kind of holders who treat all people right, regardless of nation, station or color; and all men and women who love their Redeemer, will do this without confining themselves to any one name to make themselves conspicuous."
>
> *(249)*

In fact, what Potter rails against is white hypocrisy and self-serving devotion to "worthy causes." Any number of slave narratives include stories of the narrator's being helped by a sympathetic white southerner, if not by an actual slave owner; well the hairdresser knows that it doesn't take northern residence or membership in an antislavery society to make one a friend to the slave. Potter scorns those who sympathize with the oppressed of Europe while turning away from the millions held in American perpetual servitude; she indignantly rejects a client's suggestion that she donate money to Kossuth's American campaign for Hungarian liberty: "before we go abroad to pluck the mote out of our brethren's eye, let us pick the beam out of our own eye. . . . At this very time, when there was so much sympathy excited for the oppressed Hungarians, there was, in the very midst of our city, a man being tried for running away from cruel bondage and oppression" (212, 213). Both of these passages demonstrate Potter's commitment to liberty for all. Her condemnation of "abolitionists" might raise eyebrows, but it underscores her earlier objections to easy sympathy for oppressed whites living thousands of miles away. She also echoes her contemporary Harriet Wilson, who describes the heroine of her novel as "maltreated by professed abolitionists, who didn't want slaves at the South, nor niggers in their own houses, North. Faugh!

to lodge one; to eat with one; to admit one through the front door; to sit next one; awful!"[41] Writing as free blacks in a country still committed to slavery, Wilson and Potter chose the veil of anonymity in order to present an uncensored critique. A postbellum successor, though thirty years a slave, decided against the veil—yet in doing so elected attendant rhetorical and real-life consequences.

Elizabeth Keckley provides us with more personal information than does Potter, whose book was published without so much as an author's name on the title page (her name appeared on the reverse, as holder of the copyright). Harriet Jacobs, like Potter, eschewed publishing under her own name; as Joanne Braxton says, Jacobs "speaks as a disguised woman, a woman whose identity remains partly obscured."[42] Keckley, on the other hand, has long been known to historians of the Civil War as the author of a significant primary source on the Lincolns and wartime Washington society. She tells us much about herself—if not the entire story.[43] Like innumerable former slaves, she begins her narrative with the words "I was born," but interpolates a moderately boastful first sentence: "My life has been an eventful one" (17). We know from her own telling that she was the only child of devoted slave parents, and that her early life in slavery was rather the norm than the exception: that is, she was separated from her father (although she remained with her mother) as a young girl, began working as a nursemaid while still a toddler, and while an attractive teenager was subject to violent physical and sexual abuse, the latter of which resulted in the birth of her son, George. Keckley's son, a credit to her as a martyred hero of the war, is also a living reminder of her abasement; like a veil, his memory both adorns and protects.[44] Yet after she makes the acquaintance in 1860 of Mrs. Jefferson Davis and Mrs. Abraham Lincoln, the private life of Elizabeth Hobbs Keckley recedes almost permanently into the background. Perhaps her silence stems from that culture of dissemblance black women have had to construct to shield their individual selves from a larger society that would sexually abuse and personally disrespect them. Certainly she seems to have believed her postbellum audience would have more interest in her unveiling of White House "back regions" than in her own "black back regions"; after the requisite self-imprimatur provided by her depiction of her genuine life in slavery, verisimilitude affirmed, she can go on to write the scenes her white audiences crave. Keckley knew well that her audience's attention span for things African was ending: the war was over, the slaves were freed, the controversial acts of Reconstruction were underway—although already under attack. She needed no degree in economics to gauge her own value as a black female *ex-slave* commodity in the book-buying market, and allotted space to her own life accordingly. That sense of the buyer's market, in terms of herself as a black female seller, forms or de-forms her book accordingly.

From the time we pick up the volume we see a contest between competing and unconscious beliefs, between the desire to tell her own story and that of another—one who could very well tell her own. Keckley's title reflects this struggle between private and public life, between a life lived for oneself and one displayed for whites. For a reader familiar through the advertisement with Keckley's relationship to the Lincoln family, the first three words—*Behind the Scenes*—would seem to promise insights, if not titillating tidbits, about life as a consort to America's First Family; the subtitle, *Thirty Years a Slave, and Four in the White House,* seems to undermine that promise, for one could reasonably assume that the first section would exceed the second by some dozens of chapters. This is not the case, for the thirty years are told in three chapters comprising not even fifty pages; the four years in the White House, and three following that, take up twelve chapters—nearly three hundred pages.[45] Although William Andrews has convincingly argued that in the postbellum slave narrative we can see a decreasing emphasis on "what happened *then*" and an increasing emphasis on "what *makes* things, good things, happen now," the Reconstruction-era black's pragmatism alone cannot explain the muting of certain events and emotions. Patterns of deference and of dissemblance take more than manumission to eliminate.

Like Olaudah Equiano, Keckley begins her career by careful management and self-purchase, shrewdly manipulating her capital to buy freedom for her son and self. In a chapter entitled "How I Gained My Freedom," the future seamstress-confidante of Mary Todd Lincoln recounts how she attained a slave's most precious prize. Prior to this, as did many slave narrators, Keckley details scenes from her early life, particularly the devotion of her parents to each other and the various kinds of abuse she suffers as an attractive young woman. Somewhat surprisingly, Keckley refers to obtaining her liberty as "the most interesting part of my story" (43) rather than the most interesting part *so far*—for her book continues for another dozen chapters, sans appendix. Thus unqualified, her remark indicates that freedom remains, at least for Keckley, the supreme moment of the book— which means that in some sense the following events comprise an anticlimax. The white reader, perhaps racing through these earlier, personal revelations of life in slavery to the stories "behind the scenes" about Mary

Todd and Abraham Lincoln, can miss this subtle weighing-in of substance and significance. For Keckley's black contemporaries, however, the story that follows might well function not just as a reminder of the end of slavery, with its triumphant ending of bondage by the author's own enterprise, but as an indicator of what is *most* important in the entire narrative: freedom. The abrupt silencing of the personal in subsequent chapters can thus be read as more than diffidence: William L. Andrews has noted Keckley's savviness in placing her work within a materialist discourse that substitutes for the womanly "virtue" of a prebellum woman narrator like Jacobs the marketplace know-how of a postbellum author like herself: "she expends much of her narrative in claiming credit for herself as an upholder of bourgeois economic standards."[46] In publishing her book, Keckley seeks not only to redress slanders directed against her friend and former employer, Mary Todd Lincoln, but also to recoup her own financial losses due to her championing the assassinated president's widow. She furthermore seeks "the internal sense of order and control" Nellie McKay has seen as characteristic of those belonging to "a group whose external world demanded subservience and dependence on others."[47]

Keckley, like many another slave narrator, finds herself relocated when she is given, along with other trousseau items, to Miss Ann Burwell upon her wedding to a Mr. Garland. The "family, myself included, joined him in his new home on the banks of Mississippi" (44) in St. Louis, where they find him nearly impoverished. Because of his financial reverses the whites plan to send Keckley's mother, who has also been brought along, out to service, a degradation that her only child indignantly refuses: "The idea was shocking to me. Every gray hair in her old head was dear to me, and I could not bear the thought of her going to work for strangers" (44). Her anger at the white family's lack of gratitude—earlier, in Virginia, her owners had scorned her ceaseless efforts with a cruel, "you'll never be worth your salt"—spurs her to entrepreneurial heights:

> In a short time I had acquired something of a reputation as a seamstress and dress-maker. The best ladies in St. Louis were my patrons, and when my reputation was established I never lacked for orders. With my needle I kept bread in the mouths of seventeen persons for two years and five months. While I was working so hard that others might live in comparative comfort, and move in those circles of society to which their birth gave them entrance, the thought often occurred to me whether I was really worth my salt or not; and then perhaps the lips curled with a bitter sneer. *(45–46)*

The abrupt shift from the first-person "my patrons" to the indefinite "the lips" gives away her suppressed rage and "displacement of emotion."[48] Keckley sublimates her anger and relative powerlessness in an explosion of work, showing us how she sewed her way to freedom, much as Douglass would have us believe that he wrote or thought his way out.

Although Keckley's health eventually fails under the strain of supporting an entire household (she appears to have been providing sustenance for both her white owners and her fellow slaves), her success gives her further inspiration and she proposes to buy herself. She is, of course, rejected at first: would any slave-holder so fortunate in a chattel personal let her go? But, she writes, "I would not be put off thus, for hope pointed to a freer, brighter life in the future." In fact, she wants to free not just herself, but her son as well: "He came into the world through no will of mine, and yet, God only knows how I loved him." Keckley here shows her impeccable maternal credentials, for although George is the product of a four-year-long "persecution" (39), she will not leave him behind. Curiously, she does not appear to seek her mother's liberty, and does not even discuss whether the issue is raised. Perhaps she did not attempt it because her mother "had been raised in the [Burwell] family ... and she was wound round about [the children of the family] as the vine winds itself about the rugged oak. They had been the central figures in her dream of life—a dream beautiful to her, since she had basked in the sunshine of no other" (44). For this reason, perhaps, Keckley leaves her behind. Or did her mother urge her to go, feeling it best to give liberty to those young enough to enjoy it?[49] By not telling us, Keckley begins here to bring down the veil on her personal life and to bring up the curtain on her life as a modiste and confidante to Mrs. Lincoln.

The manner in which she gains her freedom shows how Keckley's strategies differ from those of Jacobs, Bibb, and Douglass. Andrews, without pointing specifically to such possible models as Benjamin Franklin or Frederick Douglass, sees Keckley's book as "an unabashed and often plainly self-congratulatory success story. . . . Keckley portrays herself inexorably climbing the social and economic ladder to intimacy with the First Family of the United States based on her work as a modiste."[50] She wants, Andrews asserts, acknowledgment for her adherence to prevailing norms of "making it." With this in mind it seems less bizarre that Keckley, speaking of the harsh treatment she suffered as a very young slave, represents such abuse as "youth's important lesson of self-reliance" (19–20).[51] Doing so, she echoes the language of Douglass, who by the time *Behind the Scenes* appeared was already known for his speech on "Self-Made Men," and was numbered among Keckley's circle of acquaintances.

Keckley, confronting her master a second time, is surprised to have him turn to her and, "in a petulant manner," offer her money for passage on the ferry to free territory for herself and her child; she "earnestly replied: 'No, master, I do not wish to be free in such a manner. If such had been my wish I should never have troubled you. . . . By the laws of the land I am your slave . . . and I will only be free by such means as the laws of the country provide' " (48–49). Keckley longs for freedom but wants her liberty approved of by the very man who deprives her of it; this desire counts as a weird and inverse parallel to the blandishments of Dr. Norcom, who doesn't want to force himself sexually on Harriet Jacobs, but instead craves her acquiescence. Slavery warps the very "common sense" of its human participants, leading sexual predators to want to appear as ardent lovers and enjoining slaves who would be free to believe themselves equal traders in a rational marketplace. Houston Baker Jr., writing on the "adept mercantilism" of Olaudah Equiano, asserts that a large part of a slave's journey into freedom is his or her recognition of "the rudiments of economics that condition his very life"; the slave must turn from "spiritual meditations to canny speculations" in order to gain freedom (38, 33, 35). So too does Keckley turn from domestic drudgery as the sole, overworked "girl" of the Reverend Burwell household—where, she says, "we had to practice the closest economy" (32)—to the relative freedom of an urban slave who can hire her own time and gain "something of a reputation as a seamstress and dress-maker." Although she again must support a household of whites (one certainly can wonder from her telling where the epithet "shiftless black" came from), her skills at sewing and designing, like Equiano's talents trading in small items, earn her enough to buy herself and her child. Both manumissions depend on whites who are as good as their word, for slave narratives catalogue many tales of masters who swindle hardworking slaves out of their money, freedom, or sanity. Keckley goes so far as to include the documents granting her freedom within her memoir, much as did Equiano. Yet that liberty is built on sand, subject to the whims of local governments, envious whites, and the greed of others who would falsely sell them into slavery. Harriet Jacobs, on learning that she had been bought by her northern employer in order to spare her from the continual efforts of her southern "owners" to recapture her, had this to say about dealing with the devil:

So I was *sold* at last! A human being *sold*. . . . The bill of sale is on record, and future generations will learn from it that women were articles of traffic. . . . I well know the value of that bit of paper; but

much as I love freedom, I do not like to look on it. . . . I despise the mis-
creant who demanded payment for what never rightfully belonged to
him or his.
(200)

Entrepreneurship becomes a boomerang, whizzing back to strike the
player from behind. To buy one's freedom is a fine thing, Equiano and
Keckley attest—but to do so and report of one's success creates another
quandary: does doing so underwrite the slave economy, as Baker and others might suggest? Does this imply that those who don't purchase themselves have not the will to do so, and are therefore in some way less
deserving of our notice? Does Keckley subscribe to such notions herself,
or does she unwittingly play into beliefs about the "deserving" oppressed?
Her apparent soft-pedaling of human bondage, "Slavery had its dark side
as well as its bright side" (30), follows a chapter in which she remembers
being brutally whipped as a child of four, her adoring parents forever separated, a cook's son sold away to settle a debt, and her uncle hanging himself rather than face torture for a lost set of reins. Such a sentence cannot
simply be an understatement, "surprising and taciturn," as James Olney
has remarked (xxx); coming where it does in the chapter it serves as a profound full stop, and holds a mirror to the system of chattel slavery. If we
compare Keckley's statement to Frederick Douglass's *apparently* laconic
remark following his recounting of his aunt's brutal beating—"I wish I
could commit to paper the feelings with which I beheld it" (*Narrative*,
28)—and place it within a context of black narrational "undertell," we can
comprehend the restrained severity of Keckley's irony.[52]

The scenes in which Keckley recounts mourning, whether Mary Todd
Lincoln's or her own, tell us more about her autobiographical strategies. In
the chapter "Willie Lincoln's Death-Bed," Keckley demonstrates curious,
successive, and almost contradictory—if not actually competing—revelations of a child's death and his mother's grief. She begins the account within
a generalized context of mourning, setting the scene within a nation being
rent asunder, "where new graves were being made every day, where brother
forgot a mother's early blessing and sought the life-blood of brother. . . . Oh,
the front with its ghastly heaps of dead! The life of the nation was at stake;
and when the land was full of sorrow, there could not be much gayety at the
capital" (91–92). Although she then abruptly switches to a (renewed)
defense of the Lincolns—"evil report had said much of him and his wife"
(91)—in doing so she limns the skullduggery of an actress who plans to
infiltrate the household and write a tell-all book. Keckley's words—"her
object was to enter the White House as a servant, learn its secrets, and then

publish a scandal to the world" (95)—must seem peculiar to her readers; how could they avoid linking the scandalous actress to the presumptuous black woman who dares to "aid" the Lincolns? A narrative doubling of would-be and actual narrators, of women veiled and without the veil, occurs again when Keckley introduces the infinitely delicate subject of mourning. Preceding the actual death scene with some pages on Willie's decline and ill-ness, much in the manner of stories of the death of Little Eva and countless other doomed angels of the Victorian era, Keckley closes the chapter by reprinting N. P. Willis's encomium: "A wild flower transplanted from the prairie to the hothouse, he retained his prairie habits, unalterably pure and simple, till he died" (cited in Keckley, 107).

It was early 1861, the beginning of Abraham Lincoln's first term, when William Lincoln passed away. Mary Todd Lincoln's intense mourning for her middle son seemed to some hysterical and histrionic, and whispered accusations of her unseemliness would grow to audible complaints follow-ing her husband's assassination. Four years before that national disaster, Keckley recounts that "Mrs. Lincoln's grief was inconsolable. The pale face of her [dead] boy threw her into convulsions. . . . In one of her paroxysms of grief the President [warned] . . . 'try and control your grief, or it will drive you mad, and we may have to send you [to the lunatic asylum]' " (104–5).[53] Although Keckley does not mention the fact, and indeed may not have known it, Mary Todd Lincoln had already lost one son eleven years before; this death and the losses of her early childhood established her pattern of "difficult mourning" that was to become so well known but not condoned.[54] Her double bind has been illuminated by social historian Karen Halttunen, who in delineating the social codes that governed nine-teenth-century American middle-class "sentimentalization of death" has noted "In mourning, a middle-class man or woman was believed to estab-lish very clearly the legitimacy of his or her claims to genteel social sta-tus."[55] Although women and men were encouraged to shed copious tears and pine over their losses, there were nevertheless limits and parameters to the state of mourning; among them was that the mourner should enact her or his grief in the privacy of the home. Grieving was expected to aid those left behind in their progress toward Christ and to a particular station within middle-class society: a true "Christian did not wail with despair over the death of a loved one. . . . The bourgeois quest for genteel propriety was not to be abandoned" (134). Fashionable mourning jewelry, discreet and reified tokens of loss, aided in this performance; ridding one's home of every memento of the lost soul, as Mrs. Lincoln did, was not an approved-of practice.[56] One wonders at Keckley's hubris in commenting on Mary

Todd Lincoln's admittedly unorthodox mourning behaviors: "I never in my life saw a more peculiarly constituted woman. Search the world over, and you will not find her counterpart" (182). Years after the tragic events of the 1860s, there were undoubtedly many whites who found the widowed Mary Todd Lincoln's ungovernable emotions, in addition to her close friendship with a Negro dressmaker and her spurning of more socially appropriate callers "who were denied admittance to her chamber" (196), evidence of derangement—or at best, of poor judgment.

In contrast, Elizabeth Keckley's near-total silence on her own loss seems mysterious, especially as in 1868 both women could be pitied for having lost members of their immediate families in the Union cause; such suffering in the service of the nation awarded greater status to their grieving. Yet Keckley remained discreet in her style of mourning, at least with her readers. Her modern editor, James Olney, has remarked on Keckley's apparent diffidence in regard to discussing her own son's death, as opposed to her detailed treatment of Mary Todd Lincoln's grief. She "gives a good deal of space to the death of Willie Lincoln, which she renders in language that would not be out of place in Dickens or Harriet Beecher Stowe, but only glancingly and as a kind of footnote to Willie Lincoln's death does she reveal that her own only son had been killed in battle." Olney goes on to say "it is as if the Lincolns . . . were 'important,' in Keckley's view, in a way that she would never claim for herself or for her own actions and emotions" (xxxiv). Yet Keckley's relative silence could also confirm her in white eyes as a successful performer, one who could be judged socially deserving, and worthy of higher status:

> Previous to this I had lost my son. Leaving Wilberforce [the historically black college in Xenia, Ohio], he went to the battle-field with the three months troops, and was killed in Missouri—found his grave on the battle-field where the gallant General Lyon fell. It was a sad blow to me, and the kind womanly letter that Mrs. Lincoln wrote to me when she heard of my bereavement was full of golden words of comfort. *(105)*

Rather than making her loss less profound than that of Mary Todd Lincoln, Keckley might have been asserting her own delicacy—in comparison to her employer-friend, whose "womanly delicacy" she does not fail to commend—and to be withdrawing from the possibly prurient gaze of her audience a profound grief she might well hesitate to offer up to the inspection of a white reader. John E. Washington interviewed several elderly Washingtonians who remembered the late dressmaker: "To her most intimate friends, she would at times speak about her son who was killed in the first battle of the war at Wilson Creek, but her constant talk was about Mrs. Lincoln and Tad, and very seldom about her own son George." Most appeared to have had little idea of the depth or nature of Keckley's grief: as she said on a number of occasions, "I do not like to burden others with the sorrows of my past."[57] Mrs. Lincoln, then her confidante, could however write to a cousin: "our colored mantuamaker Elizabeth, lost her only son and child in the battle of Lex. M. She is heartbroken."[58] Other whites would have been still less likely to hear of "the sorrows of my past," for what African American was unaware of the false complex of beliefs and superstitions ascribed to them by their European American compatriots? Keckley may not have read the deportment guides Halttunen has studied and numerous Victorian Americans purchased, but she could hardly have been unaware of the stereotypes whites held about blacks, false portraits that could also encompass attitudes about death. Keckley well knew African Americans were believed to be heathens, or at best nominal or emotive Christians incapable of "the emotional self-control that stamped the man of gentility" (Halttunen 135).

That Keckley was aware of white perceptions of black deportment and that she was equally desirous of skirting white prejudice can be seen in her discussion of other family members' deaths and the burial of her mother. The latter reminiscence takes place within a chapter called "Old Friends," which relates in warm detail her reunion with her "white family"—that is, her former owners and their children. Andrews has remarked upon these scenes of reunion between former slaves and former master, specifically paying attention to the final autobiography of Frederick Douglass and Keckley's narrative.[59] Both authors, he believes, expressed "optimism and a . . . desire to use their personal testimony as part of the national healing process that both hoped would follow the Civil War" although "neither Keckley nor Douglass soft-pedals the injustice of slavery" (8–9). I agree with Andrews' estimation here, but would extend it further, for her mother's death and burial place constitute an almost literal site in which these two "contending forces" combine, holding out on one hand a desire for reunion and reconciliation and on the other an attestation, however covert, that on some issues the two sides have yet to agree. When northern friends "roll" their eyes in astonishment that Keckley could have anything to do with the Garlands, the former slave rebukes them gently: "the past is dear to every one. . . . To surrender it is to surrender *the greatest part of my existence*—early impressions, friends, and the graves of my father, my mother, and my son" (241; emphasis mine). Much as she earlier says that her freedom, and the circumstances leading up to it, constitute "the most interesting part of my story" (43), she once again signals that her private life, however insignificant to her white readers and auditors, is remarkable—to her and, by implication, to whatever African American audience she might have. Keckley, in fact, does not visit her mother's grave at the time she goes down to settle the dead slave's "few effects. . . . The Garlands were much surprised, but I offered no explanation." The reason given her readers appears much in keeping with the Victorian standards for proper mourning:

> My mother was buried in a public ground, and the marks of her grave, as I learned, were so obscure that the spot could not be readily designated. To look upon the grave, and not feel certain whose ashes repose beneath, is painful, and the doubt which mystifies you, weakens the force, if not the purity, of the love-offering from the heart. Memory preserved a sunny picture of my mother's face, and I did not wish to weave sombre threads—threads suggestive of a deserted graveyard—into it, and thus impair its beauty.   *(240–41)*.

Keckley's testimonial strikingly reflects the prevailing beliefs of the day—that the deserted graveyards of early America were depressing and the genuinely sensible believed in parklike spots for the commemoration of their dead—while at the same time hinting at another depressing element: the slave system that virtually assured the permanent invisibility of black mothers whose children had escaped to the North.[60]

In death as in life, slaves were construed by whites as anonymous and worthy of little note, an attitude made literal in the monument to Colonel Robert Gould Shaw.[61] In death a slave would be shielded from the prying and ignorant eyes of whites, if a grieving narrator-relative refrained from the emotional excess that European American Christians believed indicative of the heathen or the socially low: there remained a difference between anonymity and privacy. Keckley's affectless relation of her former owner's answer to the question, how fared Keckley's maternal aunt? illustrates my point further. Mrs. Garland replies that the woman is dead, and continues by admitting the hard work she had been put to; she then closes with a story about how mistress (Garland's mother) and slave (Keckley's aunt) ended up sharing a silk dress—a story told to illustrate the emotional ties between the two women. Keckley ends the anecdote by saying "we laughed over the incident," while revealing nothing further about the aunt; she does not even tell us whether she learns exactly how and when her mother's sister died. Of her burial site we learn nothing at all.[62] Keckley's reluctance to reveal the quality of her griefs—and if she grieved—or even if she could locate her mother's supposed burying place does not mean she believes such information is insignificant. Rather, Keckley's most personal memories are so important that they cannot be offered for public consumption, not even under the auspices of an autobiography. To make such a display would not only negatively affect her image as a sincere observer of public middle-class norms but would also impinge upon her privacy as an African American writer negotiating a European American genre.

Keckley may well have thought she knew her place in history, although Frances Smith Foster has remarked that the modiste misjudged profoundly her ability to ascend to the American middle class:

> In some ways, Keckley was responsible for the tragedy [of the book's reception and Lincoln's subsequent rejection of her]. She was not unsophisticated, and she had been betrayed before, but her previous successes were her undoing. She allowed her faith in the efficacy of truth, or her belief in her own specialness, to blind her to the clear evidence that Anglo-Americans routinely resented and resisted any African American volunteering any opinion on any matter that did not focus upon slavery or racial discrimination. *(Written, 127–28)*

That social order was not lost on Eliza Potter, whom her contemporary editor maintains knew "black women workers . . . are not and could never be 'one of the family.'"[63] Despite having been born and raised a slave, Keckley failed to recognize the nearly immovable social boundaries placed on blacks—yet, perhaps because she believed in the fiction of a southern family that encompassed black and white, she did not discern the trap before her. Possessed of a loyal clientele at the time of the publication of *Behind the Scenes*, the seamstress provided her reading audience—many of whom could not have afforded her services—with a window onto another world; still, it was not an African American world. She viewed her clothing business as a way into the American middle class; did she not give employment to other, deserving, upwardly mobile black women? The social climbing she implicitly, if unconsciously, attributes to Mrs. Lincoln depends on a language of clothing she, as an arbiter of fashion, well knew. Despite the suggestion that her place was to the side of these notable figures, Keckley did more than sketch charming memories of the Lincoln family. She volunteered her opinion on more than was good for her by portraying Mary Todd Lincoln as given over to fashion—much as Potter had earlier skewered the fashion-addicted of Cincinnati. Keckley tells us, for example, that at one point Mrs. Lincoln confesses "I owe altogether about twenty-seven thousand dollars. . . . I must dress in costly materials. The people scrutinize every article that I wear with critical curiosity. The very fact of having grown up in the West, subjects me to more searching observation" (149). Potter, like many a wise female dissembler, told her story from behind the veil, proclaiming "a bird's eye view" (84) of the spectacle of white fashion; Keckley's still-compromised status rests in good part with her decision to tell all without the benefit of a pseudonym or anonymity.

Historians of nineteenth-century America, especially those studying the Civil War and social history, are familiar with "the old clothes scandal" of Mary Todd Lincoln: in 1867 she publicly sold her used finery—fashionable clothing and jewelry worn during the Lincoln administration—in order to raise money for herself while petitioning the government for a larger pension and awaiting the settlement of her husband's estate.[64] One of Keckley's professed aims in writing the book is to set the record straight about this supposed serious rupture of decorum: "Mrs. Lincoln, by her own acts, forced herself into notoriety. She stepped beyond the formal lines which hedge about a private life, and invited public criticism . . . no woman was ever more traduced in the public prints of the country. . . . An act may be wrong judged purely by itself, but when the motive that prompted the act is understood, it is construed differently" (xiii). Joanne Braxton believes Keckley's "depict[ion of] Mrs. Lincoln as an emotionally unstable and financially destitute woman, who sold her wardrobe in order to meet her expenses" was motivated in part by Keckley's desire to "authenticate her work and professed intimacy with the former First Lady" (43). Frances Smith Foster attests to the tragedy of Keckley's mistaken belief that white audiences would give credence to her version of White House affairs; further difficulties stemmed from the dressmaker's advancing in a national forum her thoughts on the behavior of a famous white woman, however "peculiar" she might well be.

Keckley's stated desires—to set the record straight, to polish the tarnished image of a president's widow—become more complicated when one probes deeper "behind the scenes." Foster points out that "Keckley believed the [old clothes] slander affected both their reputations," for the black entrepreneur "enjoyed a reputation, particularly within the black community, as a lady of impeccable taste and high standards" (127). Her highly publicized involvement in the affair could affect her business. Consciously the dressmaker no doubt hoped to return Mary Todd Lincoln, if not to her former pedestal, then certainly to a position above the mud to which ignorant and scandalmongering journalists would consign her. Yet Mrs. Lincoln's egotistical behavior, and inescapable evidence of her having used Keckley as a go-between and unpaid servant, must have led to a sense of betrayal on the dressmaker's part. Mary Todd Lincoln's most recent biographer adduces that in publishing *Behind the Scenes* Keckley "undertook her own means of repayment" (Baker 280). Unfair as this may sound, we must bear in mind that Keckley was never remunerated for the weeks she spent in New York helping Lincoln with the planned sale of her clothes, although Congress had made her some compensation for settling the widow into her new home following the assassination. To have suspended the operations of her successful business and not been offered anything in the way of payment for her lost time must have galled Keckley. The two women's acrid parting can be seen as an example of the racial fault lines running through the "female world of love and ritual": the privilege Lincoln imbibed as a well-off white woman who grew up with black servants (whether or not her family actually possessed slaves) compromised what equality there could be between the white First Lady and her black dressmaker. Race and class relations inevitably contaminated interpersonal female friendships in mid-nineteenth-century America, as historian Nell Painter recognizes: "wealthy white women saw themselves in competition with women who were black and poor and powerless."[65] How aggravated these feelings of competition must have become if the black woman were perceived as being even relatively powerful! Despite the fact that Keckley's book followed weeks of slanderous reports in the white-owned newspapers, following its publication Mrs. Lincoln broke off relations with her dressmaker-confidante forever.

Keckley's sense of herself as, if not above reproach, on a par with whites, led her to make errors of judgment. For a black woman in her time, such errors could be fatal; as it was, her career collapsed, with blacks and whites alike aghast that she could tattle as she did (whites undoubtedly muttered about her "ingratitude," while African Americans worried about her making it hot for the rest of them). Foster intimates that pride led to Keckley's downfall, noting that Keckley truly believed that she, a black woman, "was a witness to and a participant in historic occasions and that she had become an example and an exemplar. She cherished her reputation for its personal vindication of her against a former mistress who predicted that Keckley would never 'be worth her salt' " (127) Keckley believes, in short, that masks and veils are unnecessary, that an honest recapitulation of events is sufficient to guard her against accusations of infamous behavior and subsequent retribution. Washington's society women might gossip about the president's wife, and even agree with Keckley's estimation of the Lincoln household and disagree with the tabloids, but they could not and would not publicly side with a black. Neither would they run the risk of being pilloried by Keckley in a later tell-all enterprise: what if the modiste, emboldened by her success, chose to tell more episodes "behind the scenes," more of the "back regions" of wealthy Potomac homes? Few whites could countenance a black woman's presumption of equality, a parity implicit in the existence of a former slave who announces herself to be a powerful white woman's "friend." Writing in the decade after the safeguarded productions of Harriet Wilson, Eliza Potter, and Harriet Jacobs, Elizabeth Keckley learned too late of the social death waiting for a black woman who would forthrightly discard the nonpersonhood of her race and sex. But African American women could sometimes find empowerment behind a class invisibility initially imposed by whites—especially when they added their own, strategically placed veil.

Potter's book, filled with small talk and dressing-room confessions, "convinces us that gossip is history,"[66] yet there's more than mere curiosity in this black female entrepreneur's look at white "high life." Keckley's revelations about the White House backstage also offer insights that white readers would have done well to regard. We, reading their works from a vantage point of over a century later, can profit too. These two memoirists, hairdresser and dressmaker, reveal complicated, contradictory strategies. If Harriet Wilson and Harriet Jacobs began a tradition of invisible black females, self-concealed in attics and crawlspaces, farm outbuildings and snaky swamps, Keckley and Potter explore fully the paradox of obscurity in full view. Speaking from even farther behind the veil, the modiste and the stylist accomplish the intriguing feat of writing African American literature with scarcely a sight of African Americans. A century later, Ralph Ellison's anonymous protagonist builds on their ambiguous achievements: "Being invisible and without substance, a disembodied voice, as it were, what else could I do? What else but try to tell you what was really happening when your eyes were looking through?"[67] Keckley and Potter, unseen autobiographers, proleptically announce a modern black narrator.

ॐ

CONCLUSION

The Beginning of African American Literature

Adopting, conforming to, and ultimately transcending mainstream attitudes and literary genres through strategies of mimicry, masking, and
invisibility preoccupied black America's first authors. Their use of captivity and conversion narratives demonstrated an ability to absorb, consciously or otherwise, the prevailing Puritan modes of expression; their
adoption of a Calvinist ethos, however, did not imply the adoption of a
white self.[1] A great difference exists between borrowing a neighboring
culture's "means and techniques" and assenting to that culture's particular goals.[2] That a slave cast his story in the medium of the slave narrative,
one specifically aimed at a white audience, does not establish his wholesale acceptance of that "white" society's attitudes; attentive readings of
such works refute an either/or position, even as they complicate the issue
of authorial stance. The rhetorical, if not political, choices of early black
writers demonstrate their steadfast attempts to comprehend and triumph
over an uninterested or hostile audience. That they strove to write an
"American" literature does not obviate or cancel their creation of an
African American consciousness; in fact, such striving may have to precede, or even operate in concert with, such a consciousness. To expand,

stretch, and build on existing elements as these authors did affirms their creativity: cultures build on cultures, whether they be diasporic African or New World European.[3] Our era's emphasis on unique, individualistic creation, without reference to surrounding intellectual currents, seems an ahistoric desideratum: we too frequently forget that before the Romantic revolution of the late eighteenth and nineteenth centuries, imitation and borrowing were not seen as evidence of creative insufficiency.

The goals of the earliest African American writers differed from those writing in the post-Reconstruction era, or even in the immediate antebellum period. Viewing themselves as cultural ambassadors with allegiances to two worlds, one European and one African, they deliberately linked their political, intellectual, and social destiny with that of their white compatriots. Native-born or not, these "Africans" had their own idealized images of that homeland, which lacked the expressly ideological aspect of subsequent authors. To them Africa was more than a trope: not just a mythical abstraction but an Edenic memory, the lost continent that could be celebrated simultaneously with their adopted Anglophone culture. Many of Phillis Wheatley's poems, not to mention the picaresque intrigues and capitalistic beliefs of Olaudah Equiano, illustrate this strangely unambiguous doubled stance. Such a position became progressively more difficult for successive generations of African American authors to maintain. Wheatley was able rather straightforwardly to see herself, and write, as an African moving in American society. Casting herself as a sable patriot, Wheatley strove to develop a rhetoric of independence that conflated her own desires as an outsider in the Boston community with the colonial struggle for separation; thus her poems speak for black *and* white emancipation while participating in a general literary discourse. Striking chords similar to those touched by white poets like Joel Barlow and Ann Eliza Bleecker, Wheatley injected an African sensibility, if not sensitivity, into revolutionary America's liberation rhetoric.

The black narrators who chose to follow most closely the form of captivity and conversion narratives had perhaps the most difficult road. For those who could not write their stories themselves, the outcome had to have been less than satisfactory. With their works screened, weighed, edited, and censured by "helpful" whites, it is a wonder that the personalities of individuals like the African-born Venture Smith come through at all. Even white female captives like Mary Rowlandson had to contend with the assistance of well-meaning but authoritarian males. Recent archival work tells us the religious enthusiasms of John Marrant were retained by his white clergyman editor, while his experiences as a free black missionary in the slave South were not. We are fortunate that the nearly blank visage of Briton Hammon, hemmed in by his editor and the conventions of the captivity narrative, was not the sole face of eighteenth-century African America shown to us.

In the next century, narrators like Henry Bibb and William Wells Brown forced their own dynamic personalities upon a preset, circumscribed pattern. The possession of literacy, of the ability to flourish "written by himself" on their title pages, enabled men like Bibb and Brown to escape much of the genre's strictures. Yet in breaking with conventional expectations, each revealed to readers a personality that contradicted the white abolitionist view of black men as noble sufferers. In displaying a truer self than the one whites wanted to see, Brown and Bibb also showed a masculine disregard for the equally real sufferings, emotional and physical, of slave women. Their tales of lying and lied-to women may be no worse than thousands of others told by blacks and whites. But in designating the slave narrative the founding text of African American literature we must be aware of what attitudes we may canonize as well.

Of all the male narrators of this period, Frederick Douglass has left the greatest mark. Yet he did so by incorporating still another formula into his autobiography. By combining the myth of the self-made man with the slave narrative, "Franklinian" Douglass created an individual African American life story out of prefabricated elements. In his first narrative and subsequent writings, Douglass alerted the nation to another kind of representative man—and the specificity of this new man to the United States. Examining how Douglass cast his success in terms familiar to whites, we should not lose sight of the other influences he deliberately concealed and repressed; his New World African had been anticipated by Venture Smith and Olaudah Equiano. And as in the narratives of Bibb and Brown, his masculine strategies for self-revelation remind us of the dearth of antebellum black women's divergent and parallel stories of freedom and success.

By the eve of the Civil War both northern and southern African Americans would have considerable difficulties with Wheatley's strategy of *rapprochement* or Douglass's apparent endorsement of the Franklinian man. The success of *Uncle Tom's Cabin* and the partial revision of that tale by a black male counterpart spurred at least two black women to engage directly with the subsequent and near-instantaneous codification of racial and domestic roles. The slave Harriet Jacobs had found individualism and determination nearly useless in securing freedom. Once liberated, she still had to fit the sentimental, middle-class model of "women's fiction" to a story that most of its proponents would never want to hear: the repeated sexual harassment of a nearly powerless black woman and the virtual impossibility of an African American mother's attaining her own home. In doing so, she implied that William Wells Brown's *Clotel* barely improved on Stowe when it came to depicting the lot of the black woman in fiction. Harriet Wilson, relating the doubly disastrous situation of being a black orphan in a small New England town, deflated the twin myths of a raceless sympathetic bond between women and the superior sensibilities of northern whites. Whereas earlier writers had first to identify their roles, mid-century writers had to define themselves against rapidly hardening stereotypes.

Bracketing the Civil War, the memoirs of Eliza Potter and Elizabeth Keckley point to the predicament of the black woman who would tell the truth about American society. Keckley, self-liberated like Douglass, sought to place herself on the stage of American history by telling the story of Mary Todd Lincoln, a heroine with human failings. Although Keckley knew enough to place herself in the background, she failed to realize that her very attempt to place in context the foibles of white Washington would mean her social death. Potter, slyer and more critical, published her scenes of "high life" at her own expense and with the crucial cover of anonymity. The visibly invisible confidante of the white boudoir's inhabitants thus creates an African American literature almost without blacks. Potter's evasions anticipate by decades some of the illusive, elusive strategies of the twentieth-century author.

Nevertheless, by the last third of the nineteenth century, black writers realized that none of the pre-existing forms would quite serve their purposes. They thus extended the process of literary appropriation, fashioning a literature distinctly their own, much as African American musicians incorporated African musical traditions into European styles. This shift occurred, I suggest, because of a political moment that underscored a historical one: the failure of transculturalization. The spurning of "Africans" by "American" society was made cruelly evident by the transient gains of Reconstruction. Black Americans could not and would not be accepted on terms of equal status in society, and so had to create their own society, a nation within a nation.[4] Significant shifts in authorial consciousness occurred after the Civil War, in good part because of the change of status of black writers: from 1868 forward, people of African descent born in the United States were to be considered citizens; in effect the Fourteenth Amendment, granting the native-born certain rights and privileges, also conferred the status of African *American* on native-born blacks. For although individual writers born in the United States of African descent may have considered themselves Americans, they could not be legally identified as such until the Fourteenth Amendment was ratified. The passing of the Fifteenth Amendment in 1870, granting suffrage to black males, seemed to advance the move toward equality. Yet these Constitutional amendments, granting long-desired civil and political rights to African Americans, paradoxically demonstrated the inefficacy of legislative solutions alone: almost immediately individual state governments began to attack these radical changes in United States racial ideology, while vigilante groups and local terrorists sought to return African Americans to near-chattel status. Although this failure had probably long been anticipated by the masses of black rural folk without recourse to intellectual gambits or urban liminality, the elite group who had attempted to write themselves into America may have taken somewhat longer to come to the same conclusion: that the dream of equality was just that—a dream.[5]

For the all-too-brief period of Reconstruction did not change very much in the life of the average American of African descent. Slavery remained, in the guise of debt peonage; overseers and patrollers reigned anew as the Ku Klux Klan and other vigilante groups; and beginning in the 1890s, various southern state constitutional conventions worked toward disfranchising the black electorate, essentially nullifying the Fifteenth Amendment.[6] Any protection offered by slavery's "paternalism" disintegrated in the tornadolike spiral of Jim Crow laws, decreased opportunity, and intensifying oppression. The period between 1865 and 1896 shows apparent successes followed by swift losses. African American attention turned first to the enormous tasks of Reconstruction, then to the Great Disappointment of 1877, and then to the utter selling-out of black interests by the white Republican establishment.[7] By 1896, when the Supreme Court ruled in *Plessy v. Ferguson* that "separate but equal" would be the nation's standard, the period Rayford Logan termed "the nadir" of race relations had begun. Yet the ever-receding achievements of Reconstruction, systematic lynchings, and nonstop civil and social sanctions against African Americans seemed to spark a resurgence of writing and publication. Literary strategies changed from the attempt to include blacks in the American mainstream by claiming familiar genres to the construction of an African American identity acknowledging its differences from white Americans. The increasing use of African American vernacular, folk motifs, points of view, and publishing firms could almost have been predicted by the swift rise and fall of African American hopes of the postwar period. That a good deal of this postbellum literature was produced by black women like Frances Harper and Pauline Hopkins led to the further irony of a woman's era taking place within a historical nadir.

The situation at the end of the nineteenth century in fact promoted necessary changes in the literary tactics of African Americans. The turn from white audience toward black readers[8] heralded the arrival of African American literature as we know it in the late twentieth century. This shift, stemming from black responses to the Civil War and the raised, then dashed hopes of Reconstruction, divides, although not very neatly, the writers whose works I have discussed here from those who follow them in the late nineteenth century. The writers of the nadir and immediately after, increasingly turning to attitudes and forms unique to their group, strove to create a more culturally specific literature within a structurally rigid society. Although this signified the coming of age of an African American sensibility, that sensibility was in fact uniquely American, with roots in the eighteenth century. Distinctly North American in their peculiarities of language, adaptations of literary styles, and meldings of diverse cultural elements, African American writers of this period can truly be said to embody that new man Crèvecoeur had described as "neither an European nor the descendant of an European, hence that strange mixture of blood, which you will find in no other country."[9] Crèvecoeur had no idea how resolutely new, how non-European, that American would be.

Understanding the achievements, variety, and complexity of African American literature requires surveying a long and apparently discontinuous field that begins within the domain of the New England colonists. The accomplishments of African Americans within and without American literary culture form an expanse not often heralded for its multicultural aspects. African American writers of the late eighteenth and early nineteenth centuries attempted to span the chasm between white America and themselves by appropriating the models of that mainstream. Within decades, their initial approach of participation had turned to the adaptation, subversion, and indirection of masks, imitation, and veiled remarks; these strategies were neatly expressed by Frederick Douglass's canny adoption of the self-made American's autobiography, Harriet Wilson's damning inversion of *Uncle Tom's Cabin*, and Eliza Potter's practiced acerbic ventriloquism. A distinctly African American literature, operating both in and beyond the context of Anglophone American society, originated in the successive literary campaigns of late-eighteenth- to mid-nineteenth-century authors. The United States eventually produced what has come to be seen as two national literatures. And while we now understand this development was inevitable, we should know too that the unavoidable may not necessarily be the undesirable.

NOTES

ð

INTRODUCTION: OF MASKS, MIMICRY, AND INVISIBILITY

1. Wheatley and Wright may be linked by more than the fact of being writers of African descent in the United States; both found confirmation of their talents in the course of transatlantic travel. What M. Lynn Weiss has said about Wright may apply to them both: "Wright's journey . . . may have revealed how slavery had severed him from the traditions of his ancestral past. But it also revealed how closely it aligned him with his American origins and his special role in America's literary history." M. Lynn Weiss, *"Para Usted*: Richard Wright's *Pagan Spain,*" 225. Paul Gilroy's *The Black Atlantic: Modernity and Double Consciousness* develops a compelling, extended argument for the inescapable modernity of what he might term a transatlantic African diaspora.

2. Richard Wright, "The Literature of the Negro in United States," in *White Man, Listen!*, 145. Further references will appear in the text.

3. That neither Dumas nor Pushkin was abducted from West Africa as a child, and both were freeborn of free parents, sets them apart from Wheatley. Furthermore, their phenotypical "whiteness," however relative, may have eased their acceptance into French and Russian society. Winthrop Jordan's *White Over Black: American Attitudes Toward the Negro, 1550–1812* demonstrates, by pointing out the racism embedded in American culture, how quixotic is any belief that Wheatley could be "one" with eighteenth-century Anglo-American culture. As important, I do not mean to say that the poet did not strive to breach the gap, and even succeed in some ways; see the next chapter. For a concise overview of this issue see Henry Louis Gates Jr.'s "Editor's

Introduction: Writing 'Race' and the Difference It Makes" in *"Race," Writing, and Difference*, especially 1–14.

4. Phillip M. Richards, "Phillis Wheatley and Literary Americanization," 163.

5. Eric Sundquist, *To Wake the Nations: Race in the Making of American Literature*, 22.

6. Paul Laurence Dunbar, "We Wear the Mask," in *Lyrics of Lowly Life: The Poetry of Paul Laurence Dunbar*, 167.

7. J. Saunders Redding, *To Make A Poet Black*, xix.

8. Of the authors discussed in this study I might take as an exception Phillis Wheatley, much of whose extant work does not *overtly* raise the issues of African equality or liberty.

9. Nathan Irvin Huggins, *Harlem Renaissance*, 261, 263.

10. This line, without my italic interpolation, may be found in W. E. B. Du Bois, *The Souls of Black Folk: Essays and Sketches*, 13.

11. See Phillip Brian Harper, "Nationalism and Social Division in Black Arts Poetry of the 1960s."

12. Arlene A. Elder, *The "Hindered Hand": Cultural Implications of Early African-American Fiction*, xiii.

13. Elizabeth McHenry, " 'Dreaded Eloquence': The Origins and Rise of African American Literary Societies and Libraries," 32.

14. Two well-known works from a previous era of literary criticism that grapple with the dilemma of black writers in white America are Redding, *To Make a Poet Black*, and Sterling Brown, *The Negro in American Literature*.

15. See, for example, Houston A. Baker Jr., *Blues, Ideology, and Afro-American Literature: A Vernacular Theory* and Henry Louis Gates Jr., ed., *Black Literature and Literary Theory*.

16. Baker Jr., *Blues, Ideology*, 1.

17. Houston A. Baker Jr., *The Journey Back: Issues in Black Literature and Literary Criticism*, 29, 30.

18. Houston A. Baker Jr., *Workings of the Spirit: The Poetics of Afro-American Women's Writing*, 66.

19. See Henry Louis Gates Jr., "Criticism in the Jungle," especially 1–13, and *The Signifying Monkey: A Theory of African-American Literary Criticism*, xxv–xxvii and *passim*.

20. See Henry Louis Gates Jr., "The blackness of blackness: a critique of the sign and the Signifying Monkey" in *Black Literature and Literary Theory*, 316.

21. Fredrik Barth, introduction to *Ethnic Groups and Boundaries: The Social Organization of Culture Difference*, 9.

22. See ibid., especially 14–15.

23. Sterling Stuckey's "Identity and Ideology: The Names Controversy" provides an excellent survey of the continually contested terrain of self-representation in the African American community. See *Slave Culture: Nationalist Theory and the Foundations of Black America*, 193–244.

We all tend to use terms like "European" and "African" without enough attention to their content, conveniently forgetting that the various groups included in these categories are hardly synonyms for "white" or "black." For the purposes of my argument, "African American" refers to individuals who can trace some, if not all, of their ancestry back to Africa and are thus legally defined as "black" (I also use "black" as a descriptor interchangeably with the above, in keeping with my own generation's usage). The relevance of Stuckey's discussion of naming will continue into the twenty-first century. By "European Americans," I mean those who not only can trace ancestry back to Europe, but are also legally identified as descendants of that world and therefore as "white."

24. Compare Morrison's remark, cited in Edwin McDowell, "Grass vs. Bellow over U.S. at PEN," with her book-length essay *Playing in the Dark: Whiteness and the Literary Imagination*.

25. When she uses the word "transculturation," critic Mary Louise Pratt writes that she follows the use "coined in the 1940s by Cuban sociologist Fernando Ortiz in a pioneering description of Afro-Cuban culture"; specifically, Pratt looks at "how subordinated or marginal groups select and invent from materials transmitted to them by dominant or metropolitan culture" (6). Although I started with anthropologist A. Irving Hallowell's use of the term to indicate the genuine adoption of an individual into a group, as opposed to one group becoming part of another, I have found Pratt's literary-critical use pertinent as well. See Mary Louise Pratt, *Imperial Eyes: Travel Writing and Transculturation*, 6 and 228n4, and A. Irving Hallowell, "American Indians, White and Black."

26. A classic essay on borrowing cultural forms and styles is George Devereux and Edwin M. Loeb, "Antagonistic Acculturation," 133–47.

27. Robert A. Lystad, "Tentative Thoughts on Basic African Values," 187–88.

28. For an exposition on the theory of "Afrocentricity" see Molefi Kete Asante, *The Afrocentric Idea*.

29. Sacvan Bercovitch suggested this phrasing.

30. See, for example, Ann duCille discussing the marriage contract as an example of this in *The Coupling Convention: Sex, Text, and Tradition in Black Women's Fiction*.

31. See Werner Sollors, *Beyond Ethnicity: Consent and Descent in American Culture*, especially 3–5 and 149–55.

32. Valerie Smith, *Self-Discovery and Authority in Afro-American Literature*, 6.

33. Carla Peterson, *"Doers of the Word": African-American Women Speakers and Writers in the North (1830–1880)*, 7.

34. Hazel M. Carby, *Reconstructing Womanhood: The Emergence of the Afro-American Woman Novelist*, 16–17.

35. See Lawrence Levine's *Black Culture, Black Consciousness: Afro-American Folk Thought from Slavery to Freedom* for an excellent study of African American cultural forms exclusive of published literary texts. Also see Stuckey's very fine, nearly monograph-length introduction, "Slavery and the Circle of Culture," to *Slave Culture*, 3–97.

36. The phrase is Albert Murray's.

37. See Shelley Fisher Fishkin, *Was Huck Black? Mark Twain and African American Culture* and Sundquist, *To Wake the Nations*.

38. "Among the blacks is misery enough, God knows, but no poetry. . . . Religion indeed has produced a Phyllis Whately [sic]; but it could not produce a poet. The compositions published under her name are below the dignity of criticism." Thomas Jefferson, *Notes on the State of Virginia*, 267.

39. Annette Kolodny, *The Land Before Her: Fantasy and Experience of the American Frontiers, 1630–1860*, xv.

40. Robert Stepto has written provocatively on this issue of "shared texts." See *From Behind the Veil: A Study of Afro-American Narrative*, 3–16.

41. See John Sekora, "Black Message/White Envelope," *passim*, on the idea of white hegemony/white "authority" versus black "authenticity."

42. For a discussion of "resistance to borrowing," see Devereux and Loeb, "Antagonistic Acculturation," 134–35. The latter quotation is from Frederick Douglass, *Narrative of the Life of Frederick Douglass, An American Slave, Written by Himself*, 59.

43. Franklin's *Autobiography* did not appear in an official edition until 1818, and then only in an incomplete version. A first edition, consisting of the first part only, appeared in France in 1791; the earliest English language versions were translated from the French volume. Not until 1868 was a complete text prepared and published. See R. Jackson Wilson, "A Note on the Text," xxxv.

44. See Karen Sánchez-Eppler's excellent article, "Bodily Bonds: The Intersecting Rhetorics of Feminism and Abolition," 28–59, and Jean Fagan Yellin's *Women and Sisters: The Antislavery Feminists in American Culture*, especially her chapter on the abolitionist emblem.

45. For views of Stowe's African American contemporaries, see Richard Yarborough, "Strategies of Black Characterization in *Uncle Tom's Cabin*," and Robert Stepto, "Sharing the Thunder: The Literary Exchanges of Harriet Beecher Stowe, Henry Bibb, and Frederick Douglass."

46. Jean Fagan Yellin, who prepared the scholarly edition of Jacobs's story, may be the first among many readers who noted this connection. See her introduction to Harriet Jacobs, *Incidents in the Life of a Slave Girl, Written by Herself*, xii–xxxiv.

1. SABLE PATRIOTS AND MODERN EGYPTIANS: PHILLIS WHEATLEY, JOEL BARLOW, AND ANN ELIZA BLEECKER

1. John C. Shields, "Phillis Wheatley and Mather Byles: A Study in Literary Relationship"; Carolivia Herron, "Milton and Afro-American Literature"; and Richards, "Phillis Wheatley and Literary Americanization" are among many current discussions of English and Anglophone colonial influences on Wheatley.

2. Mukhtar Ali Isani, "Phillis Wheatley and the Elegiac Mode," 208–14 discusses the importance of this form for an appreciation of Wheatley. William H. Robinson's anthology, *Critical Essays on Phillis Wheatley*, testifies to the shifts in thinking on Wheatley between the beginning and the end of the twentieth century.

3. When I say Wheatley was "the lonely first," I do not mean she was the first black whose writings appeared in print—Briton Hammon and Jupiter Hammon precede her, for example. However, she is notable for her steps toward a specifically African American literary consciousness.

4. Julian D. Mason Jr. has pointed out that the British did not set store in black achievement much more than their North American relatives. See Mason Jr., ed., *The Poems of Phillis Wheatley*, 6 and 186n2.

5. See William H. Robinson, *Phillis Wheatley in the Black American Beginnings*, 53.

6. John C. Shields discusses which verses were kept back from the first edition of *Poems* in *The Collected Works of Phillis Wheatley*, 232–34. Unless noted, all page references to Wheatley's work are to this edition.

7. See chapters 5 and 6 for discussions of the literary veil of black women writers at mid-century.

8. Redding, *To Make a Poet Black*, 9.

9. Terrence Collins, "Phillis Wheatley: The Dark Side of the Poetry," 155–57.

10. I believe Professor Henderson would allow me to posit that early American black male authors share this position of multivoicedness she implicitly locates beyond W. E. B. Du Bois's double-consciousness. See Mae Gwendolyn Henderson,

"Speaking in Tongues: Dialogics, Dialectics, and the Black Woman Writer's Literary Tradition," 119.

11. Sondra O'Neale, "A Slave's Subtle War: Phillis Wheatley's Use of Biblical Myth and Symbol," 144, 145. Her monograph on Jupiter Hammon extends this line of thinking: much "criticism . . . is devoid of two scholarly considerations: (1) the rise of egalitarian Christianity as the predominant moral and aesthetic force in eighteenth-century America and its pervasive influence on the literary expression of the age; and (2) the biblical fabric of contemporary slave expression—in worship, sermon, art, and song—as the almost exclusive mode of protest expression." See O'Neale, *Jupiter Hammon and the Biblical Beginnings of African American Literature*, 7–8.

12. I am grateful for John Saillant's recent work on John Marrant and "black" Calvinism, e.g., " 'Wipe Away All Tears From Their Eyes': Religion and An African American Exodus to Sierra Leone, 1785–1808," unpublished manuscript, and "Slavery and Divine Providence in New England Calvinism: The New Divinity and a Black Protest." Being a Christian does not preclude identification with and pride in one's African heritage, as any member of a black denominational church can attest.

13. As I noted earlier, the punning use of "refin'd" here has a salutary effect on criticism that seeks to flatten poems like "On being brought" to one-dimensional status.

14. See Shields's scholarly detective work in *The Collected Works of Phillis Wheatley*, 195.

15. Phillip M. Richards, "Phillis Wheatley, Americanization, the Sublime, and the Romance of America." Richards would say that Wheatley does indeed laud Moorhead in Christian terms.

16. As Shields points out, a number of critics have made this observation; see for example his "Phillis Wheatley's Subversive Pastoral," 634, and chapter 1 of my Harvard University dissertation, *White Call, Black Response: Adoption, Subversion, and Transformation in American Literature, 1760–1860.*

17. See Betsy Erkilla, "Phillis Wheatley and the Black American Revolution," 231–34. Wendy Motooka, personal communication, 15 February 1996.

18. One only has to read John Winthrop's address en route to the Massachusetts Bay Colony or Samuel Danforth's stirring "Errand into the Wilderness" sermon to see the conflation of white European enterprise with Christian mission. See also my chapter, "Capturing the Captivity," which follows.

19. For the first extensive discussion of Wheatley's "Africanisms" see Mukhtar Ali Isani, " 'Gambia on My Soul': Africa and the African in the Writings of Phillis Wheatley."

Much recent work on African American syncretism, while not on Wheatley specifically, supports my belief: see, for example, David Howard-Pitney, "Introduction: Civil Religion and the Anglo- and Afro-American Jeremiads," in *The Afro-American Jeremiad: Appeals for Justice in America*, 11–13.

20. E.g., "But Britain is the parent country, say some. Then the more shame upon her conduct. Even brutes do not devour their young, nor savages make war upon their families." Thomas Paine, *Common Sense*, 84. That the American colonists frequently cast their conflict in familial terms is considered a given. For the now-standard discussion of this discourse see Jay Fliegelman, *Prodigals and Pilgrims: The American Revolution Against Patriarchal Authority, 1750–1800.*

21. See my pages 8 and 9, above; Barlow, *The Columbiad*, book 8, 689–99, ll. 179–406, in *Collected Works of Joel Barlow. Volume 2: Poetry.*

22. This proposed volume was a precursor of *Poems on Various Subjects*. John C. Shields has noted the necessity of Wheatley's dropping "poems chronicling events in

the growing colonial resistance" for her first, British edition. See *The Collected Works of Phillis Wheatley*, 159–60.

23. For a sample bibliography on Occom and Native American literature, see Dana Nelson, "Reading the Written Selves of Colonial America: Franklin, Occom, Equiano, and Palou/Serra," 258–59. Little is known of Obour Tanner; see William H. Robinson, *Phillis Wheatley and Her Writings*, 24, 40–43, and 314*n*2.

24. Donna Landry, *The Muses of Resistance: Laboring-Class Women's Poetry in Britain, 1739–1796*, 243.

25. Werner Sollors reminded me of this parallel. See Levine, *Black Culture and Black Consciousness*, 30–55, for an excellent discussion of this connection.

26. Cynthia J. Smith, " 'To Maecenas': Phillis Wheatley's Invocation of an Idealized Reader," 589–90.

27. Hortense J. Spillers, "Moving on Down the Line," 94.

28. My apologies to Audre Lorde. Read her essay "The Master's Tools Will Never Dismantle the Master's House" in *Sister Outsider: Essays and Speeches*.

29. For the record: Phillis Wheatley, ca. 1754–1784; Joel Barlow, 1754–1812; Ann Eliza Bleecker, 1752–1783. Biographical information on Wheatley can be found in many places now; see, for example, Mason Jr., introduction to *The Poems of Phillis Wheatley*, 1–22. Biographical sources on Barlow and Bleecker will follow.

30. O'Neale, citing the 1855–56 *Proceedings of the Massachusetts Historical Society*, says Wheatley was the first American author to refer to America as "Columbia" ("A Slave's Subtle War," 153). The term had already been used by other colonial writers, however. Julian D. Mason Jr., personal communication, September 1996.

31. Phillip M. Richards's work on Phillis Wheatley represents a quantum leap in *literary* scholarship on the poet. His essays provide both a fair review of previous criticism and acute insights of his own; see, in particular, "Phillis Wheatley and Literary Americanization." His "Phillis Wheatley, Americanization, the Sublime and the Romance of America" develops and expands on ideas presented in the earlier essay. The quote above is from "Literary Americanization," 165.

Richards was anticipated by Henry Louis Gates Jr., who had called for an analysis like Richards's several years before. See Gates Jr., "Phillis Wheatley and the Nature of the Negro," 215–33. I reviewed some of these ideas as well in my dissertation, *White Call, Black Response*.

32. For biographical information on Joel Barlow's political and social maturation, see Leon Howard's *The Connecticut Wits*, especially the chapter "Citizen Joel Barlow," 271–341.

33. Wheatley's long-missing second volume of poems, sought by her widower in newspaper advertisements following her death, would likely have demonstrated different sentiments from the first: between volumes, she had married, given birth to and lost children, and witnessed the formation of the United States. Not long ago, scholar Richard Newman told an audience at the W. E. B. Du Bois Institute that he firmly believes the manuscript still exists, is somewhere in the Philadelphia area, and will reappear. Personal communication, 8 May 1996.

34. Howard, *The Connecticut Wits*, 309.

35. John Griffith is but one critic who has commented on Barlow's changing ideological affections. See his "*The Columbiad* and *Greenfield Hill*: History, Poetry, and Ideology in the Late Eighteenth Century."

36. Joel Barlow, *The Columbiad*, in *Collected Works*, 379. All parenthetical references are to this edition.

37. Howard, *The Connecticut Wits*, 408. One could smile at this relegation of formerly "high culture" writers to the category of "intellectual history," a move analogous to the designation of Wheatley as African American literary curiosity.

38. Isani, in "Phillis Wheatley and the Elegiac Mode," discusses the importance of this form for an appreciation of Wheatley.

39. See Mason Jr., introduction to *The Poems of Phillis Wheatley*, 6.

40. Compare this to Wheatley's General Wooster, who alleges freedom will not come to those who enslave others; he dies on the field of battle, proclaiming the error of slavery-condoning patriots. A discussion of this poem follows later in this chapter.

41. Pierre Grimal, *The Dictionary of Classical Mythology*, 68–69.

42. Joel Barlow, "The Hasty Pudding," in *Collected Works*, 85–99. Further references are to this edition and will be cited parenthetically.

43. Wendy Motooka reminded me that "the mock epic tradition is larger than Pope . . . there are dozens of mock epics through the mid-18th c. that call themselves 'iads' . . . including the *Lousiad*." Motooka, personal communication, 15 February 1996. For an extended discussion of "The Hasty Pudding" and gastronomic nationalism, see Rafia Zafar, "The Proof of the Pudding: Of Haggis, Hasty Pudding, and Transatlantic Influence."

44. Robert D. Arner, "The Smooth and Emblematic Song: Joel Barlow's *The Hasty Pudding*." Further references will be cited parenthetically.

45. Without the advice of my colleague and friend Julie Ellison, this chapter would not have included the little-known Bleecker; to Julie goes my gratitude for an excellent scholarly tip. See her fine essay, "Race and Sensibility in the Early Republic: Ann Eliza Bleecker and Sarah Wentworth Morton," further references to which are within the text.

46. Emily Stipes Watts, quoted in Pattie Cowell, *American Women Poets in Pre-Revolutionary America 1650–1775: An Anthology*, 139. Also see Cowell's estimation, *American Women Poets*, 138.

47. Ann Eliza Bleecker, *The Posthumous Works of Ann Eliza Bleecker, in Prose and Verse. To which is added, A Collection of Essays, Prose and Poetical, by Margaretta V. Faugeres*. This volume also contains a biography, "Memoirs of Mrs. Ann Eliza Bleecker" (i–xviii), by her daughter, Margaretta Faugeres. Further references are in the text.

48. Wheatley wrote frequently about grief and loss, if not specifically her own. See Isani, "Phillis Wheatley and the Elegiac Mode."

49. An examination of each poet's letters, appended to the editions of both writers' verse, illuminates further each woman's thought. See *The Collected Works of Phillis Wheatley*, 162–87, and Bleecker, *The Posthumous Works*, 115–84.

50. "L," quoted in *The Poems of Phillis Wheatley*, 142.

51. One of Wheatley's modern editors has argued for the importance of recognizing Jungian archetypes—unconscious memory, if you will—in much of the poet's oeuvre; he refers to a "partially unconscious response to her personal predicament" as working in tandem with her "fully conscious responses." See Shields, "Phillis Wheatley's Struggle for Freedom in Her Poetry and Prose," in *The Collected Works of Phillis Wheatley*, 240.

52. In an oft-quoted letter to the Reverend Samson Occom, Wheatley refers to whites as "our modern Egyptians." See *The Poems of Phillis Wheatley*, 204.

53. See Joanne M. Braxton, *Black Women Writing Autobiography: A Tradition Within a Tradition*, 19.

54. Although this would seem a likely subject for the creator of so many elegies, no poems by Wheatley about maternal loss survive, despite the deaths of all three of her children as infants.

55. According to Grimal, Clio represents history and Calliope, epic poetry. Mnemosyne, memory, was the mother of the muses and Zeus, the leader of the Gods, their father. The other muses were Polyhymnia (mime), Euterpe (flute), Terpsichore (light verse and dance), Erato (lyric choral poetry), Melpomene (tragedy), Thalia (comedy), and Urania (astronomy). By the classical period, this list of nine, with their relative associations, was standard. See Grimal, *Dictionary*, 297–98. Mneme is a synonym for Mnemosyne.

56. The rather gruesome "The History of Maria Kittle," a captivity narrative written by Bleecker and said by her to be completely true, is in Bleecker's *Posthumous Works*, 19–87. As I note in a later chapter, it can be difficult to ascertain which group Protestant authors of captivity narratives thought worse—Indians or Catholics.

57. Montgomery was killed during the assault on Quebec in December 1775.

58. As Julie Ellison has noted, "Race is inseparable from the politics of war . . . Bleecker's mourning for Abella [is] inseparable from her Indian-hating commitment to national unity"; see "Race and Sensibility," 469.

59. Bleecker refers to a mulatto servant, if not a slave; also see Ellison's reference to a weird sympathy in ibid.

60. Walt Nott, "From "uncultivated Barbarian" to "Poetical Genius": The Public Presence of Phillis Wheatley," 25.

61. Wright, *White Man, Listen!*, n. [7].

2. CAPTURING THE CAPTIVITY: AFRICAN AMERICANS AMONG THE PURITANS

1. Phillips D. Carleton, "The Indian Captivity," 176.

2. Ibid., 170, 180.

3. Despite this invocation of earlier Puritan models, few modern critics have commented on the similarities between captivity and slave narratives. Annette Kolodny, in *The Land Before Her*, represents one exception: commenting on their "structural and stylistic affinities," she notes that both kinds of narratives relate "accounts of captivity amid powerful Others" (xv). Richard Slotkin, to whom I will refer directly, is another.

4. Nellie Y. McKay, "Nineteenth-Century Black Women's Spiritual Autobiographies: Religious Faith and Self-Empowerment," 140.

5. James Albert Ukawsaw Gronniosaw, *A Narrative of the Most Remarkable Particulars in the Life of James Albert Ukawsaw Gronniosaw, An African Prince, as Related by HIMSELF*, 21. The copy held in Houghton Library, Harvard University has been speculatively dated. Further references are to this edition.

6. See Edmund S. Morgan, *Visible Saints: The History of a Puritan Idea*, 58–62.

7. See Richard Slotkin's discussion of the captivity narratives as "genuine, first person accounts of actual ordeals . . . [the] first coherent myth-literature of the United States" in "Israel in Babylon: The Archetype of the Captivity Narratives (1682–1700)" in *Regeneration Through Violence*, 94–115.

8. Ann Kibbey's discussion of the interlocked nature of violence and Puritan religion is invaluable to a comprehension of early American rhetorical strategies; see *The Interpretation of Material Shapes in Puritanism*.

9. See Richard Slotkin, "Narratives of Negro Crime in New England, 1675–1800," especially 24–25, and Daniel A. Cohen, *Pillars of Salt, Monuments of Grace*, particularly "An Overview: The Succession of Genres, 1674–1860," 3–38.

10. Similar constructions of "white" versus "black" were seen toward the end of the seventeenth century in stratagems and strictures against miscegenation in the southern colonies. With the rise of black chattel slavery, laws and statutes began to equate or substitute "white" with "Christian." Such hair-splitting became an economic necessity when black slaves began to embrace the gospel of Jesus Christ and pre-existing laws specifically forbade the enslavement of Christians. See Winthrop D. Jordan, "Unthinking Decision: Enslavement of Negroes in America to 1700," in *Shaping Southern Society*, 111–15.

11. Mary Rowlandson, *The Sovereignty and Goodness of God* (1682), 36; in *Held Captive by Indians: Selected Narratives, 1642–1836*, Vaughan and Clark, eds. Further references are to this edition and will be cited parenthetically.

12. Kibbey, *The Interpretation of Material Shapes*, 2, 100. Kibbey sees this kind of violent rhetoric in Puritan male rhetoric about women and about Native Americans. Her study, focusing on men, chiefly John Cotton, does not account for white Protestant *female* participation in such rhetorical strategies. Rowlandson's testimony demonstrates such violent prejudice, as does, to a somewhat different extent, the poetry of Eliza Bleecker. White women writers were not immune to xenophobic flights.

13. At least the American edition of 1682 was so entitled. Subsequent editions, such as the English edition of the same year, were titled for a more secular audience. See note following.

14. "Per amicum," "The Preface to the Reader" in *A True History of the Captivity and Restoration of Mrs. Mary Rowlandson, A Minister's Wife in New England* (London: Joseph Poole, 1682), n.p. In the collection of Chapin Library, Williams College.

15. Ibid.

16. Ibid.

17. Kibbey, in *The Interpretation of Material Shapes*, finds "the simultaneity of the [Pequot] war and the [Hutchinson] religious controversy" suggestive of a link between the "prejudices of race and gender," but that "the relationship is a complicated one." She notes, for example, that "the Pequot women at Mystic were the objects of both kinds of prejudice" (2), but avoids discussing Rowlandson's narrative. Gender solidarity was frequently subsumed by racial alignments, as the struggles between white mistresses and black slave women would demonstrate.

18. Mitchell Breitwieser, *American Puritanism and the Defense of Mourning*, 142.

19. Pierre Bourdieu, *Distinction: A Social Critique of the Judgement of Taste*, 466–67, emphasis mine.

20. Elizabeth Hanson, *God's Mercy Surmounting Man's Cruelty*, 230–44. In *Held Captive by Indians*, Vaughan and Clark have reprinted the 1728 edition published at Philadelphia. All further references in the text are to this edition.

21. Rowlandson does witness the murders of several relatives and friends, including her sister Elizabeth and her nephew William.

22. Sandra Gunning wondered whether crushing defeats of Native Americans in both the Pequot War and King Phillip's War enabled this insight; with Indians no longer a threat, whites could afford to "understand" them. S. Gunning, personal communication, 1995. Also see Kathryn Derounian, "Puritan Orthodoxy and the 'Survivor Syndrome' in Mary Rowlandson's Indian Captivity Narrative."

23. Vaughan and Clark, *Puritans Among the Indians: Accounts of Captivity and Redemption, 1676–1724*, 230.

24. Pratt, *Imperial Eyes*, 84.

25. He later ascribes an illness to his mistreatment of Hanson's son, and she wonders at "the Lord's doing, and it was marvelous in my eyes" (240).

26. Hanson's other prejudices remain intact, however, as can be seen in her remarks about the French who ransom her: "I now having changed my landlord [her Indian captor], table, and diet, as well as my lodgings, the French were civil beyond what I could either desire or expect" (241). This anti-Catholic bias is evident in other early American narratives, including John Williams's *A Redeemed Captive Returned to Zion* and Mrs. Susannah Johnson's *A Narrative of the Captivity of Mrs. Johnson: Containing an Account of her Sufferings, during Four Years with the Indians and French*.

27. Michael Warner, *The Letters of the Republic: Publication and the Public Sphere in Eighteenth-Century America*, 11.

28. John Saillant, " 'Remarkably Emancipated from Bondage, Slavery, and Death'," 123.

29. Kolodny, *The Land Before Her*, xv. Other writers before me have noted these similarities, among them William L. Andrews, "The First Fifty Years of the Slave Narrative," in *The Art of the Slave Narrative*, 6–24, and Richard Slotkin (see note following).

30. Slotkin, *Regeneration Through Violence*, 441. Slotkin briefly, though cogently, discusses the continuum running from the seventeenth-century captivities to the slave narratives of the mid-nineteenth century; he extends the line through *Uncle Tom's Cabin*. See *Regeneration*, 441–44.

31. Although writing on "authenticating documents," critic Robert Stepto does not extend his analysis to include the captivity narratives, although as we will see, the stories of white captives, be they relatively powerless females or males, just as frequently appeared with the imprimatur of an "objective" editor. See *From Behind the Veil*, 5.

32. Literacy rates varied by region; New England had the highest rate in the new nation at the end of the eighteenth century. Somewhat ironically, the South only legislated for universal public education after the Civil War. It would be poor whites, not poor African Americans, who would largely benefit from these Reconstruction-era reforms. See Du Bois, *Black Reconstruction*.

33. See Benedict Anderson, *Imagined Communities: Reflections on the Origin and Spread of Nationalism*, especially 67–79. The birth and proliferation of African American newspapers from the 1830s on attests to similar strategies of self-identification and creation.

34. In fact, Africans from the same language group were frequently split up on their arrival in America; the ability to communicate with one another was rightly seen as an aid to insurrection.

35. Wright, *White Man, Listen!*, 115.

36. Sekora, "Black Message/White Envelope," 483. Further references to this essay are cited parenthetically.

37. Marion Wilson Starling demonstrates that embedded belief in black inferiority was in large part responsible for this question. See Starling, *The Slave Narrative: Its Place in American History*, 2nd ed., notably "The Trustworthiness of the Slave Narrative," 221–48.

38. One might then say that captivity narratives boast female authors but not female authority, a highly debatable issue I will not now take up.

39. Lydia Maria Child said that she had done little but rearrange Harriet Jacobs's manuscript. See Child's introduction in Jacobs, *Incidents*, 3.

40. The perennially debated verisimilitude of Nat Turner's "Confessions" stems in good measure from the evident tension between the scribe/inquisitor, William Gray, and the subject/narrator, Turner.

41. As the folk saying goes, "got one face for the white man to see, got another for what I know is me . . . he don't know my mind."

42. Briton Hammon, *Narrative of the Uncommon Sufferings and Surprising Deliverance of Briton Hammon, a Negro Man, Servant to General Winslow, of Marshfield, in NEW-ENGLAND; Who returned to Boston, after having been absent almost Thirteen Years*. Further references are to this edition.

43. Andrews, "The First Fifty Years of the Slave Narrative," 8.

44. In general, I have avoided discussing "co-authored" texts, such as the one by Hammon and Marrant's narrative as released by Aldridge, precisely because of the difficulty of teasing out how much would have been told, how much would have been taken down without editorial intervention, and so forth. These problems arise with many of the earliest extant narratives—e.g., Venture Smith's life, published in 1798, was narrated to a (presumably) white amanuensis and is another example of a co-"related" text—but by the mid-nineteenth century African American literacy had progressed to such an extent that a large number of African American texts were indeed "written by themselves." I should point out that limited slave literacy, bisected by gender, further narrows the field of black female authors, which leaves the scholar of early black women's writing in something of a quandary. See my discussion of Jarena Lee, following, and of Keckley's "authenticity" in note 53, chapter 6.

45. Sekora has closely compared Hammon's narrative with that of Thomas Brown, the white male whose captivity narrative was published just a few months earlier; the latter's preface, "As I am but a Youth, I shall not make those Remarks on the Difficulties I have met with . . . and [I shall] relate Matters of Fact as they occur to my Mind" is almost repeated word for word by Hammon. This shared "boilerplate" points to their similar low social status, or class (though the word "class" is mine, not Sekora's). See Sekora, "Red, White, and Black," 98.

46. The white Jonathan Dickinson, like Hammon a seventeenth-century survivor of shipwreck and Indian captivity, had similar forebodings: "We sat ourselves down, expecting cruelty and hard death, except it should please the Almighty God to work wonderfully for our deliverance." *Jonathan Dickinson's Journal; or, God's Protecting Providence*, 29.

47. Hallowell described the phenomenon of transculturalization as "the process whereby *individuals* under a variety of circumstances are . . . detached from one group, enter the web of social relations that constitute another society, and come under the influence of its customs ideas, and values to a greater or lesser degree." See "American Indians, White and Black," 523.

48. Ibid., *passim* and especially 526–27.

49. Sekora, "Red, White, and Black," especially 98–102. Sekora's essay was preceded in the previous year by a published version of this chapter; although we come to similar conclusions about Hammon and the development of captivity and slave narratives, Sekora's essay concentrates on the print politics of eighteenth-century colonial America.

50. Gronniosaw, *A Narrative*, 15. Note the "trope of the talking book," noted as a significant early African American literary device by Henry Louis Gates Jr. I believe

this emphasizes rather the gap between literate and nonliterate or Christian and non-Christian than between black and white, as my discussions of Indian-African American contact in this and the next chapter show. See also Zafar, "Capturing the Captivity," 33–34n14.

51. See Venture Smith, *A Narrative of the Life and Adventures of Venture, A Native of Africa, But Resident Above Sixty Years in the United States of America, Related by Himself*. Although Smith's narrative was originally published in 1798, Arna Bontemps reprints the Haddam, Connecticut 1896 edition in *Five Black Lives* "revised and republished with Traditions by H. M. Selden."

52. As had other Protestant captives during the seventeenth century, Williams expended much energy in his narrative on denigrating his Catholic hosts/imprisoners. See John Williams, *The Redeemed Captive Returning to Zion*. The Vaughan and Clark reprint is a "slightly modified version of Edward W. Clark's edition of Williams's *Redeemed Captive* [probably the 1707 edition which appeared in Boston], published in 1976 by the University of Massachusetts Press."

53. Compare the version of John Marrant, *A Narrative of the Lord's Wonderful Dealings with John Marrant, a Black (Now going to Preach the Gospel in Nova-Scotia)* reprinted in Richard VanDerBeets, *Held Captive By Indians: Selected Narratives, 1642–1836* with John Marrant, *A Narrative . . . Fourth Edition, Enlarged by Mr. Marrant and Printed (with permission), for his sole benefit* (Rare Book Room, Boston Public Library). I am profoundly grateful for the scholarship of my friend John Saillant, who directed me to the crucial differences between editions of the *Narrative* edited by Aldridge only, and those amended and approved by Marrant himself; John Saillant, personal communication, 5 June 1995. Discussions of these differences will follow. In the recently published *Black Atlantic Writers of the Eighteenth Century: Living the New Exodus in England and the Americas*, Adam Potkay and Sandra Burr, eds., readers will find a scholarly edition faithful to Marrant's intentions. My earlier published essay, "Capturing the Captivity: African Americans Among the Puritans" relies on the VanDerBeets volume, which reproduces an edition not authorized by Marrant; while my conclusions there are essentially the same as herein, I extrapolated Marrant's black consciousness from other, extratextual evidence. I rely also on Saillant's unpublished essay, " 'Wipe Away All Tears from their Eyes': Religion and an African American Exodus to Sierra Leone, 1785–1808," an early version of which was given at the Institute for Early American History and Culture Annual Conference, 3 June 1995, Ann Arbor, Michigan.

54. Marrant's sermon to the Prince Hall Masons was published as *A Sermon preached on the 24th day of June 1789, being the Festival of St. John the Baptist, at the request of the right worshipful the grand master Prince Hall, and the rest of the brethren of the African Lodge of the Honorable Society of Free and Accepted Masons in Boston* (Boston: The Bible and Heart, 1789?).

55. Marrant received his training and ordination at the religious school run by the Countess, to whom the Reverend George Whitefield had earlier served as chaplain. See VanDerBeets, *Held Captive By Indians*, 177–78.

56. As evidence of this common strain of black Christianity, Adam Potkay and Sandra Burr point out that "the appearance of [the evangelical preacher George] Whitefield, as character and symbol, had become an important motif of [early] black autobiography." Wheatley, whose contemporary fame rested in part on her eulogy to Whitefield; Equiano; Ukawsaw Gronniosaw; and Marrant: all of these eighteenth-century Africans writing Anglophone literature incorporate the charismatic English min-

ister, whether "as 'truth' [or] 'fact' " (9). See Potkay and Burr, introduction to *Black Atlantic Writers*.

57. See Gates Jr., "Writing 'Race' and the Difference It Makes," 12.

58. Adam Potkay, "Olaudah Equiano and the Art of Spiritual Autobiography," 678 and *passim*.

59. Homi K. Bhabha, "Signs Taken for Wonders," 168, 174.

60. Although he does not make his argument about Marrant in these exact terms, John Saillant's reading of Marrant as formulator of a specifically Africanist Calvinism would certainly apply.

61. Without question some Puritans thought Native Americans redeemable—the "praying Indians," the "Indian school" that became Dartmouth College, and Samson Occom's ministry tell us so. But there were numerous wartime instances of converted or "friendly" Indians being lumped in with their ethnic group rather than with their white allies or fellow Christians—and paying with their lives for such racial identification. See Kibbey, *The Interpretation of Material Shapes*, 100–1.

62. See also Angelo Constanzo, *Surprizing Narrative: Olaudah Equiano and the Beginnings of Black Autobiography*, 96–104 on Marrant's typology, as well as my discussion in "Capturing the Captivity," 30. I did not know of the existence of Marrant's own edition of his narrative when writing, and neither, presumably, did Costanzo.

63. Compare Jesus's parable of the lost son in St. Luke, chapter 15:24: "For this my son was dead, and is alive again; he was lost, and is found." Benilde Montgomery also discusses some of these typological moments in "Recapturing John Marrant."

64. Curiously, the Aldridge editions omit the elder sister's beating the younger for insisting that Marrant is indeed their brother; also changed is the way in which the younger sister recognizes her brother: in the Aldridge edition she knows Marrant "the moment she saw me" (VanDerBeets, *Held Captive by Indians*, 196); in Marrant's authorized edition, she thinks the stranger is her brother but steals peeks at him twice more before insisting that it is indeed him (Potkay and Burr, *Black Atlantic Writers*, 90). Thanks again to John Saillant.

65. Also see my related discussion of Indian-African American contact in the next chapter.

66. Potkay and Burr, *Black Atlantic Writers*, 73.

67. See my discussion of Henry Bibb in the next chapter.

68. Marrant, *A Sermon*, 21.

69. Compare Acts 17:26: "And [God] hath made of one blood all nations of men for to dwell on all the face of the earth." See Sollors, *Beyond Ethnicity*, especially 61–62, for a discussion of the use to which Afro-Americans put this particular New Testament passage.

70. Potkay and Burr, in their discussion of Marrant, aver that "Marrant undeniably delivered the sermon, but his authorship is questionable. . . . There is reason to believe that Prince Hall [the Boston-based black activist and Freemason] at least edited the *Sermon* before its publication" (74). Although they make a case for Marrant's not being the sole author, his delivery of the speech does not preclude a proto-African nationalism, which I claim here and which is demonstrated in subsequent work on Marrant by John Saillant.

71. This comes from a letter Phillis Wheatley wrote to the Mohegan minister Samson Occom (*The Collected Works of Phillis Wheatley*, 177).

72. Both versions of Lee's autobiography are available in modern editions; the 1849 version is titled *Religious Experience and Journal of Mrs. Jarena Lee, Giving an*

Account of Her Call to Preach the Gospel. See William L. Andrews, ed., *Sisters of the Spirit: Three Black Women's Autobiographies of the Nineteenth Century*, 25–48, for the 1836 edition; Susan Houchins, ed., *Spiritual Narratives*, 1–97 reprints the 1849 version. Further references are to the Houchins volume.

73. Gilroy, *The Black Atlantic*, 19, 133, and throughout.

74. Saillant has concisely discussed Marrant's efforts to build an Afrocentric Calvinist community in Sierra Leone (" 'Wipe Away All Tears from Their Eyes' "). After gathering together in Nova Scotia a flock of black, Tory veterans of the Revolutionary War, Marrant died in London before reaching the Promised Land.

75. C. Eric Lincoln and Lawrence H. Mamiya, *The Black Church in the African American Experience*, 56–57.

76. Frances Smith Foster, " 'Great Liberty in the Gospel': Jarena Lee's Religious Experiences, Life, and Journal" in *Written By Herself*, 56–75; Nellie Y. McKay, "Nineteenth-Century Black Women's Spiritual Autobiographies," and Carla Peterson, " 'Humble Instruments in the Hands of God': Maria Stewart, Jarena Lee, and the Economy of Spiritual Narrative" in *"Doers of the Word"*, 56–87.

77. Jean McMahon Humez, introduction to *Gifts of Power*, 4, 43n41. We know the two met; see the entry for January 1, 1857, in which Jackson records having met Jarena Lee (262).

78. Foster does not say that Lee had read Marrant's narrative but does, in suggesting that a tradition of African American narrative was already "discernible," imply that such influence could exist; see " 'Great Liberty in the Gospel' " 68, and 64–66.

79. In a recent conference paper, Martha L. Wharton reports Julia Foote's damning response to black male resistance to female inclusion within the [AME] church hierarchy by flinging the rhetoric of the Dred Scott decision in the faces of her black, male readers; Wharton quotes Foote's scathing critique: "Even ministers of Christ did not feel that women had any rights which they were bound to respect." Wharton, " 'I Remember Hearing My [Mother] Tell . . .': Memory's Redeeming Power in Julia Foote's *A Brand Plucked from the Fire* [1879 and 1886]."

80. Although I do not address them here, other early African American religious narratives reflect a multifold engagement of issues; see, for example, Graham Hodges, ed., *Black Itinerants of the Gospel: The Narratives of John Jea and George White* and the works of Maria W. Stewart and Julia Foote reprinted in Houchins, *Spiritual Narratives*.

3. ENSLAVING THE SAVED: THE NARRATIVES OF HENRY BIBB AND WILLIAM WELLS BROWN

1. I use "African" here in the self-ascriptive sense that Wheatley and others used it until well into the nineteenth century—to indicate Americans of African descent.

2. The rhetoric of constitutional rights, of course, was similarly seized upon by black writers in this period; for a particularly thorough discussion of such strategies see Fishkin and Peterson, " 'We Hold These Truths to Be Self-Evident': The Rhetoric of Frederick Douglass's Journalism."

3. See Greg Siemenski, "The Puritan Captivity Narrative and the Politics of the American Revolution," especially 37–42, and Slotkin, *Regeneration Through Violence*, especially chapter 2, "Cannibals and Christians: European vs. American Indian Culture," 25–56.

4. Ibid., 440–43.

5. See Stepto's essay, "Sharing the Thunder," particularly 136–41.

6. Cotton Mather, "A Narrative of Hannah Dustan's Notable Deliverance from Captivity," in Vaughan and Clark, *Puritans Among the Indians*, 164.

7. "The Preface to the Reader" in Mary Rowlandson, *A True History*, no pagination. One can assume that Rowlandson's text had a male editor for two reasons: the extreme scarcity of women writing and publishing at this time; and the reference to her "modesty," which a woman editor would have been unlikely to make without a similar plea on her own behalf (compare Child's preface to Harriet Jacobs, *Incidents*, 3–4). A final seal of male approval was placed on Rowlandson's narrative by the addition of an appendix containing her husband's last sermon.

8. Devereux and Loeb, "Antagonistic Acculturation," 133.

9. Sekora, "Black Message/White Envelope," 496.

10. Annette Niemtzow, "The Problematic of Self in Autobiography: The Example of the Slave Narrative," 107.

11. Henry Bibb, *Narrative of the Life and Adventures of Henry Bibb, an American Slave, Written by Himself*, 13. Further references are to this edition and will be cited parenthetically.

12. Rowlandson, *Sovereignty and Goodness*, 52.

13. Douglass, *Narrative*, 52.

14. See William L. Andrews, "The Performance of Slave Narrative in the 1840s," in *To Tell a Free Story*, especially 151–52.

15. St. Augustine, *Confessions*, 47. This passage appears in the fourth section of book 2.

16. Bibb gained fame, if not notoriety, for the number of escape attempts he made and his perilous returns to slave country in order to free his wife and child.

17. The appendix of Douglass's *Narrative* is devoted to the differences between "the Christianity of [America] and the Christianity of Christ." Douglass, *Narrative*, 155.

18. Kibbey, *The Interpretation of Material Shapes*, 2.

19. Although the gamblers and Bibb meet his last owner among Cherokees at a gathering in the Indian Territory, Bibb never says definitively whether his last purchaser hails from that nation; I will refer to him as an "Indian" as well, rather than by a specific group identity.

20. Compare the Puritan Rowlandson's wish to "have been a servant to a Christian" (75).

21. See Hallowell, "American Indians, White and Black" and James Axtell, "The Indian Impact on English Colonial Culture."

22. I refer in the following discussion to Pratt, *Imperial Eyes*, 7.

23. Tzvetan Todorov, *The Conquest of America*, 101.

24. See ibid., 100, for a discourse on the provenance of the epithet "La Malinche."

25. Jacobs, *Incidents*, 37.

26. Andrews, *To Tell a Free Story*, 158.

27. Deborah McDowell, "In the First Place: Making Frederick Douglass and the Afro-American Tradition," 200. In the passage from which the above quotation is taken, McDowell goes on to cite Sánchez-Eppler's "Bodily Bonds." As the latter critic says, "the ability to have 'a wife and children' like the ability to 'go and come' or 'buy and sell' serves to define freedom" (48)—but this is a species of freedom arrogated to males. See also V. Smith for a related discussion of black male adoption of white masculine "norms" in *Self-Discovery and Authority*, 20–34.

28. Slotkin, *Regeneration Through Violence*, 441.

29. The expression comes from Sekora, "Black Message/White Envelope."

30. For the purposes of this discussion I am using the text of the second, expanded edition of 1848.

31. William L. Andrews, "Towards a Poetics of Afro-American Autobiography," 81.

32. William Wells Brown, *Narrative of William W. Brown, A Fugitive Slave, Written by Himself*, 70. Further references will be cited parenthetically.

33. Spillers, "Moving on Down the Line," 162ff.

34. Richard Yarborough, "The First-Person in Afro-American Fiction," 115.

35. Ibid., 112. Yarborough's essay focuses on fictional strategies of the nineteenth-century African American writer as generally differing from autobiographical ones: "given the abiding concern of early black writers with establishing the credibility of their literary voices and thus of their views of reality, fiction as a mode of self-expression must have generated some extremely ambivalent feelings. That is, why use *fiction* as a weapon in the battle to gain a hearing for the *true* version of the Afro-American experience?" *Clotel*, as Yarborough would agree, in some ways speaks to this authorial ambivalence by incorporating both "fictional" and "factual" incidents.

36. The poem had also appeared in *The Liberty Bell* of 1848. See Brown, *Narrative*, and "A Lecture Delivered before the Female Anti-Slavery Society of Salem, 1847," 50–52.

37. The picaresque side of Brown is not entirely excised from the later version: his escapades as a barber and wildcat banker in Monroe, Michigan, do not paint him as faultless. On the other hand, the pluck necessary to follow through on such schemes casts him more as an entrepreneur than as an exploiter. See William Wells Brown, "Narrative of the Life and Escape," 28–31.

38. This error could be attributed to another, editorial hand in the compilation/revision of the narrative—the now well-known author probably preferred to have Eliza sink entirely into obscurity.

39. Robert Stepto, "Distrust of the Reader," 303–4 and elsewhere.

40. Ralph Ellison, "Change the Joke and Slip the Yoke," 55.

41. James Olney, " 'I Was Born': Slave Narratives, Their Status as Autobiography and as Literature," 167. Further references will be cited parenthetically.

4. "IT IS NATURAL TO BELIEVE IN GREAT MEN."

1. Ralph Waldo Emerson, *Representative Men*, 615.

2. John Seelye, "The Clay Foot of the Climber: Richard M. Nixon in Perspective," 125.

3. The African American revision of the paradigmatic self-made man continues into the late twentieth century, as at least one reviewer of General Colin Powell's autobiography has noted; see the Boston *Globe* review by Gaddis Smith, "His Life So Far," B39:3.

4. Myra Jehlen, "Imitate Jesus and Socrates: The Making of a Good American," 503.

5. Elizabeth Keckley and Eliza Potter, the latter of whom published anonymously, scripted their how-tos of self-advancement and -promotion within a culture that severely curtailed the success, if not stifled the actual voices, of black women. While I do not want to unfairly segregate my discussion of self-made narrators by gender, I believe the nature of their achievements calls for a separate chapter.

6. Sterling Stuckey has carefully delineated the influence Douglass's own, African American family had upon the young slave's life, suggesting reasons the grown man would not want such influence publicized. See Stuckey, " 'Ironic Tenacity': Frederick

Douglass's Seizure of the Dialectic," in Sundquist, *Frederick Douglass*, 23–46. Although Equiano's best-selling autobiography had appeared decades before Franklin's, Douglass and other nineteenth-century writers could well have been familiar with it through the two American printings of 1829 and 1837; see Potkay and Burr, *Black Atlantic Writers*, 163.

7. Nathan Huggins, referring to the Benjamin Quarles biography of Frederick Douglass; personal communication, 13 July 1988. Alain Locke is quoted in Rayford Logan's introduction to the *Life and Times of Frederick Douglass*, 16. See also Peter F. Walker, "Frederick Douglass: Orphan Slave," 213.

8. James Olney, "The Founding Fathers—Frederick Douglass and Booker T. Washington," 3.

9. J. A. Leo Lemay, quoted in Bruce Granger, "Benjamin Franklin," 275.

10. Many scholars besides the just-cited James Olney have noted the adoption of the American model of self-made man by African Americans; few outline the details of black-white correspondence as I do. One early, close analysis of such congruences is in Sidonie Smith's comparison of Franklin and Booker T. Washington; see *Where I'm Bound*, especially 30–37, and David Van Leer, "Reading Slavery: The Anxiety of Ethnicity in Douglass's *Narrative*," 118–40. An earlier version of this chapter, "Franklinian Douglass," appeared in 1990 in the same volume as Van Leer's essay.

11. James M. Cox, "Autobiography and America," 252. Further references will be cited parenthetically.

12. Benjamin Franklin, *The Autobiography*, in *Writings*, 1383. Further references will be cited parenthetically.

13. V. Smith, *A Narrative*, 3. Compare the disclaimer in B. Hammon, *Narrative*, 3. Michael Berthold has said of a later, similarly co-authored text, "although the control of representation in *Silvia Dubois* is hardly unidirectional, it is the intentionality of Larison, the recorder, that dominates. Because of his authorial superimpositions, we have to wonder to what degree, finally, we hear Dubois's voice at all"; see " 'The peals of her terrific language'," 13.

14. Both narratives are now available in one volume; see Potkay and Burr, *Black Atlantic Writers*.

15. Keith A. Sandiford, *Measuring the Moment*, 150.

16. For a discussion of the abolitionist-derived pattern of early black narrative see Sekora, "Black Message/White Envelope."

17. Olaudah Equiano, *The Interesting Narrative of the Life of Olaudah Equiano, or Gustavus Vassa, the African, Written by Himself*, 54. Other references are to this edition and will be cited within the text.

18. For two discussions of Equiano within the picaro tradition see Angelo Costanzo, *Surprizing Narrative*, and Raymond Hedin, "The American Slave Narrative: the Justification of the Picaro."

19. Peterson, *"Doers of the Word"*, 5.

20. See O'Neale, *Jupiter Hammon and the Biblical Beginnings of African-American Literature*, and Phillip M. Richards's essay, "Nationalist Themes in the Preaching of Jupiter Hammon."

21. Andrews, *To Tell A Free Story*, 60.

22. Baker Jr., *Blues, Ideology*, 38 and 31–50 *passim*.

23. I and many other others have debated how "American" Equiano's autobiography truly is; perhaps the relative brevity of my discussion of this remarkable text signals my continued fence-sitting.

24. Marion Wilson Starling has identified "only four autobiographies of American Negro Slaves containing accounts of the author's own experiences in Africa": those of James Albert Ukawsaw Gronniosaw, Olaudah Equiano, Venture Smith, and Zamba. See *The Slave Narrative*, 59 and 319*n*.

25. Whether there is a direct influence on Douglass and other American slave narrators remains open to debate, though some critics claim such a connection. Among others who discuss explicit and implicit influence of Equiano on Douglass are David Van Leer, "The Anxiety of Ethnicity in Douglass's *Narrative*," 122–23, and Baker Jr., *Blues, Ideology*, 39–44.

26. Robert Allison, "Introduction: Equiano's Worlds," in Equiano, *The Interesting Narrative*, 8. I found his historical overview very helpful.

27. Toward the end of his life, the Connecticut freedman Venture Smith viewed his achievements in terms of capital accumulation: "Notwithstanding all the losses I have suffered . . . I am now possessed of more than one hundred acres of land, and three habitable dwelling houses. It gives me joy to think that I *have* and that I *deserve* so good a character, especially for *truth* and *integrity*." V. Smith, *A Narrative*, 24.

28. Robert Allison, introduction to *The Interesting Narrative*, 23.

29. In the original manuscript Franklin had written "fame" instead of "reputation." When reading over the pages again he may have decided to follow his own advice: "I can not boast of much Success in acquiring the *Reality* of this Virtue [Humility]; but I had a good deal with regard to the *Appearance* of it" (1393). See *The Autobiography of Benjamin Franklin: A Genetic Text*, 1, and Franklin, *Writings*, 1307, to compare the texts of the opening address.

30. His mother rates a handful of words, and his wife, adoptive mother to the addressed son, several mentions.

31. Although Franklin's eldest son was not with Deborah Read but from an earlier liaison "with an unidentified mother" (LeMay, in Franklin, *Writings*, 1474), he was nevertheless the presumptive heir. Following the Revolutionary War, however, Franklin and his eldest child split over the issue of loyalties, with the son remaining Tory; this matter of misplaced patriotism cost William Franklin his legacy.

32. Douglass, *Narrative*, 24. Further references are to the Quarles edition and will be cited parenthetically.

33. The Douglass's first child, Rosetta, was born in 1839; Anna Murray Douglass then bore three sons before 1845: Lewis Henry (1840), Frederick Jr. (1842), and Charles Remond (1844). See Waldo E. Martin, *The Mind of Frederick Douglass*, 15.

34. Orlando Patterson, *Slavery and Social Death: A Comparative Study*, 5.

35. Douglass was still a fugitive slave at the time of the *Narrative*'s publication. His children, paradoxically, did "exist" because their mother and his wife, Anna Murray Douglass, was a free black. On the concept of natal alienation, see ibid., 5–9.

36. See Franklin, *Writings*, 1324.

37. Once in New Bedford, Douglass subscribes to William Lloyd Garrison's *The Liberator*: "The paper became my meat and my drink. My soul was set all on fire" (153).

38. Douglass may have intended a critique of white Christianity here, for the passage reads as an inversion of Ezekiel 3:1: "Son of man, eat that thou findest; eat this roll [of scripture], and go speak unto the house of Israel." Thanks to Michael Carter for this insight.

39. Frederick Douglass knew that his poor white friends would be free "when they got to be men." An Irish immigrant whom Douglass had aided urged the young boy to

run off, once he realized that such "a fine little fellow as [yourself] should be a slave *for life*" (emphasis added; Douglass, *Narrative*, 65, 69).

40. The young Franklin might well have been a bit much for his brother to swallow. On his first return to Boston, Franklin notes: "I was better dress'd than ever while in his Service, having a genteel new Suit . . . a Watch, and my Pockets lin'd with near Five Pounds Sterling in Silver. He receiv'd me not very frankly, look'd me all over, and turn'd to his Work again." Franklin finished off his visit by producing a handful of silver coins and giving the journeymen money for a drink. *Writings*, 1333–1334.

41. Werner Sollors, " 'Never Was Born': The Mulatto, An American Tragedy?," 305 and *passim*.

42. For two discussions of this scene, see Deborah McDowell, "In the First Place: Making Frederick Douglass and the Afro-American Tradition," especially 201–4, and Jenny Franchot, "The Punishment of Esther: Frederick Douglass and the Construction of the Feminine."

43. In the last chapter I refer again to Douglass's rhetorical assumption of the "sentimental" when discussing the figure of his abandoned elderly grandmother.

44. See Dickson J. Preston's *Young Frederick Douglass*, especially 22–40, for a discussion of the relationship between Frederick Douglass and his alleged father Aaron Anthony.

45. V. Smith, *Self-Discovery and Authority*, 33–34.

46. In Jenkins's defense one might add that the root conjuror had a free wife. Having enslaved—or relatively defenseless—relatives and friends kept many slaves from open participation in either rebellions or escape plans.

47. Frederick Douglass, *My Bondage and My Freedom*, 245.

48. Compare ibid., 244–46 with his *Narrative*, 102–3.

49. Valerie Smith has remarked that although Douglass's *Narrative* criticized "American cultural practices . . . [he affirmed] its definitions of manhood and power." *Self-Discovery*, 21.

50. "I should have no Objection to a Repetition of the same Life from its Beginning, only asking the Advantage Authors have in a second Edition to correct some Faults of the first. So Would I if I might . . . change some sinister Accidents & Events of it for others more favourable." Franklin, *Writings*, 1307.

51. This particular sentence was brought to my attention by Orlando Patterson in *Slavery and Social Death*, 13; the complete passage can be found in *The Life and Times of Frederick Douglass*, 143. The popular antebellum illustrated emblem of an enchained, supplicating slave—"Am I not a man and a brother?"—may have served to incite as much disdain at the bondsman's unmanliness as sympathy with his lot.

52. Douglass, *Life and Times*, 217.

53. Frederick Douglass, "Self Made Men" (n.d.), in the papers of Frederick Douglass, Library of Congress, volume 29, microform reel 18, page 5. Of the many variants of this speech I used the version in a pamphlet commemorating an address of Douglass to the students of the Carlisle Indian School. Further references will be cited parenthetically.

54. For further discussion of Douglass's postbellum speeches see David Blight, " 'For Something Beyond the Battlefield': Frederick Douglass and the Struggle for the Memory of the Civil War," 1156–1178. Waldo E. Martin's intellectual biography of Douglass explores at length the great black abolitionist's relation to the ideology of self-made men; see "Self-Made Man, Self-Conscious Hero," in *The Mind of Frederick Douglass*, 253–78.

55. McDowell, "In the First Place," 198. See also Wilson J. Moses on Douglass's "self-projection" in "Where Honor Is Due: Frederick Douglass as Representative Black Man," 177–89, and Rafia Zafar, "Franklinian Douglass."

56. I take the term "androcentric" from McDowell, "In the First Place," 198.

57. Douglass, *Narrative*, 104–5.

58. Douglass, "Self-Made Men," 7.

59. Compare Gates Jr., "[Phillis Wheatley and the Nature of the Negro]," 224.

60. Douglass, *Narrative*, 113.

61. See Albert Murray, *The Omni-Americans: Some Alternatives to the Folklore of White Supremacy*, 13–38, for his lively argument on the essential "American-ness" of the American Negro.

62. Du Bois, *The Souls of Black Folk*, 3.

63. Victor Turner, "Liminality and Communitas," in *The Ritual Process: Structure and Anti-Structure*, 110.

64. Ibid.

65. Anderson, *Imagined Communities*, 40.

66. In the formulation of Devereux and Loeb, Douglass's autobiography can be viewed as a supreme feat of antagonistic acculturation, for it adopts the literary genres of the white mainstream the better to denounce that hegemony. See "Antagonistic Acculturation," *passim*.

67. Robert Pattison, *On Literacy*, 62.

5. THE BLACKWOMAN IN THE ATTIC

Although the first draft of this section was already written when I took up my duties as coeditor of *Harriet Jacobs and Incidents in the Life of a Slave Girl: New Critical Essays*, the scholarship of and intellectual exchange with my colleagues on the project helped with the final shaping of this chapter. To them, my sincerest thanks.

The epigraph to this chapter comes from Richard Yarborough's "Strategies of Black Characterization," 72. Further references to this essay will be made parenthetically.

1. Werner Sollors first expressed this belief to me some years ago; he furthermore helped me to this chapter's title. That Stowe can now be seen as a virtual part of black American literature is underscored by Harryette Mullen's statement: "*Uncle Tom's Cabin* can be regarded as an important precursor of the African American novel." See "Runaway Tongue," 244.

2. We do well to contemplate the longevity of Stowe's creation: "Stowe, the writer, casts a long shadow, becomes an implacable act of precursor poetics that the latter-day black writer would both outdistance *and* 'forget.' " Hortense J. Spillers, "Changing the Letter: The Yokes, the Jokes of Discourse, or, Mrs. Stowe, Mr. Reed," 30.

3. William Wells Brown's *Clotel; or the President's Daughter* (1853) appeared in its first, English version the year after the book publication of *Uncle Tom's Cabin*. Frank Webb's *The Garies and Their Friends* (1857), like *Clotel*, was published in England, finding an American publisher only in the twentieth century. Martin R. Delany's *Blake, or the Huts of America* appeared only in serial form during the nineteenth century, first in the *Anglo-African Magazine* (1859) and later in the *Weekly Anglo-African* (1861–1862). For further information see "A note on this edition" in Floyd J.

Miller, ed., *Blake, or the Huts of America*, ix, as well as Bernard Bell, *The Afro-American Novel and Its Tradition*, 38.

4. The second and modern edition of *Our Nig* contains what little biographical information on Wilson as was then (during the 1980s) extant; born around 1827, Wilson survived until sometime after the publication of her little volume. See David A. Curtis, "Chronology of Harriet E. Adams Wilson," in Harriet E. Wilson, *Our Nig; or, Sketches from the Life of a Free Black, in a Two-Story White House, North, Showing that Slavery's Shadows Fall Even There*, xiii–xxvii. On treating the work as an autobiography, see Barbara A. White's " 'Our Nig' and the She-Devil: New Information about Harriet Wilson and the 'Bellmont' Family"; White has unearthed additional, compelling information about Wilson. Peterson also refers to this aspect of Wilson in *"Doers of the Word"*, 165. Further references will be provided within the main text.

5. Jean Fagan Yellin's scrupulous edition of Jacobs's *Incidents* has provided this generation with a wealth of biographical detail on Jacobs; see her introduction to *Incidents*, xiii–xxxiv. Further references are to this edition and will be cited parenthetically.

6. See Andrews's discussion of Jacobs and other writers in " 'Free at Last': From Discourse to Dialogue in the Novelized Autobiography," in *To Tell a Free Story*, 265–91.

7. Compare Lydia Maria Child's "The Quadroons," in *Fact and Fiction: A Collection of Stories*, 61–76, which Brown essentially includes wholesale within *Clotel*.

8. P. Gabrielle Foreman, "The Spoken and the Silenced in *Incidents in the Life of a Slave Girl* and *Our Nig*," 313.

9. Although *Clotel* was published in England, reviews, if not copies, of the novel appeared in the United States within months. William Edward Farrison refers to two such articles, one in the *Liberator* and one in the *National Anti-Slavery Standard*. See Farrison, " 'Clotel; or the President's Daughter' " in *William Wells Brown: Author & Reformer*, 259. A case might also be made for Jacobs's, if not Wilson's, influence on later versions of this novel (revised and republished three times during the 1860s), but such an examination lies beyond the purview of this chapter. See note 71, this chapter.

10. Melvin Dixon, *Ride Out the Wilderness*, 27. Sidonie Smith also refers to the "homelessness," literal and figurative, of Harriet Jacobs. Although I didn't come across her thoughtful essay until the final revisions of this chapter, our discussions differ somewhat. See "Resisting the Gaze of Embodiment: Women's Autobiographies in the Nineteenth Century," 98–102.

11. See Valerie Smith, " 'Loopholes of Retreat': Architecture and Ideology in Harriet Jacobs's *Incidents in the Life of a Slave Girl*"; Mullen, "Runaway Tongue"; Hortense J. Spillers, "Mama's Baby, Papa's Maybe: An American Grammar Book"; and Sandra M. Gilbert and Susan Gubar, *The Madwoman in the Attic*. Further references will be cited parenthetically.

12. Peterson, *"Doers of the Word"*, 23.

13. Harriet Beecher Stowe, *Uncle Tom's Cabin; or, Life Among the Lowly*, 1:73–74. I have referred here and in the following to the 1852 Jewett edition, which appeared in two volumes.

14. Robyn Warhol, *Gendered Interventions*, vii.

15. Robyn Warhol explains this as an instance of Stowe's authorial cross-dressing, noting that Stowe simultaneously "engages" and "distances" her reader, that she "crosses gender," as it were, rhetorically; Stowe's "Concluding Remarks" especially demonstrate this. See *Gendered Interventions*, 101–15.

16. As I have discussed both versions of his autobiography in an earlier chapter I will not go into them in detail once more, but I do want to highlight again the deliberate decisions Brown made when writing and publishing his works.

17. Stepto, *From Behind the Veil*, 30–31.

18. Dana Nelson, *The Word in Black and White*, 144, 145.

19. For various discussions of Wilson and her appeal to black readers see Gates Jr.'s introduction to *Our Nig*, xi–lv; Peterson, *"Doers of the Word"*, 147–75; Ernest "Economies of Identity"; and White, " 'Our Nig' and the She Devil."

20. Barbara A. White establishes the primacy of economic motives to Wilson in ibid.

21. The McFeely biography of Douglass tells us otherwise—that Betsey Bailey was not abandoned—thus demonstrating the wielded artifice in Douglass; see William S. McFeely, *Frederick Douglass*, 28, 294.

22. Barbara A. White says her research almost certainly proves that "Harriet Wilson . . . lived in Boston from 1856 to 1863" (22), but that period follows the lonely years spent as an indentured servant.

23. See Foreman, "The Spoken and the Silenced," 317 and *passim*; for an intriguing discussion of "the undertell" read her "Manifest in Signs: The Politics of Sex and Representation in *Incidents in the Life of a Slave Girl*" in Garfield and Zafar, *Harriet Jacobs and* Incidents in the Life of a Slave Girl: *New Critical Essays*, 76–99.

24. Among the many scholars who have wrestled with the complexities of Child's status as an abolitionist editor I have here noted Bruce Mills, "Lydia Maria Child and the Endings to Harriet Jacobs's *Incidents in the Life of a Slave Girl*" and Sandra Gunning, "Reading and Redemption" in Garfield and Zafar, *Harriet Jacobs and* Incidents. Jean Fagan Yellin's discussion, "L. Maria Child," in *Women and Sisters* (58–76) has greatly aided my comprehension of Child's influence.

25. The story of Margaret Garner, the real-life slave mother who killed a daughter rather than return her to slavery, takes on radically different forms in two retellings, one by a white contemporary, the other by a black twentieth-century novelist: compare the story of Cassy's last child in Stowe with that of the lost girl in Toni Morrison's *Beloved*. In contrast to the story told by Child and repeated by Wells Brown in *Clotel* ("The Quadroons"), where tragic mulattas seek death rather than sexual defilement, Jacobs plots other ways out, even if it means "willing" sexual behavior. And unlike Stowe's Cassy, Jacobs neither goes mad nor kills her children.

26. Foreman, "The Spoken and the Silenced," 323.

27. See Elizabeth Ammons, "Stowe's Dream of the Mother-Savior: *Uncle Tom's Cabin* and American Women Writers Before the 1920s."

28. As Linda Kerber has demonstrated, "The Republican Mother's life was dedicated to the service of civic virtue: she educated her sons for it." See *Women of the Republic*, 229.

29. Stowe does include a list of independent black entrepreneurs in "Concluding Remarks" (2:320).

30. As she concludes, Stowe's "matriarchal ideal does not finally alter the basic structure of the patriarchy" (802); see Askeland, "Remodeling the Model Home in *Uncle Tom's Cabin* and *Beloved*," 785–805. Compare this argument with that of Elizabeth Ammons or Jane Tompkins, for example.

31. Claudia Tate discusses this likelihood in the most detail, saying that Wilson's narrative "calls our attention to its effaced sexual discourse" time and again; see Tate, *Domestic Allegories of Political Desire*, 47–48, as well as Peterson, *"Doers of the Word"*, 167.

32. Contrast this to Jacobs's explanation that "Linda Brent" took Sands on as a lover to avoid the abuse of her owner, Dr. Flint—not because she aspired to fancy clothing.

33. And it is Mary, Currer's granddaughter, white by any description but that of a slave owner, who attains the true mark of white womanhood: legal marriage (albeit first to a Frenchman, and later to the equally "white" George Green, another voluntary Negro).

34. See duCille, *The Coupling Convention*, 24–25. DuCille in this section also refers to the dialogue between Brown, Stowe, and other authors of the day.

35. In reality, Jacobs's grandmother was named Molly Horniblow. Even though Jean Fagan Yellin's edition has determined the actual names of virtually all of the main characters in Jacobs's narrative, I have in general stayed with the names the autobiographer herself gave them, with the exception of Jacobs herself; see *Incidents*, xv.

36. Frederick Douglass "expected to meet with . . . the most Spartan-like simplicity [in the North, with none] of the ease, luxury, pomp, and grandeur of southern slaveholders." Instead, he found "splendid churches, beautiful dwellings, and finely-cultivated gardens"; his new African American friend Nathan Johnson "lived in a neater house; dined at a better table . . . than nine tenths of the slaveholders in Talbot county, Maryland." Douglass, *Narrative*, 148–50.

37. Baker Jr., *Blues, Ideology*, 35, and Gillian Brown, "Sentimental Possession," 42.

38. The reference is to Lydia Maria Child's "Slavery's Pleasant Homes: A Faithful Sketch."

39. William Wells Brown, quoted in Yarborough, "Strategies of Black Characterization," 68.

40. See duCille, *The Coupling Convention*, 24–25, and Carolyn Karcher, "Lydia Maria Child's *A Romance of the Republic*," 101n6. For other discussions of Child's tragic mulatto plots see Jean Fagan Yellin, *The Intricate Knot*, 171–76; Carolyn Karcher's earliest essay on this subject, "Rape, Murder, and Revenge in 'Slavery's Pleasant Homes',", 323–32, and Peterson, *"Doers of the Word"*, 160. All discuss the small yet significant changes Brown made when incorporating the Child story into his own work.

41. Spillers, "Changing the Letter," 27.

42. Compare this behavior to that of Hester Prynne in *The Scarlet Letter* when she insists on coming back to her original house of disgrace: "And Hester Prynne had returned, and taken up her long-forsaken shame. . . . Here had been her sin; here, her sorrow; and here was yet to be her penitence." Nathaniel Hawthorne, *The Scarlet Letter*, 343, 344.

43. The phrase "black back regions" is from P. Gabrielle Foreman, "Manifest in Signs," 78.

44. See Gillian Brown's "Someone's in the Kitchen with Dinah: Domestic Politics in *Uncle Tom's Cabin*," 503, and Lynn Wardley's "Relic, Fetish, Femmage: The Aesthetics of Sentiment in the Work of Stowe," 203, for interesting analyses of domestic economy and slavery in Stowe.

45. Wilson in fact intimates that as long as Mrs. Bellmont has been in charge any domestic worker has been doomed: she quotes Mag Smith as saying " 'She can't keep a girl in the house over a week' " (*Our Nig* 18).

46. Her early residence in a little house with her slave parents was, as she finds, no more secure than Uncle Tom's: although her family "lived together in a comfortable home" its permanence was already compromised by the fact of their being chattel (*Incidents* 5). Upon her parents' death the young Jacobs, like the "living furniture" she is, is transferred to her owner's abode. See Gillian Brown, *Domestic Individualism*, 49–50.

47. Although not chiefly examining homes in Jacobs's narrative, Sandra Gunning does analyze the "American cultural setting that defines black feminity as . . . publicly exposed, sexualized, unable or unwilling to create a domestic space of its own." See "Reading and Redemption," 151, 134.

48. During her long stay in the garret, Jacobs once goes "up stairs to the room I used to occupy" for a clandestine meeting with her daughter Ellen (139); her friend Fanny, who escapes north with her on the same vessel, hides in "a small tenement belonging to my grandmother, and built on the same lot with her own house" (149).

49. We should remember that affection for Aunt Marthy led a white woman slaveholder to hide Jacobs in her own home, a point I will return to shortly.

50. Kolodny, *The Land Before Her*, 9.

51. Slave narrators from Henry Bibb to Harriet Jacobs could recall their own experiences living in the woods, sojourns that were anticipated by the travels of the itinerant John Marrant.

52. The above-named slaves were interviewed in 1910 by Mary White Ovington; the transcript is reprinted in John Blassingame, *Slave Testimony*, 537.

53. Nathan Irvin Huggins, *Black Odyssey*, 209.

54. Let us recall that Eliza Harris, Stowe's runaway mother, risks her own and her small child's lives crossing a raging, ice-jammed river rather than face recapture.

55. From William Cowper's "The Task," book 4, lines 88–90; Jean Fagan Yellin must be credited with the identification. Yellin notes also that "Jacobs was not the first Afro-American to use Cowper's phrase. In 1838 . . . [it] appeared as an epigraph to 'The Curtain,' . . . in *Freedom's Journal*." Yellin, introduction to *Incidents*, 277n1.

56. Cowper's verse was well known to American abolitionists; with Robert Southey, he has been called one of "the two major English poets who commanded considerable [American] recognition for their antislavery views." See Isani, "Far 'From Gambia's Golden Shore'," 368. An examination of Child's *An Appeal in Favor of That Class of Americans Called Africans* and her subsequent, edited volume of Afro-American biography and essays, *The Freedman's Book*, reveals several citations of Cowper. See *An Appeal*, 1, 188, and *The Freedman's Book*, 23.

57. V. Smith, "Introduction," xxxiii–xxxiv.

58. Spillers, "Mama's Baby," 77.

59. Jacobs, *Incidents*, 28.

60. From the evidence available, it appears Stowe did not learn definitely of Jacobs's self-incarceration until she was writing her *Key to Uncle Tom's Cabin*. Nevertheless, the unclear dating of the first Jacobs letter to Amy Post discussing Stowe's possible involvement, as well as Jacobs's being known in antislavery circles during the decade or so preceding the publication of *Incidents*, does not rule out Stowe's having used Jacobs's sojourn in the crawl space as the model for Cassy's stay in Legree's attic. See *Incidents*, 231–32.

61. I am indebted to Jean Fagan Yellin's introduction and notes to *Incidents* for my chronology; see xiii–xxxiv and 253–92, *passim*.

62. That black women could view without being seen is no accident. In the next chapter I return to this notion of a black female watcher; the idea follows Michel Foucault's discussion of Surveillance in *Discipline and Punish* (200).

Werner Sollors once suggested the possibility that Stowe's *rendition* of Cassy's imprisonment affected the way Jacobs depicted her own. An interesting thought: Stowe, having perhaps learned of Jacobs's imprisonment and recast it into fictional form, must then be corrected by the original captive. Werner Sollors, personal communication, May 1989.

63. Douglass, *Narrative*, 105.

64. Karla F. C. Holloway, "Economies of Space: Markets and Marketability in *Our Nig* and *Iola Leroy*," 134.

65. One might consider that Stowe's Eliza Harris, the proud inhabitant of a room she considers "her home; and . . . a happy one it had been to her" (1:60), nevertheless is subject to the economic fortunes of the Shelby family. That home, we should keep in mind, was given to her by the people most likely to deprive her of it.

66. Beth Maclay Doriani, "Black Womanhood in Nineteenth Century America: Subversion and Self-Construction in Two Women's Autobiographies," 219.

67. As Gibson says, "the ideal domestic state was somewhat achieved in the living situation of her grandmother, but not quite. Her grandmother possessed the house, but her children were never able to share 'the snug little home.' " See Donald B. Gibson, "Harriet Jacobs, Frederick Douglass, and the Slavery Debate," 172.

68. For information on George Mason Wilson's foster home and death, see *Our Nig*, 139, xxi, xxiv–v; and White, " 'Our Nig' and the She-Devil," 24–26.

69. Askeland, "Remodeling the Model Home," 786.

70. Sánchez-Eppler, "Bodily Bonds," 31.

71. Brown's later versions of the novel may in fact show the influence of Jacobs, if not Wilson, for the novel appeared several times in altered form during the 1860s. Jacobs's fictionalized autobiography appeared during the publication of *Miralda*—the serialized version of *Clotel*, which came out during the winter of 1860–61—and before the last two versions, which appeared in 1864 and 1867. M. Giulia Fabi discusses Brown's various textual changes during the Civil War and postbellum period, as well as Jacobs's more forthright depiction of sexualized slavery in *Incidents*; she does not, however, link *Clotel*'s changes directly to the influence of *Incidents*. See " 'Unguarded Expressions of the Feelings of the Negroes': Gender, Slave Resistance, and William Wells Brown's Revisions of *Clotel*."

72. Carby, *Reconstructing Womanhood*, 61.

73. Barbara White's research indicates that Wilson very probably lived in Boston for seven years; it seems likely she had contact with the activist black antislavery community there after her husband's abandonment and death. See " 'Our Nig' and the She-Devil" 26.

74. John Ernest, "Economies of Identity: Harriet E. Wilson's *Our Nig*," 429.

75. Jean Fagan Yellin discusses the vicissitudes of the publication and reviews of *Incidents* in her introduction to Jacobs's narrative; see *Incidents*, xxi–xxv.

76. Due to the vagaries—or racism—of the marketplace, *Our Nig* did not make much of an impact: Henry Louis Gates Jr., writing in his introduction to the modern edition of *Our Nig*, suggests that it may be the "boldness" of Wilson's themes (miscegenation, northern racism, free black duplicity) that kept the work from being reviewed and noticed. See *Our Nig*, xxvi–xxxi.

6. DRESSING UP AND DRESSING DOWN: ELIZABETH KECKLEY'S *BEHIND THE SCENES AT THE WHITE HOUSE* AND ELIZA POTTER'S *A HAIRDRESSER'S EXPERIENCE IN HIGH LIFE*

I would like to acknowledge in particular the support of my colleagues at the Charles Warren Center for Studies in American History during the year 1995–96; their response to, and advice on, an early version of this chapter was very helpful— even if I did not follow all of their good suggestions! Sandra Gunning, as has been happily the case with a good part of this book, remains my ideal reader: thank you, dear friend.

1. Deborah McDowell, letter to the author, 27 July 1992.

2. Peterson, *"Doers of the Word"*, 5.

3. We should consider why twentieth-century readers continue to view Jacobs's success in terms of her remaining sexually "intact"—that is, that we read her not having spoken of rape as her not having been raped. For two discussions of sexual "virtue" in Jacobs, read Foreman, "Manifest in Signs" and Gunning, "Reading and Redemption."

4. V. Smith, *Self-Discovery and Authority*, 27. Still, few writers adhered strictly to one genre and Douglass, among the many I discuss in this book, is no exception. See the previous chapter for brief remarks on Douglass's marshaling of the sentimental.

5. See Joanne Braxton, *Black Women Writing Autobiography*, for a discussion of Jacobs and the black women's archetype of "outraged motherhood." For further discussion of Jacobs and her role in the development of African American literary identity, see the preceding chapter.

6. The essays on Keckley by William L. Andrews and Frances Smith Foster, noted subsequently, are virtually alone in current literary scholarship.

7. Keith Walker, of Dartmouth's Afro-American Studies department, wished I would more fully treat the implications of the "wedding veil" in this discussion; instead, I direct my readers to duCille's excellent analysis of black signifying on conventional "marriage plots" in *The Coupling Convention*.

8. Peterson, "Doers of the Word", 23.

9. See Foreman's "Manifest in Signs," 78. Sánchez-Eppler's essay, "Bodily Bonds," on black/white women is justly well known for her discussion of these issues.

10. Elsa Barkley Brown, "African-American women's quilting," 929.

11. Carla Peterson has called for the end of an African American literary history that takes the slave narrative as its primary early genre, a point seconded by Sandra Gunning. See Peterson, *"Doers of the Word"*, 5; Gunning, personal communication, 12 May 1996.

12. See Darlene Clark Hine, "Rape and the Inner Lives of Black Women in the Middle West," 915.

13. Yarborough, "The First-Person in Afro-American Fiction," 112.

14. See Stepto, "Distrust of the Reader," 304, 309.

15. Foreman uses this phrase in "Manifest in Signs" (77 and elsewhere) to refer to the narrative subterfuges of Harriet Jacobs; I will refer to her use of "undertell" shortly.

16. Zora Neale Hurston, *Their Eyes Were Watching God*, 28. Hurston's character refers to the reigning, hierarchical power structure in the United States, which places white men at the top and black women at the bottom.

17. See Elsa Barkley Brown, "Negotiating and Transforming the Public Sphere," 144.

18. An important early work on the corrupted relations between white mistresses and black women slaves is Catherine Clinton's *The Plantation Mistress*; three recent discussions of the complicated and suspicion-fraught relations between black and white women, slave or free, include Sánchez-Eppler's "Bodily Bonds"; Yellin's *Women and Sisters*, especially 3–26; and Gunning, "Reading and Redemption." I here refer, of course, to Carroll Smith-Rosenberg's "The Female World of Love and Ritual." I also direct readers to Nell Painter's recent work on white and black female relations in the context of the southern patriarchy; see "Soul Murder and Slavery: A Fully-Loaded Cost Accounting" and "Of *Lily*, Linda Brent, and Freud."

19. Eliza Potter, *A Hairdresser's Experience in High Life,* and Elizabeth Keckley, *Behind the Scenes; or, Thirty Years a Slave and Four in the White House.* All references to these works will be noted within the text.

20. Noliwe M. Rooks's *Hair Raising: Beauty, Culture, and African-American Women* came to my attention too late for me to discover whether she appraises the meaning of nineteenth-century hairdressers such as Potter.

21. See Andrews, "Reunion in the Postbellum Slave Narrative."

22. James Olney, in his introduction to *Behind the Scenes,* says that "After the first three chapters, the book could best be described as 'memoirs' " (xxxiii); the modern editor of *A Hair-dresser's Experience,* Sharon G. Dean, remarks in her introduction that Potter's "autobiography lacks an overt interest in defining a black self" (lvii).

23. Some of my readers have by now recognized the reference in P. Gabrielle Foreman's punning phrase "black back regions"; she signifies on Karen Halttunen's "back regions" discussion in *Confidence Men and Painted Women.* In regard to entrepreneurship, the Jamaican hotel-keeper Mary Seacole is still another nineteenth-century black female autobiographer whose work I do not here have the space to explore. Her autobiography, *Wonderful Adventures of Mrs. Seacole in Many Lands* (1857), is available in two editions: one American, edited by William L. Andrews; and the other British, edited by Audrey Dewjee and Ziggi Alexander. The latter edition contains valuable historical and biographical information. Sandra Gunning first drew my attention to Seacole, and her "Maternity, Economy and Mobility in *Wonderful Adventures of Mrs. Seacole in Many Lands*" discusses issues related to the ones I explore here.

24. Although not national figures, Potter and Keckley speak openly about their activities for their oppressed fellows: Potter announces that she had only performed a "Christian" deed in telling a slave how to get to Canada, an act for which she goes to jail (17–19); Keckley discusses her role in organizing a relief program for former slaves of the Confederacy (113—16). See Peterson, *Doers of the Word,* on black women speakers.

25. Baker Jr., *Blues, Ideology,* 35. But by not including the works of black women in his discussion Baker overlooks an implied dichotomy therein: "The economics of slavery not only reduced the African man to laboring chattel, but also reduced African women to sexual objects" (37). As black women also labored, and black men could be and were sometimes sexually exploited (if more rarely or less openly than females), this either/or explanation seems unlikely.

26. Both women, like Equiano, were well-traveled, and as such represent the peripatetic, if not transatlantic, black American Paul Gilroy and Carla Peterson have described in their work.

27. Dean, introduction to *A Hair-dresser's Experience,* xxxiii. I rely on her excellent introduction to the secrets and subterfuges of Eliza Potter; for example, Dean points out that among other facts of the author's life not revealed in the narrative are her two children (li).

28. Dean points briefly to Keckley's and Potter's similar observer status: "Eliza Potter stage manages the social melodrama around her, much as Elizabeth Keckley seems to do in her 1868 autobiography" (iv).

29. Frederick Douglass's break with the Garrisonian wing of abolitionism came in large measure because of their differences over what was fitting, and what was not, for an ex-slave to say: he recalls a white "Friend" saying "Give us the facts . . . we will take care of the philosophy." Douglass, *My Bondage and My Freedom,* 220.

30. Jean Fagan Yellin's edition of Jacobs tells us that other African Americans used this metaphor as early as 1838; she also reproduces the key lines from the abolitionist poet:

"'Tis pleasant, through the loopholes of retreat, / To peep at such a world,—to see the stir / Of the great Babel, and not feel the crowd." See Yellin, notes to *Incidents*, 277n1.

31. Moira Ferguson, *Subject to Others*, 127.

32. Compare William Boelhower's reading of the "ethnic gaze" in *Through a Glass Darkly*, especially 17–40.

33. Michel Foucault discusses the notion of being viewed as surveillance in *Discipline and Punish*; see his chapter "Panopticism," 195–228, especially 200.

34. Claudia Tate, in her chapter on Harriet Wilson's *Our Nig* and Jacobs's *Incidents*, discusses the economic necessity that led many near-impoverished free blacks to have their still-young children take up paying jobs, or enter into indentured servitude. See Tate, "Maternal Discourse as Antebellum Social Protest," in *Domestic Allegories of Political Desire*, especially 25–26 and 33–38.

35. In an encouraging change of pace, the Delany sisters, two centenarian African American professionals from Mt. Vernon, New York, became celebrities in the 1990s for their pithy, as-told-to joint autobiography. See the Delany sisters, *Having Our Say*.

36. Potter enumerates "at this time, four distinct circles of fashionables: first, is the real old aristocracy; second, the monied aristocracy; third, the church aristocracy, and fourth, the school aristocracy" (196). By "school aristocracy" she means the parents who send their children to particular schools in order to gain access to higher social circles.

37. In Keckley's very first exchange with Lincoln she finds that her previous work for a lady of *ton* (Mrs. Jefferson Davis) helps land her the job; Lincoln even then expressed anxieties about their relative lack of money vis-a-vis the necessities of fashionable dress: "We are just from the West" (85).

38. Ellen Craft not only passed for white but cross-dressed, impersonating both a white and a man; her daring story has made her the latter-day heroine of critics investigating liminality and gender. See her dictated slave autobiography, co-authored with her husband William, *Running a Thousand Miles for Freedom*.

39. Commenting on interracial unions in Cincinnati, Potter notes that some women who are married to white men "pass for white, and some, again, are so independent they will be thought nothing but what they are" (155).

40. Joanne Braxton determines "sass" to be characteristic of black women's autobiography; see *Black Women Writing Autobiography*, 30–31.

41. Susan Graber, "*A Hair-dresser's Experience in High Life* by Mrs. Eliza Potter: Cincinnati Society in the Mid-Nineteenth Century," 217. Graber, as can be deduced from the title of her essay, is more concerned with the light Potter shed on whites in mid-nineteenth-century Ohio; she does acknowledge that "in several instances" Potter demonstrates "strong anti-slavery" sentiment (217).

42. Harriet E. Wilson, *Our Nig*, 129.

43. Despite my repeated references in the previous chapter to Harriet Jacobs as the protagonist-author of *Incidents in the Life of a Slave Girl*, I well remember that *Incidents* appeared as the work of one "Linda Brent." Also see Braxton, *Black Women Writing Autobiography*, 24.

44. See Kathleen Thompson's entry on Keckley in *Black American Women: An Encyclopedia*, 672–73.

45. I refer to Darlene Clark Hine, "Rape and the Culture of Dissemblance." I will return shortly to George Keckley and his mother's revealing and concealing of his body and her mourning. Interestingly enough, the younger Keckley enlisted as a *white* man and was killed in 1861 (John Washington, *They Knew Lincoln*, 208). Many of

Keckley's readers would have known that black soldiers did not enter the war until late the following year, with the formation of the famous Fifty-Fourth Massachusetts Volunteers—and that tells us even more about Keckley's veiled account.

46. I do not count the forty-page appendix following the years with Mrs. Lincoln, as the correspondence contained therein was published without Keckley's consent or approval. See Foster, *Written by Herself*, 128, and Washington, *They Knew Lincoln*, 239–40.

47. William L. Andrews, "The Changing Moral Discourse of Nineteenth-Century African American Women's Autobiography," 232.

48. Nellie Y. McKay, "Nineteenth-Century Black Women's Spiritual Auto-biographies," 140.

49. Sandra Gunning, personal communication, 4 May 1996.

50. Years later, after the war, Keckley returns to the South. But it is not to visit her mother, who died earlier at some unspecified point following the family's removal to Mississippi; she goes to visit the *white* Burwell-Garland clan. I will return to the deaths of Keckley's mother and son. See Andrews, "Reunion in the Postbellum Slave Narrative," 5–16, for a reading of postbellum slave/master reunions.

51. Andrews, "Changing Moral Discourse," 234. Interestingly, Andrews sees Keckley as a precursor of Booker T. Washington, rather than an heir to the economically skilled Equiano Houston Baker has described.

52. Keckley is whipped for rocking her white charge clear out of the cradle and then attempting to pick the baby up with a shovel: what seems peculiar and aggressive behavior becomes pathetically explicable when we recall she was at the time a four-year-old assigned to care for an infant. See Keckley, *Behind the Scenes*, 18–21.

53. The locution "undertell" is P. Gabrielle Foreman's; while she uses it to refer to black women's narratives, specifically that of Harriet Jacobs, her examination of the "readings of the relation between coded silences and 'truth,' between signs and literal script" is useful to black autobiographical criticism in general. See Foreman, "Manifest in Signs," 79 and *passim*.

54. Mary Todd Lincoln's most recent biographer disputes somewhat Keckley's version of the event, especially the president's pointing to the asylum. Despite Jean H. Baker's denigrating the authority of *Behind the Scenes* because it was "ghost-written," she relies on the dressmaker-entrepreneur's autobiography throughout her own book. John E. Washington acknowledges that James Redpath took down Keckley's dictation, but adds "It is no surprise that an expert should assist Mrs. Keckley to arrange her facts and make her book a good narrative"; he points out that whites did not say Jefferson Davis's autobiography was equally doubtful, for he had the same helper—James Redpath (239). We can assume that the literate Keckley would have more control over her memoirs than an illiterate fugitive slave.

See also Frances Smith Foster, "Resisting *Incidents*," for a discussion of the continuing doubts about another mid-nineteenth century writer's authenticity.

55. See Jean H. Baker, *Mary Todd Lincoln*, 126–28; Baker asserts that Todd Lincoln's early life, plagued by deaths and abandonments, created a persona of public grief that went against the grain of nineteenth-century dictates of Christian submission (xiv and elsewhere). Todd Lincoln's habit of destroying or giving away the effects of her deceased loved ones perhaps contributed to Keckley's ignorance or silence on the subject; see *Mary Todd Lincoln*, 213–14.

56. Halttunen, *Confidence Men*, 124; her "Mourning the Dead: A Sentimental Ritual," 124–52, is important to the discussion that follows.

57. Mrs. Lincoln's tortured outbursts and other behaviors deemed unacceptable in a proper middle-class widow would later help her surviving son in his very public battle to have her judged insane. See Baker, *Mary Todd Lincoln*, 315–50.

58. Washington, *They Knew Lincoln*, 213, 217.

59. Mary Todd Lincoln to Elizabeth Todd Grimsley, cited in ibid., 208.

60. Andrews, "Reunion in the Postbellum Slave Narrative."

61. Halttunen makes this connection clear: "Colonial graveyards, not surprisingly, were regarded as unpleasant places to be avoided by the living. By the late eighteenth century . . . burial grounds were deteriorating into weedy fields filled with fallen tombstones and the offensive odor of decay" (*Confidence Men*, 127).

62. The Shaw memorial on Boston Common, created by the noted sculptor Augustus Saint-Gaudens, commemorated the white leader of the renowned African American Civil War regiment, and by extension the Massachusetts Fifty-fourth. Shaw is depicted on horseback above a group of anonymous black soldiers.

63. Jacobs speaks in more detail about her parents' last resting places: she obliquely refers to the surviving African tradition of planting a tree at the foot of a grave (her father, before his death, plants a tree at the head of his wife's plot), and makes her decision to resist her master while kneeling near her parents' burial sites (this vow perhaps marks a second African survival—the belief in a continuity between the living world and the realm of the dead). Jacobs, *Incidents*, 90–91. For information on African American graveyards and ritual beliefs see John Michael Vlach, *The Afro-American Tradition in Decorative Arts*, 139–47.

64. Dean, introduction to *A Hair-dresser's Experience*, xxxiv.

65. Along with her "uncontrollable grief after Lincoln's assassination," shopping sprees, and other "peculiarities," Robert Lincoln used this breach of conduct to convict his mother of insanity. See Baker, *Mary Todd Lincoln*, 321. We may consider how such beliefs in proper female mourning continue: only recall how Jacqueline Kennedy was universally praised for her stoicism following her husband's martyrdom.

66. Although primarily focused on sexual competition, Painter's essay includes further suggestions for reading on this subject. See "Of *Lily*, Linda Brent, and Freud," 259.

67. Dean, introduction to *A Hair-dresser's Experience*, lvii.

68. Ralph Ellison, *Invisible Man*, 503.

CONCLUSION: THE BEGINNING OF AFRICAN AMERICAN LITERATURE

1. Various of John Saillant's essays on African Calvinism and early black authors and divines discuss this apparent contradiction; I here refer specifically to " 'Wipe Away All Tears From Their Eyes.'"

2. Devereux and Loeb, "Antagonistic Acculturation," *passim*.

3. In different eras and different disciplines various scholars have come to this same conclusion; see, for example, Mechal Sobel, *The World They Made Together*, and Melville Herskovits, preface to *The Myth of the Negro Past*, xxi.

4. Stuckey's analysis locates the roots of this nation-within-a-nation in the political activism and theory of antebellum thinkers such as David Walker and Henry Highland Garnet; see *Slave Culture*, especially 98–192.

5. I have therefore confined this study to individuals publishing full-length works before 1870 although, as should be evident, no chronological line can be drawn that effectively demarcates such a change.

6. I have relied here on W. E. B. Du Bois's still-standard discussion; see *Black Reconstruction*, 670–710.

7. For example, although the former slave George Teamoh became a Virginia state senator during Reconstruction, the manuscript, completed at the urgings of friends, was not published until more than a century later. See Teamoh's narrative, *God Made Man, Man Made the Slave*.

8. Andrews, *To Tell A Free Story*, 29–30 and closing chapter.

9. J. Hector St. John de Crèvecoeur, *Letters from an American Farmer*, 43.

BIBLIOGRAPHY

Ammons, Elizabeth. "Stowe's Dream of the Mother-Savior: *Uncle Tom's Cabin* and American Women Writers Before the 1920s." In Eric J. Sundquist, ed., *New Essays on* Uncle Tom's Cabin, 155–95. New York: Oxford University Press, 1986.

Anderson, Benedict. *Imagined Communities: Reflections on the Origin and Spread of Nationalism.* London: Verso Editions, 1983.

Andrews, William L. "The Changing Moral Discourse of Nineteenth-Century African American Women's Autobiography: Harriet Jacobs and Elizabeth Keckley." In Sidonie Smith and Julia Watson, eds., *De/Colonizing the Subject: The Politics of Gender in Women's Autobiography,* 225–41. Minneapolis: University of Minnesota Press, 1992.

——. "The 1850s: The First Afro-American Literary Renaissance." In William L. Andrews, ed., *Literary Romanticism in America,* 38–60. Baton Rouge: Louisiana State University Press, 1981.

——. "The First Fifty Years of the Slave Narrative." In John Sekora and Darwin T. Turner, eds., *The Art of the Slave Narrative: Original Essays in Criticism and Theory,* 6–24. Macomb: Western Illinois University Press, 1982.

——. "Reunion in the Postbellum Slave Narrative: Frederick Douglass and Elizabeth Keckley." *Black American Literature Forum* 23, no. 1 (Spring 1989): 5–16.

——. *Sisters of the Spirit: Three Black Women's Autobiographies of the Nineteenth Century.* Bloomington: Indiana University Press, 1986.

——. *To Tell a Free Story: The First One Hundred Years of the Slave Narrative.* Urbana and Chicago: University of Illinois Press, 1986.

——. "Towards a Poetics of Afro-American Autobiography." In Houston A. Baker Jr. and Patricia Redmond, eds., *Afro-American Literary Studies in the 1990s*, 78–91. Chicago: University of Chicago Press, 1989.

Arner, Robert D. "The Connecticut Wits." In Everett Emerson, ed., *American Literature, 1764–1789: The Revolutionary Years*, 233–52. Madison: University of Wisconsin Press, 1977.

——. "The Smooth and Emblematic Song: Joel Barlow's *The Hasty Pudding*." *Early American Literature* 7, no. 2 (Spring 1972): 76–91.

Asante, Molefi Kete. *The Afrocentric Idea*. Philadelphia: Temple University Press, 1987.

Askeland, Lori. "Remodeling the Model Home in *Uncle Tom's Cabin* and *Beloved*." *American Literature* 64, no. 4 (December 1992): 785–805.

Axtell, James. "The Indian Impact on English Colonial Culture," in *The European and the Indian: Essays in the Ethnohistory of Colonial North America*, 272–315. New York: Oxford University Press, 1981.

Baker Jr., Houston A. *Blues, Ideology, and Afro-American Literature: A Vernacular Theory*. Chicago: University of Chicago Press, 1984.

——. "In Dubious Battle." *New Literary History*, 18, no. 2 (Winter 1987): 363–69.

——. *The Journey Back: Issues in Black Literature and Criticism*. Chicago: University of Chicago Press, 1980.

——. *Modernism and the Harlem Renaissance*. Chicago: University of Chicago Press, 1987.

——. *Workings of the Spirit*. Chicago: University of Chicago Press, 1991.

—— and Patricia Redmond. *Afro-American Literary Study in the 1990s*. Chicago: University of Chicago Press, 1989.

Baker, Jean H. *Mary Todd Lincoln: A Biography*. New York: Norton, 1987.

Barlow, Joel. *Collected Works of Joel Barlow. Volume 2: Poetry*. Facsimile reproductions with an introduction by William K. Battorff and Arthur L. Ford. Gainesville, FL: Scholars' Facsimiles & Reprints, 1970.

Barth, Fredrik. Introduction to *Ethnic Groups and Boundaries: The Social Organization of Culture Difference*, 9–38. Boston: Little, Brown, 1969.

Baym, Nina. *Woman's Fiction: A Guide to Novels by and About Women in America, 1820–1870*. Ithaca: Cornell University Press, 1978.

Bell, Bernard. "African-American Writers." In Everett Emerson, ed., *American Literature, 1764–1789: The Revolutionary Years*, 171–93. Madison: University of Wisconsin Press, 1977.

——. *The Afro-American Novel and Its Tradition*. Amherst: University of Massachusetts Press, 1987.

Bercovitch, Sacvan. *The American Jeremiad*. Madison: University of Wisconsin Press, 1978.

——. "The Problem of Ideology in American Literary History." *Critical Inquiry* 12 (Summer 1986): 631–53.

——. *The Puritan Origins of the American Self*. New Haven: Yale University Press, 1975.

——, ed. *Reconstructing American Literary History*. Cambridge: Harvard University Press, 1986.

——. "The Ritual of American Autobiography: Jonathan Edwards, Benjamin Franklin, Henry David Thoreau." In *Revue Française des Etudes Americaines* 7, no. 14 (May 1982): 139–50.

Berthold, Michael C. " 'The peals of her terrific language': The Control of Representation in *Silvia Dubois, a Biografy of the Slav Who Whipt Her Mistres and Gand Her Fredom*." *MELUS* 20, no. 2 (Summer 1995): 3–14.

Bibb, Henry. *Narrative of the Life and Adventures of Henry Bibb, an American Slave, Written by Himself*. Third Stereotype Edition, 1850. New York. Published by the author.

Bhabha, Homi K. "Signs Taken for Wonders: Questions of Ambivalence and Authority under a Tree Outside Delhi, May 1817." In Henry Louis Gates Jr., ed., *"Race," Writing, and Difference*, 163–84. Chicago: University of Chicago Press, 1986.

Blassingame, John, ed. *Slave Testimony*. Baton Rouge: Louisiana State University Press, 1977.

Bleecker, Ann Eliza. *The Posthumous Works of Ann Eliza Bleecker, in Prose and Verse. To which is added, A Collection of Essays, Prose and Poetical, by Margaretta V. Faugeres*. New York: T. and J. Swords, 1793.

Blight, David. " 'For Something Beyond the Battlefield': Frederick Douglass and the Struggle for the Memory of the Civil War." *Journal of American History* 75, no. 4 (March 1989): 1156–1178.

Bontemps, Arna, ed. *Five Black Lives: The Autobiographies of Venture Smith, James Mars, William Grimes, The Rev. G. W. Offley, and James L. Smith*. Middletown, CT: Wesleyan University Press, 1971.

——. "The Slave Narrative: An American Genre." In *Great Slave Narratives*. Boston: Beacon Press, 1969.

Bourdieu, Pierre. *Distinction: A Social Critique of the Judgement of Taste*. Trans. Richard Nice. Cambridge: Harvard University Press, 1984.

Bradstreet, Anne. *The Works of Anne Bradstreet*. Jeannine Hensley, ed. Cambridge: Harvard University Press, 1967.

Braxton, Joanne. *Black Women Writing Autobiography: A Tradition Within a Tradition*. Philadelphia: Temple University Press, 1989.

——. "Harriet Jacobs' *Incidents in the Life of a Slave Girl*: The Re-definition of the slave." *Massachusetts Review* 27, no. 2 (Summer 1986): 379–87.

Breitwieser, Mitchell Robert. *American Puritanism and the Defense of Mourning: Religion, Grief, and Ethnology in Mary White Rowlandson's Captivity Narrative*. Madison: University of Wisconsin Press, 1990.

Brown, Elsa Barkley. "African-American Women's Quilting: A Framework for Conceptualizing and Teaching African-American Women's History." *SIGNS: Journal of Women in Culture and Society* 14, no. 4 (1989): 921–29.

——. "Negotiating and Transforming the Public Sphere: African American Political Life in the Transition from Slavery to Freedom." *Public Culture* 7 (1994): 106–46.

Brown, Gillian. *Domestic Individualism: Imagining Self in Nineteenth-Century America*. Berkeley: University of California Press, 1990.

——. "Getting in the Kitchen with Dinah: Domestic Politics in *Uncle Tom's Cabin*." *American Quarterly* 36, no. 4 (Fall 1984): 502–23.

Brown, Sterling. *The Negro in American Fiction*. 1937. Reprint, Port Washington, NY: The Kennikat Press, 1968.

Brown, William Wells. *Clotel, or the President's Daughter*. London: Partridge & Oakey, 1853.

——. "Narrative of the Life and Escape of William Wells Brown." In Henry Louis Gates Jr., ed., *Three Classic African-American Novels*, 7–44. New York: Vintage, 1990.

——. *The Narrative of William W. Brown, A Fugitive Slave [1848] and A lecture delivered before the Female Anti-Slavery Society of Salem, 1847*. Larry Gara, ed. Reading, MA: Addison-Wesley, 1969.

Bruss, Elizabeth. *Autobiographical Acts: The Changing Situation of a Literary Genre*. Baltimore: The Johns Hopkins University Press, 1976.

Caldwell, Patricia. *The Puritan Conversion Narrative*. Cambridge: Cambridge University Press, 1983.

Carby, Hazel. *Reconstructing Womanhood: The Emergence of the Afro-American Woman Novelist*. New York: Oxford University Press, 1987.

Carleton, Phillips D. "The Indian Captivity." *American Literature* 15 (1943): 169–80.

Chametzky, Jules. *Our Decentralized Literature: Cultural Mediations in Selected Jewish and Southern Writers*. Amherst: University of Massachusetts Press, 1986.

Chesnutt, Charles W. *The Conjure Woman*. 1899. Reprint, Ann Arbor: University of Michigan Press, 1969.

——. *The Wife of His Youth and other stories*. 1899. Reprint, Ann Arbor: The University of Michigan Press, 1968.

Child, Mrs. [Lydia Maria]. *An Appeal in Favor of that Class of Americans Called Africans*. Boston: Allen and Ticknor, 1833.

——. *Fact and Fiction: A Collection of stories*. New York: C. S. Francis & Co., 1846.

——. *The Freedman's Book*. Boston: Ticknor and Fields, 1866.

——. "Slavery's Pleasant Homes. A Faithful Sketch," *The Liberty Bell* 4 (1843): 147–60.

Clinton, Catherine. *The Plantation Mistress: Woman's World in the Old South*. New York: Pantheon Books, 1982.

Cohen, Daniel A. *Pillars of Salt, Monuments of Grace: New England Crime Literature and the Origins of American Popular Culture, 1674–1860*. New York: Oxford University Press, 1993.

Collins, Terrence. "Phillis Wheatley: The Dark Side of the Poetry." In William H. Robinson, ed., *Critical Essays on Phillis Wheatley*. Boston: G. K. Hall, 1982. Reprinted from *Phylon* 36, no. 1 (March 1975): 147–58.

Costanzo, Angelo. *Surprizing Narrative: Olaudah Equiano and the Beginnings of Black Autobiography*. Westport, CT: Greenwood Press, 1987.

Cowell, Pattie. *American Women Poets in Pre-Revolutionary America, 1650–1775: An Anthology*. Troy, NY: Whitson Publishing Company, 1981.

Cowper, William. *The Works of William Cowper, Esq. comprising His Poems, Correspondence, and Translations. With a Life of the Author, by the Editor, Robert Southey, Esq. LL.D*. Volumes 9 and 10. 1837. Reprint, New York: AMS Editions, 1971.

Cox, James M. "Autobiography and America." *Virginia Quarterly Review* 47, no. 2 (Spring 1971): 252–77.

Craft, Ellen and William Craft. *Running a Thousand Miles for Freedom; or the Escape of William and Ellen Craft from Slavery*. 1860. Reprint, New York: Arno Press, 1969.

Crévecoeur, J. Hector St. John de. *Letters from an American Farmer*. 1782. Reprint, London and New York: Everyman's Library, 1971.

Culley, Margo, ed. *American Women's Autobiography. Fea(s)ts of Memory*. Madison: University of Wisconsin Press, 1992.

Danforth, Samuel. *A Brief Recognition of New Englands Errand into the Wilderness*. In A. W. Plumstead, ed., *The Wall and the Garden*, 53–77. 1671. Reprint, Minneapolis: University of Minnesota Press, 1968.

Dauber, Kenneth. "Benjamin Franklin and the Idea of Authorship." *Criticism* 28, no. 3 (Summer 1986): 355–86.

Davis, Arthur P. "The Personal Elements in the Poetry of Phillis Wheatley." In William H. Robinson, ed., *Critical Essays on Phillis Wheatley*. 93–101. Boston: G. K. Hall, 1982.

Davis, Elizabeth. "Events in the Life and the Text: Franklin and the Style of American Autobiography." *Revue Française d'Etudes Americaines* 7, no. 14: 187–97.

Dawson, Hugh J. "Fathers and Sons: Franklin's "Memoirs" as Myth and Metaphor." *Early American Literature* 14 (1979–80): 269–92.

Dean, Sharon G. Introduction to Eliza Potter, *A Hairdresser's Experience in High Life*. New York: Oxford University Press, 1988.

Delany, Sarah and Elizabeth A. with Amy Hill Hearth. *Having Our Say: The Delany Sisters' First Hundred Years*. New York: Kodansha International, 1993.

Delany, Martin R. *Blake, or the Huts of America*. 1859, 1861. Reprint, Boston: Beacon Press, 1970.

Derounian, Kathryn Zabelle. "Puritan Orthodoxy and the 'Survivor Syndrome' in Mary Rowlandson's Indian Captivity Narrative." *Early American Literature* 22, no. 1 (Spring 1987): 82–93.

Devereux, George and Edwin M. Loeb. "Antagonistic Acculturation." *American Sociological Review* 8, no. 2 (April 1943): 133–47.

Dickinson, Jonathan. *Jonathan Dickinson's Journal; or, God's Protecting Providence Man's Surest Help and Defence*. Evangeline Walker Andrews and Charles McLean Andrews, eds. 1699. Reprint, New Haven: Yale University Press, 1945.

Dixon, Melvin. *Ride Out the Wilderness: Geography and Identity in Afro-American Literature*. Urbana: University of Illinois Press, 1987.

Doriani, Beth Maclay. "Black Womanhood in Nineteenth Century America: Subversion and Self-Construction in Two Women's Autobiographies." *American Quarterly* 43, no. 2 (June 1991): 199–221.

Douglas, Ann. *The Feminization of American Culture*. 1977. Reprint, New York: Anchor Press, 1988.

Douglass, Frederick. *The Life and Times of Frederick Douglass*. 1892. Reprint, New York and London: Collier Macmillan, 1962.

——. *My Bondage and My Freedom*. 1855. Reprint, New York: Arno Press and *The New York Times*, 1968.

——. *Narrative of the Life of Frederick Douglass, An American Slave. Written by Himself*. Benjamin Quarles, ed. 1845. Reprint, Cambridge: Harvard University Press, 1960.

——. "Self-Made Men" (n.d.). Printed text in the Frederick Douglass Papers, Library of Congress, volume 29, microfilm reel 18.

——. "What to the Slave is the Fourth of July?: An Address Delivered in Rochester, New York, on 5 July 1852." In John W. Blassingame, ed., *The Frederick Douglass Papers. Series I: Speeches, Debates, and Interviews; Volume 2: 1847–1854*, 359–88. New Haven: Yale University Press, 1982.

Du Bois, W. E. B. *Black Reconstruction in America, 1860–1880*. 1935. Reprint, New York: Atheneum, 1983.

——. *The Souls of Black Folk: Essays and Sketches*. Chicago: A. C. McClurg and Company, 1903.

duCille, Anne. *The Coupling Convention: Sex, Text, and Tradition in Black Women's Fiction*. New York: Oxford University Press, 1993.

Dunbar, Paul Laurence. *Lyrics of Lowly Life: The Poetry of Paul Laurence Dunbar.* 1896. Reprint, New York: The Citadel Press, 1984.

Elder, Arlene A. *The "Hindered Hand": Cultural Implications of Early African-American Fiction.* Westport, CT: Greenwood Press, 1978.

Ellison, Julie. "Race and Sensibility in the Early Republic: Ann Eliza Bleecker and Sarah Wentworth Morton." *American Literature* 65, no. 3 (September 1993): 445–74.

Ellison, Ralph. "Change the Joke and Slip the Yoke." In *Shadow and Act,* 45–59. 1953, 1964. Reprint, New York: Vintage, 1972.

———. *Invisible Man.* New York: Random House, 1952.

Emerson, Ralph Waldo. "Representative Men." In Joel Porte, ed., *Essays and Lectures,* 611–761. 1850. Reprint, New York: Library of America, 1983.

Erkilla, Betsy. "Phillis Wheatley and the Black American Revolution." In Frank Shuffleton, ed., *A Mixed Race: Ethnicity in Early America,* 225–40. New York: Oxford University Press, 1993.

Ernest, John. "Economies of Identity: Harriet E. Wilson's *Our Nig.*" *PMLA* 109, no. 3 (May 1994): 424–38.

Equiano, Olaudah. *The Interesting Narrative of the Life of Olaudah Equiano, or Gustavus Vassa, the African, Written by Himself.* 1792. Reprint, Leeds, England: James Nichols, 1814.

———. *The Interesting Narrative of the Life of Olaudah Equiano, Written by Himself.* Robert J. Allison, ed. Boston and New York: Bedford Books of St. Martin's Press, 1995.

Fabi, M. Giulia. "The 'Unguarded Expressions of the Feelings of the Negroes': Gender, Slave Resistance, and William Wells Brown's Revisions of *Clotel.*" *African American Review* 27, no. 4 (1993): 639–54.

Farrison, William Edward. *William Wells Brown: Author & Reformer.* Chicago: University of Chicago Press, 1969.

Ferguson, Moira. *Subject to Others: British Women Writers and Colonial Slavery, 1670–1834.* New York: Routledge, 1992.

Fiedler, Leslie. "New England and the Invention of the South." In James Nagel and Richard Astro, eds., *American Literature: The New England Heritage,* 101–12. New York: Garland Publishers, 1981.

Fisher, Dexter and Robert B. Stepto, eds. *Afro-American Literature: The Reconstruction of Instruction.* New York: Modern Language Association, 1979.

Fisher, Philip. *Hard Facts: Setting and Form in the American Novel.* New York: Oxford University Press, 1987.

Fishkin, Shelley Fisher. *Was Huck Black? Mark Twain and African American Culture.* New York: Oxford University Press, 1993.

——— and Carla L. Peterson. " 'We Hold These Truths to Be Self-Evident': The Rhetoric of Frederick Douglass's Journalism." In Eric J. Sundquist, ed., *Frederick Douglass: New Literary and Critical Essays,* 189–204. New York: Cambridge University Press, 1990.

Fliegelman, Jay. *Prodigals and Pilgrims: The American Revolution Against Patriarchal Authority, 1750–1800.* New York: Cambridge University Press, 1982.

Foreman, P. Gabrielle. "Manifest in Signs: The Politics of Sex and Representation in *Incidents in the Life of a Slave Girl.*" In Deborah Garfield and Rafia Zafar, eds., *Harriet Jacobs and Incidents in the Life of a Slave Girl: New Critical Essays,* 76–99. New York: Cambridge University Press, 1996.

———. "The Spoken and the Silenced in *Incidents in the Life of a Slave Girl* and *Our Nig.*" *Callaloo* 13, no. 2 (Spring 1992): 313–24.

Foster, Frances Smith. "Autobiography After Emancipation: The Example of Elizabeth Keckley." In James Robert Payne, ed., *Multicultural Autobiography: American Lives*, 32–63. Knoxville: University of Tennessee Press, 1992.

——. " 'In Respect to Females . . .': Differences in the Portrayals of Women by Male and Female Narrators." *Black American Literature Forum* 15 (Summer 1981): 66–70.

——. "Resisting *Incidents*." In Deborah Garfield and Rafia Zafar, eds., *Harriet Jacobs and Incidents in the Life of a Slave Girl: New Critical Essays*, 57–75. New York: Cambridge University Press, 1996.

——. *Witnessing Slavery: The Development of Ante-bellum Slave Narratives*. Westport, CT: Greenwood Press, 1979.

——. *Written by Herself: Literary Production by African American Women, 1746–1892*. Bloomington: Indiana University Press, 1993.

Foucault, Michel. *Discipline and Punish*. Trans. Alan Sheridan. New York: Pantheon, 1977.

Fox-Genovese, Elizabeth. Epilogue to *Within the Plantation Household: Black and White Women of the Old South*, 372–96. Chapel Hill: University of North Carolina Press, 1988.

——. "To Write My Self. The Autobiographies of Afro-American Women." In Shari Benstock, ed., *Feminist Issues in Literary Scholarship*, 161–80. Bloomington: Indiana University Press, 1987.

Franchot, Jenny. "The Punishment of Esther: Frederick Douglass and the Construction of the Feminine." In Eric J. Sundquist, ed., *Frederick Douglass: New Literary and Historical Essays*, 141–65. New York: Cambridge University Press, 1990.

Franklin, Benjamin. *The Autobiography*. In J. A. Leo Lemay, ed., *Writings*, 1307–1469. New York: The Library of America, 1987.

——. *The Autobiography of Benjamin Franklin: A Genetic Text*. J. A. Leo Lemay and P. M. Zall, eds. Knoxville: University of Tennessee Press, 1981.

Frederickson, George M. "Self-Made Hero." Rev. of *Young Frederick Douglass: The Maryland Years* and *The Mind of Frederick Douglass*. *The New York Review of Books*, June 27, 1985, 3–4.

Fromm, Harold. "Real Life, Literary Criticism, and the Perils of Bourgeoisification." *New Literary History* 20, no. 1 (Autumn 1988): 49–64.

Garfield, Deborah and Rafia Zafar. *Harriet Jacobs and Incidents in the Life of a Slave Girl: New Critical Essays*. New York: Cambridge University Press, 1996.

Gates Jr., Henry Louis, ed. *Black Literature and Literary Theory*. New York and London: Methuen, 1984.

——. "Criticism in the Jungle." In *Black Literature and Literary Theory*, 1–24. New York and London: Methuen, 1984.

——. " 'A Negro Way of Saying.' " Rev. of *Moses, Man of the Mountain* and *Dust Tracks on a Road*. *The New York Times Book Review*, April 21, 1985, 45.

——. "[Phillis Wheatley and the Nature of the Negro]." In William H. Robinson, ed., *Critical Essays on Phillis Wheatley*, 215–33. Boston: G. K. Hall, 1982.

——, ed. *"Race," Writing, and Difference*. Chicago: University of Chicago Press, 1986.

——, ed. *Reading Black, Reading Feminist*. New York: Meridian, 1990.

——. *The Signifying Monkey: A Theory of African-American Literary Criticism*. New York: Oxford University Press, 1988.

——. " 'What's Love Got To Do With It?': Critical Theory, Integrity, and the Black Idiom." *New Literary History* 18, no. 2 (Winter 1987): 345–62.

——. "Writing 'Race' and the Difference It Makes." *Critical Inquiry* 12, no. 1 (Autumn 1985): 1–20.

Gayle Jr., Addison, ed. *The Black Aesthetic.* 1971. Reprint, New York: Anchor Press, 1972.

——. *The Way of the New World: The Black Novel in America.* 1975. Reprint, New York: Anchor Press, 1976.

Gibson, Donald B. "Harriet Jacobs, Frederick Douglass, and the Slavery Debate: Bondage, Family, and the Discourse of Domesticity." In Deborah Garfield and Rafia Zafar, eds., *Harriet Jacobs and Incidents in the Life of a Slave Girl: New Critical Essays,* 156–78. New York: Cambridge University Press, 1996.

Gilbert, Sandra M. and Susan Gubar. *The Madwoman in the Attic: The Woman Writer and the Nineteenth-Century Literary Imagination.* 1979. Reprint, New Haven: Yale University Press, 1984.

Gilroy, Paul. *The Black Atlantic: Modernity and Double Consciousness.* Cambridge: Harvard University Press, 1993.

Goody, Jack and Ian Watt. "The Consequences of Literacy." In Jack Goody, ed., *Literacy in Traditional Societies,* 27–68. Cambridge: Cambridge University Press, 1968.

Graber, Susan P. "*A Hair-dresser's Experience in High Life* by Mrs. Eliza Potter: Cincinnati Society in the Mid-Nineteenth Century." [Introduction to, and excerpts from, Potter's book.] *Bulletin of the Historical and Philosophical Society of Ohio* 25, no. 3 (1967): 215–24.

Granger, Bruce. "Benjamin Franklin." In Earl N. Harbert and Robert A. Rees, eds., *Fifteen American Authors Before 1900,* 185–206. Rev. ed. Madison: University of Wisconsin Press, 1984.

Griffith, John. "*The Columbiad* and *Greenfield Hill*: History, Poetry, and Ideology in the Late Eighteenth Century." *Early American Literature* 10, no. 3 (Winter 1975/1976): 235–50.

Grimal, Pierre. *The Dictionary of Classical Mythology.* Trans. A. R. Maxwell-Hyslop. Oxford, England: Basil Blackwell, 1986.

Gronniosaw, Ukawsaw. *A Narrative of the Most Remarkable Particulars in the Life of James Albert Ukawsaw Gronniosaw, An African Prince, as Related by HIMSELF.* 2nd ed. n.d. [Bath, England: 1770]

Gunning, Sandra. "Reading and Redemption in *Incidents in the Life of a Slave Girl.*" In Deborah Garfield and Rafia Zafar, eds., *Harriet Jacobs and Incidents in the Life of a Slave Girl: New Critical Essays,* 131–55. New York: Cambridge University Press, 1996.

Hallowell, A. Irving. "American Indians, White and Black: The Phenomenon of Trans-culturalization." *Current Anthropology* 4, No. 5 (December 1963): 519–31.

Halttunen, Karen. *Confidence Men and Painted Women: A Study of Middle-Class Culture in America, 1830–1870.* New Haven: Yale University Press, 1982.

——. "Gothic Imagination and Social Reform: The Haunted Houses of Lyman Beecher, Henry Ward Beecher, and Harriet Beecher Stowe." In Eric J. Sundquist, ed., *New Essays on Uncle Tom's Cabin,* 107–34. New York: Oxford University Press, 1986.

Hammon, Briton. *Narrative of the Uncommon Sufferings and Surprising Deliverance of Briton Hammon, A Negro Man, Servant to General Winslow, of Marshfield, in NEW-ENGLAND; Who returned to Boston, after having been absent almost Thirteen Years.* Boston: Green & Russell, 1760.

Hammon, Jupiter. "An Address to Miss Phillis Wheatly, Ethiopian Poetess" (1778). In Richard Barksdale and Keneth Kinnamon, eds., *Black Writers of America: A Comprehensive Anthology,* 47–48. New York: Macmillan, 1972.

Hanson, Elizabeth. *God's Mercy Surrounding Man's Cruelty* (1728). In Richard VanDerBeets, ed., *Held Captive by Indians: Selected Narratives, 1642–1836,* 230–44. Knoxville: University of Tennessee Press, 1973.

Harper, Frances E. W. *Iola Leroy, or Shadows Uplifted.* 1893. Reprint, Boston: Beacon Press, 1987.

Harper, Phillip Brian. "Nationalism and Social Division in Black Arts Poetry of the 1960s." *Critical Inquiry* 19 (Winter 1993): 234–55.

Hawthorne, Nathaniel. *The Scarlet Letter.* In Millicent Bell, ed., *Nathaniel Hawthorne: Novels,* 115–345. 1850. Reprint, New York: Library of America, 1983.

Hayden, Robert. *Collected Poems.* Frederick Glaysher, ed. New York: Liveright, 1985.

Heard, J. Norman. *White Into Red: A Study of the Assimilation of White Persons Captured by Indians.* Metuchen, NJ: The Scarecrow Press, 1973.

Hedin, Raymond. "The American Slave Narrative: the Justification of the Picaro." *American Literature* 53 (1982): 630–45.

Hedrick, Joan D. " 'Peaceable Fruits': The Ministry of Harriet Beecher Stowe." *American Quarterly* 40, no. 3 (September 1988): 307–32.

Henderson, Mae. "Speaking in Tongues: Dialogics, Dialectics, and the Black Woman Writer's Literary Tradition." In Henry Louis Gates Jr., ed., *Reading Black, Reading Feminist,* 116–42. New York: Meridian, 1990.

Henson, Josiah. *The Life of Josiah Henson, formerly a slave, As narrated by himself.* London: Charles Gilpin, 1852.

Herron, Carolivia. "Milton and Afro-American Literature." In Mary Nyquist and Margaret W. Ferguson, eds., *Re-membering Milton: Essays on the Texts and Traditions,* 278–300. New York and London: Methuen, 1987.

Herskovits, Melville. Preface to *The Myth of the Negro Past,* xv–xxix. 1940. Reprint, Boston: Beacon Press, 1958.

Hine, Darlene Clark. "Rape and the Inner Lives of Black Women in the Middle West: Preliminary Thoughts on the Culture of Dissemblance." *SIGNS: Journal of Women in Culture and Society* 14, no. 4 (1989): 912–20.

Hodges, Graham Russell, ed. *Black Itinerants of the Gospel: The Narratives of John Jea and George White.* Madison, WI: Madison House, 1993.

Holloway, Karla F. C. "Economies of Space: Markets and Marketability in *Our Nig* and *Iola Leroy.*" In Joyce W. Warren, ed., *The (Other) American Traditions: Nineteenth-Century Women Writers,* 126–40. New Brunswick, NJ: Rutgers University Press, 1993.

Hopkins, Pauline. *Contending Forces: A Romance Illustrative of Negro Life North and South.* 1900. Reprint, New York: Oxford University Press, 1988.

Horton, James Oliver and Lois E. Horton. "Violence, Protest, and Identity: Black Manhood in Antebellum America." In *Free People of Color: Inside the African American Community,* 80–97. Washington, DC: Smithsonian Institution Press, 1993.

Houchins, Susan, ed. *Spiritual Narratives.* New York: Oxford University Press, 1988.

Howard, Leon. *The Connecticut Wits.* Chicago: University of Chicago Press, 1943.

Howard-Pitney, David. *The Afro-American Jeremiad: Appeals for Justice in America.* Philadelphia: Temple University Press, 1990.

——. "The Enduring Black Jeremiad: The American Jeremiad and Black Protest Rhetoric from Frederick Douglass to W. E. B. Du Bois, 1841–1919." *American Quarterly* 38, no. 3 (Bibliography 1986): 481–92.

Huggins, Nathan Irvin. *Black Odyssey.* New York: Oxford University Press, 1977.

——. *Harlem Renaissance*. New York: Oxford University Press, 1971.

Humez, Jean McMahon. Introduction to *Gifts of Power: The Writings of Rebecca Jackson, Black Visionary, Shaker Eldress*, 1–50. Amherst: University of Massachusetts Press, 1981.

Hurston, Zora Neale. *Their Eyes Were Watching God*. 1937. Reprint, Urbana: University of Illinois Press, 1978.

Isani, Mukhtar Ali. "Far 'From Gambia's Golden Shore': The Black in Late Eighteenth-Century American Imaginative Literature." *William and Mary Quarterly*, Third Series, 36, no. 3 (July 1979): 353–72.

——. " 'Gambia on My Soul': Africa and the African in the Writings of Phillis Wheatley." *MELUS* 6, no. 1 (Spring 1979): 64–72.

——. "Phillis Wheatley and the Elegiac Mode." In William H. Robinson, ed., *Critical Essays on Phillis Wheatley*, 208–14. Boston: G. K. Hall, 1982.

Jackson, Blyden. *The Waiting Years: Essays on American Negro Literature*. Baton Rouge: Louisiana State University Press, 1976.

—— and Louis D. Rubin Jr. *Black Poetry in America: Two Essays in Historical Interpretation*. Baton Rouge: Louisiana State University Press, 1974.

Jacobs, Harriet [a.k.a. Linda Brent]. *Incidents in the Life of a Slave Girl, Written by Herself*. Edited by L. Maria Child (1861). Jean Fagan Yellin, ed. Cambridge: Harvard University Press, 1987.

Jahn, Janheinz. *Muntu: An Outline of Neo-African Culture*. Trans. Marjorie Grene. London: Faber & Faber, 1961.

Jefferson, Thomas. *Notes on the State of Virginia* (1787). In *Writings*, 123–325. Merrill D. Peterson, ed. New York: Library of America, 1984.

Jehlen, Myra. "Imitate Jesus and Socrates: The Making of a Good American." *South Atlantic Quarterly* 89, no. 3 (Summer 1990): 501–24.

Johnson, Mrs. [Susannah Willard Hastings]. *A Narrative of the Captivity of Mrs. Johnson: Containing an Account of her Sufferings, during Four Years with the Indians and French*. Walpole, NH: David Carlisle Jr., 1796.

Jordan, June. "The Difficult Miracle of Black Poetry in America or Something Like a Sonnet for Phillis Wheatley." *Massachusetts Review* 27, no. 2 (Summer 1986): 252–62.

Jordan, Winthrop D. "Unthinking Decision: Enslavement of Negroes in America to 1700." In T. H. Breen, ed., *Shaping Southern Society*, 100–15. New York: Oxford University Press, 1976.

——. *White Over Black: American Attitudes Toward the Negro, 1550–1812*. 1968. Reprint, New York: Pelican Books, 1969.

Joyce, Joyce A. "The Black Canon: Reconstructing Black American Literary Criticism." *New Literary History* 18, no. 2 (Winter 1987): 335–44.

——. " 'Who the Cap Fit': Unconsciousness and Unconscionableness in the Criticism of Houston A. Baker Jr. and Henry Louis Gates Jr." *New Literary History* 18, no. 2 (Winter 1987): 371–84.

Karcher, Carolyn. "Lydia Maria Child's *A Romance of the Republic*: An Abolitionist Vision of America's Racial Destiny." In Deborah E. McDowell and Arnold Rampersad, eds., *Slavery and the Literary Imagination*, 81–103. Baltimore: The Johns Hopkins University Press, 1989.

——. "Rape, Murder, and Revenge in 'Slavery's Pleasant Homes': Lydia Maria Child's Antislavery Fiction and the Limits of Genre." *Women's Studies International Forum* 9, no. 4 (1986): 323–32.

Keckley, Elizabeth. *Behind the Scenes; or, Thirty Years a Slave and Four in the White House*. 1868. Reprint, New York: Oxford University Press, 1988.

Kerber, Linda. *Women of the Republic: Intellect and Ideology in Revolutionary America*. Chapel Hill: University of North Carolina Press, 1980.

Kibbey, Ann. *The Interpretation of Material Shapes in Puritanism: A Study of Rhetoric, Prejudice, and Violence*. New York: Cambridge University Press, 1986.

——. "Language in Slavery: Frederick Douglass's *Narrative*." In Jack Salzman, ed., *Prospects: The Annual of American Cultural Studies 8*, 163–82. Cambridge and New York: Cambridge University Press, 1983.

Kolodny, Annette. *The Land Before Her: Fantasy and Experience of the American Frontiers, 1630–1860*. Chapel Hill: University of North Carolina Press, 1984.

——. "Turning the Lens on the Panther Captivity: A Feminist Exercise in Practical Criticism." *Critical Inquiry* 8, no. 2 (Winter 1981): 329–45.

Kretzoi, Charlotte. "Puzzled Americans: Attempts at an American National Epic Poem." In Tibor Frank, ed., *The Origins and Originality of American Culture*, 139–48. Budapest: Akadémiai Kiaddo', 1984.

Kuncio, Robert C. "Some Unpublished Poems of Phillis Wheatley." *New England Quarterly* 18, no. 2 (June 1970): 287–97.

Landry, Donna. *The Muses of Resistance: Laboring-Class Women's Poetry in Britain, 1739–1796*. New York: Cambridge University Press, 1990.

Lawrence, D. H. "Benjamin Franklin." In Charles L. Sanford, ed., *Benjamin Franklin and the American Character*, 57–64. Boston: D. C. Heath, 1955.

Lemay, J. A. Leo. "The Contexts and Themes of 'The Hasty Pudding.' " *Early American Literature* 17, no. 1 (Spring 1982): 3–23.

Levine, Lawrence W. *Black Culture and Black Consciousness: Afro-American Folk Thought From Slavery To Freedom*. New York: Oxford University Press, 1977.

Lincoln, C. Eric and Lawrence H. Mamiya. *The Black Church in the African American Experience*. Durham, NC: Duke University Press, 1990.

Lorde, Audre. *Sister Outsider: Essays and Speeches*. Trumansburg, NY: The Crossing Press, 1984.

Lystad, Robert A. "Tentative Thoughts on Basic African Values." In *Africa and the United States: Images and Realities*, 176–89. Background Book, 8th National Conference for UNESCO, October 22–26, 1961. New York: UNESCO, 1961.

McDowell, Deborah E. "In the First Place: Making Frederick Douglass and the Afro-American Narrative Tradition." In William L. Andrews, ed., *Critical Essays on Frederick Douglass*, 192–213. Boston: G. K. Hall, 1991.

—— and Arnold Rampersad, eds. *Slavery and the Literary Imagination*. Baltimore: The Johns Hopkins University Press, 1989.

McDowell, Edwin. "Grass vs. Bellow over U.S. at PEN." *The New York Times*, January 15, 1986, Sec. C, p. 15, col. 1.

McFeely, William S. *Frederick Douglass*. New York: Norton, 1991.

McHenry, Elizabeth. " 'Dreaded Eloquence': The Origins and Rise of African American Literary Societies and Libraries." *Harvard University Library Bulletin* New Series 6, no. 2 (Spring 1995): 32–56.

McKay, Nellie Y. "The Journals of Charlotte L. Forten-Grimké: *Les Lieux de Mémoire* in African-American Women's Autobiography." In Geneviève Fabre and Robert O'Meally, eds., *History and Memory in African-American Culture*, 261–71. New York: Oxford University Press, 1994.

——. "Nineteenth-Century Black Women's Spiritual Autobiographies: Religious Faith and Self-Empowerment." In The Personal Narratives Group, eds., *Interpreting Women's Lives: Feminist Theory and Personal Narratives*, 139–54. Bloomington: Indiana University Press, 1989.

MacKethan, Lucinda H. "From Fugitive Slave to Man of Letters: The Conversion of Frederick Douglass." *The Journal of Narrative Technique* 16, no. 1 (Winter 1986): 55–71.

Marrant, John. *A Narrative of the Lord's Wonderful Dealings with John Marrant, A Black (Now going to Preach the Gospel in Nova-Scotia) Born in New-York, in North-America, Taken down from his own Relation, arranged, corrected and published, by the Rev. Mr. Aldridge* (1785). In Richard VanDerBeets, ed., *Held Captive by Indians*, 177–201. Knoxville: University of Tennessee Press, 1973.

——. *A Narrative of the Lord's Wonderful Dealings with John Marrant, A Black (Now going to Preach the Gospel in Nova-Scotia) Born in New-York, in North-America. Fourth Edition, Enlarged by Mr. Marrant and Printed (with Permission), for his Sole Benefit, with Notes Explanatory*. London: R. Hawes, 1785.

——. *A Sermon preached on the 24th day of June 1789, being the Festival of St. John the Baptist, at the request of the right worshipful the grand master Prince Hall, and the rest of the brethren of the African Lodge of the Honorable Society of Free and Accepted Masons in Boston*. [1789]. Boston: The Bible and Heart.

Mars, James. *Life of James Mars, A Slave Born and Sold in Connecticut, Written by Himself*. 1864. Reprint in Arna Bontemps, ed., *Five Black Lives*, 35–58. Middletown, CT: Wesleyan University Press, 1971.

Martin Jr., Waldo E. *The Mind of Frederick Douglass*. Chapel Hill: University of North Carolina Press, 1984.

Mason Jr., Julian D. Introduction to *The Poems of Phillis Wheatley*, 1–34. Revised and enlarged edition. Chapel Hill: University of North Carolina Press, 1989.

Mather, Cotton. "A Narrative of Hannah Dustan's Notable Deliverance from Captivity." In Alden T. Vaughan and Edward W. Clark, eds., *Puritans Among the Indians: Accounts of Captivity and Redemption, 1676–1724*, 162–64. Cambridge: Harvard University Press, 1981.

Matson, R. Lynn. "Phillis Wheatley—Soul Sister?" In William H. Robinson, ed., *Critical Essays on Phillis Wheatley*, 113–22. Boston: G. K. Hall, 1982.

Matthews, Victoria Earle. "The Value of Race Literature: An Address." 1895. Reprinted with an afterword by Fred Miller Robinson in *The Massachusetts Review* 27, no. 2 (Summer 1986): 169–91.

Miller, Perry. "Errand Into the Wilderness." In *Errand Into the Wilderness*, 1–15. Cambridge: Harvard University Press, 1956.

Mills, Bruce. "Lydia Maria Child and the Endings to Harriet Jacobs's *Incidents in the Life of a Slave Girl*." *American Literature* 61, no. 2 (June 1992): 255–72.

Minter, David. "The Puritan Jeremiad as a Literary Form." In Sacvan Bercovitch, ed., *The American Puritan Imagination: Essays in Revaluation*, 45–55. Cambridge: Cambridge University Press, 1974.

Montgomery, Benilde. "Recapturing John Marrant." In Frank Shuffleton, ed., *A Mixed Race: Ethnicity in Early America*, 105–15. New York: Oxford University Press, 1993.

Morgan, Edmund S. *Visible Saints: The History of a Puritan Idea*. Ithaca: Cornell University Press, 1965.

Morrison, Toni. *Beloved*. New York: Knopf, 1987.

BIBLIOGRAPHY

——. *Playing in the Dark: Whiteness and the Literary Imagination.* 1992. Reprint, New York: Vintage, 1993.

Moses, Wilson J. "Where Honor Is Due: Frederick Douglass as Representative Black Man." In Jack Salzman, ed., *Prospects: An Annual of American Cultural Studies 17,* 145–55. New York: Cambridge University Press, 1992.

Mullen, Harryette. "Runaway Tongue: Resistant Orality in *Uncle Tom's Cabin, Our Nig, Incidents in the Life of a Slave Girl,* and *Beloved.*" In Shirley Samuels, ed., *The Culture of Sentiment,* 244–64. New York: Oxford University Press, 1992.

Murray, Albert. *The Omni-Americans: Some Alternatives to the Folklore of White Supremacy.* 1970. Reprint, New York: Vintage, 1983.

Neal, Larry. "The Black Arts Movement." In Addison Gayle, ed., *The Black Aesthetic,* 257–74. 1968. Reprint, New York: Anchor Press, 1971.

Nelson, Dana. "Reading the Written Selves of Colonial America: Franklin, Occom, Equiano, and Palou/Serra." In *Resources for American Literary Study* 19, no. 2 (1993): 246–59.

——. *The Word in Black and White.* New York: Oxford University Press, 1992.

Nichols, Charles. *Many Thousand Gone: The Ex-Slaves' Account of Their Bondage and Freedom.* Leiden: E. J. Brill, 1963.

Niemtzow, Annette. "The Problematic of Self in Autobiography: The Case of the Slave Narrative." In John Sekora and Darwin T. Turner, eds., *The Art of the Slave Narrative,* 96–109. Macomb: Western Illinois University Press, 1982.

Nott, Walt. "From 'uncultivated Barbarian' to 'Poetical Genius': The Public Presence of Phillis Wheatley." *MELUS* 18, no. 3 (Fall 1993): 21–32.

Olney, James. "The Founding Fathers—Frederick Douglass and Booker T. Washington." In Deborah McDowell and Arnold Rampersad, eds., *Slavery and the Literary Imagination,* 1–24. Baltimore: The Johns Hopkins University Press, 1989.

——. "'I Was Born': Slave Narratives, Their Status as Autobiography and as Literature." In Charles T. Davis and Henry Louis Gates Jr., eds., *The Slave's Narrative,* 148–75. New York: Oxford University Press, 1985.

O'Neale, Sondra. *Jupiter Hammon and the Biblical Beginnings of African-American Literature.* Metuchen, NJ: The American Theological Library Association and the Scarecrow Press, 1993.

——. "A Slave's Subtle War: Phillis Wheatley's Use of Biblical Myth and Symbol." *Early American Literature* 21, no. 2 (Fall 1986): 144–65.

Paine, Thomas. *Common Sense.* 1776. Reprint, New York: Penguin, 1976.

Painter, Nell Irvin. "Of *Lily,* Linda Brent, and Freud: A Non-Exceptionalist Approach to Race, Class, and Gender in the Slaveholding South." *Georgia Historical Quarterly* 76, no. 2 (Summer 1992): 241–59.

——. "Soul Murder and Slavery: A Fully-Loaded Cost Accounting." In Kathryn Kish Sklar et al., eds., *U.S. History as Women's History,* 125–46. Chapel Hill: University of North Carolina Press, 1995.

Patterson, Orlando. "Language, Ethnicity, and Change." *Journal of Basic Writing* 3, no. 1 (Fall/Winter 1980): 62–73.

——. *Slavery and Social Death: A Comparative Study.* Cambridge: Harvard University Press, 1982.

Pattison, Robert. *On Literacy: The Politics of the Word from Homer to the Age of Rock.* New York: Oxford University Press, 1982.

Pearce, Roy Harvey. "The Significance of the Captivity Narrative." *American Literature* 19 (1947): 1–20.

235

Peterson, Carla. *"Doers of the Word": African-American Women Speakers and Writers in the North (1830–1880)*. New York: Oxford University Press, 1995.

Petry, Ann. *The Street*. 1946. Reprint, Boston: Beacon Press, 1985.

Plumstead, A. W., ed. *The Wall and The Garden*. Minneapolis: University of Minnesota Press, 1968.

Potkay, Adam. "Olaudah Equiano and the Art of Spiritual Autobiography." *Eighteenth Century Studies* 27 (Summer 1994): 677–92.

—— and Sandra Burr, eds. *Black Atlantic Writers of the Eighteenth Century: Living the New Exodus in England and the Americas*. New York: St. Martin's Press, 1995.

Potter, Eliza. *A Hair-dresser's Experience in High Life*. 1859. Reprint, New York: Oxford University Press, 1988.

Pratt, Mary Louise. *Imperial Eyes: Travel Writing and Transculturation*. London and New York: Routledge, 1992.

Preston, Dickson J. *Young Frederick Douglass*. Baltimore: The Johns Hopkins University Press, 1980.

Raboteau, Albert J. *Slave Religion: The "Invisible Institution" in the Antebellum South*. New York: Oxford University Press, 1978.

Redding, J. Saunders. *To Make A Poet Black*. With an introduction by Henry Louis Gates Jr. 1939. Reprint, Ithaca: Cornell University Press, 1988.

Reed, Ishmael. "Flight to Canada." In *Flight to Canada*, 3–5. New York: Random House, 1976.

Richards, Phillip M. "Nationalist Themes in the Preaching of Jupiter Hammon." *Early American Literature* 25, no. 2 (1990): 123–38.

——. "Phillis Wheatley, Americanization, the Sublime, and the Romance of America." *Style* 27, no. 2 (Summer 1993): 194–221.

——. "Phillis Wheatley and Literary Americanization." *American Quarterly* 44, no. 2 (June 1992): 163–91.

Richmond, M. A. *Bid the Vassal Soar: Interpretive Essays on the Life and Poetry of Phillis Wheatley (ca. 1753–1784) and George Moses Horton (ca. 1797–1883)*. Washington, DC: Howard University Press, 1974.

Robinson, William H., ed. *Critical Essays on Phillis Wheatley*. Boston: G. K. Hall, 1982.

——. *Phillis Wheatley in the Black American Beginnings*. Detroit, MI: Broadside Press, 1975.

——. *Phillis Wheatley and Her Writings*. New York: Garland Publishing, 1984.

Rowlandson, Mary. *The Sovereignty and Goodness of God* (1682). In Alden T. Vaughan and Edward W. Clark, eds., *Puritans Among the Indians: Accounts of Captivity and Redemption, 1676–1724*, 31–75. Cambridge: Harvard University Press, 1981.

——. *A True History of the Captivity & Restoration of Mrs. Mary Rowlandson, A Minister's Wife in New-England. Wherein is set forth, The Cruel and Inhumane Usage she underwent amongst the Heathens, for Eleven Weeks time: And her Deliverance from them*. London: Joseph Poole, 1682.

Saillant, John. " 'Remarkably Emancipated From Bondage, Slavery, and Death': An African American Retelling of the Puritan Captivity Narrative, 1820." *Early American Literature* 29, no. 2 (1994): 122–40.

——. "Slavery and Divine Providence in New England Calvinism: The New Divinity and a Black Protest." *New England Quarterly* 68, no. 4 (December 1995): 584–608.

——. " 'Wipe Away All Tears From Their Eyes': Religion and An African American Exodus to Sierra Leone, 1785–1808." Unpublished manuscript.

Saint Augustine. *Confessions*. Trans. R. S. Pine-Coffin. London: Penguin, 1961.

Sánchez-Eppler, Karen. "Bodily Bonds: The Intersecting Rhetorics of Feminism and Abolition." *Representations* 24 (Fall 1988): 28–59.

Sandiford, Keith A. *Measuring the Moment: Strategies of Protest in Eighteenth-Century Afro-English Writing*. Selinsgrove, London, and Toronto: Susquehanna and Associated University Presses, 1988.

Sayre, Robert F. *The Examined Self: Benjamin Franklin, Henry Adams, Henry James*. Princeton: Princeton University Press, 1964.

Seacole, Mrs. Mary. *Wonderful Adventures of Mrs. Seacole in Many Lands*. 1857. William L. Andrews, ed. New York: Oxford University Press, 1988.

———. *Wonderful Adventures of Mrs. Seacole in Many Lands*. 1857. Audrey Dewjee and Ziggi Alexander, eds. Bristol, England: Falling Wall Press, 1984.

Seaver, James E. *Life of Mary Jemison: Deh-ne-wä-mis, the White Woman of the Genesee*. 4th ed. New York and Auburn: Miller, Orton, & Mulligan, 1856.

Seelye, John. "The Clay Foot of the Climber: Richard M. Nixon in Perspective." In William L. Andrews, ed., *Literary Romanticism in America*, 109–34. Baton Rouge: Louisiana State University Press, 1981.

Sekora, John. "Black Message/White Envelope: Genre, Authenticity and Authority in the Antebellum Slave Narrative." *Callaloo* 10, no. 3 (Summer 1987): 482–515.

———. "Comprehending Slavery: Language and Personal History in Douglass's *Narrative*." *College Language Association Journal* 29, no. 2 (December 1985): 157–70.

———. "The Dilemma of Frederick Douglass: The Slave Narrative as Literary Institution." *Essays in Literature* 10, no. 2 (Fall 1983): 219–26.

———. "Red, White, and Black: Indian Captivities, Colonial Printers, and the Early African-American Narrative." In Frank Shufflelton, ed., *A Mixed Race: Ethnicity in Early America*, 92–104. New York: Oxford University Press, 1993.

——— and Darwin T. Turner. *The Art of the Slave Narrative: Original Essays in Criticism and Theory*. Macomb: Western Illinois University Press, 1982.

Sherman, Joan R. Introduction to *Invisible Poets: Afro-Americans of the Nineteenth Century*, xv–xxxii. 2nd ed. Urbana: The University of Illinois Press, 1989.

Shields, John C. "Phillis Wheatley and Mather Byles: A Study in Literary Relationship." *College Language Association Journal* 23, no. 4 (June 1980): 377–90.

———. "Phillis Wheatley's Struggle for Freedom in her Poetry and Prose." In John C. Shields, ed., *The Collected Works of Phillis Wheatley*, 229–70. New York: Oxford University Press, 1988.

———. "Phillis Wheatley's Use of Classicism." *American Literature* 52, no. 1 (March 1980): 97–111.

Siemenski, Greg. "The Puritan Captivity Narrative and the Politics of the American Revolution." *American Quarterly* 42, no. 1 (March 1990): 35–56.

Slotkin, Richard. "Narratives of Negro Crime in New England, 1675–1900." *American Quarterly* 25, no. 1 (March 1973): 3–31.

———. *Regeneration Through Violence: The Mythology of the American Frontier, 1600–1860*. Middletown, CT: Wesleyan University Press, 1973.

Smith, Cynthia. " 'To Maecenas': Phillis Wheatley's Invocation of an Idealized Reader." *Black American Literature Forum* 23, no. 3 (Fall 1989): 579–92.

Smith, Gaddis. "His Life so Far." Review of Colin Powell's autobiography, *My American Journey*. *Boston Globe*, September 17, 1995, B39:3.

Smith, Sidonie. "Resisting the Gaze of Embodiment: Women's Autobiographies in the Nineteenth Century." In Margo Culley, ed., *American Women's Auto-*

biography: Fea(s)ts of Memory, 75–110. Madison: University of Wisconsin Press, 1992.

——. Where I'm Bound: Patterns of Slavery and Freedom in Black American Autobiography. Westport, CT: Greenwood Press, 1974.

Smith, Stephanie. "Heart Attacks: Frederick Douglass's Strategic Sentimentality." Criticism 34, no. 2 (Spring 1992): 193–216.

Smith, Valerie. Introduction to Harriet Jacobs, Incidents in the Life of a Slave Girl, xxvii–xl. New York: Oxford University Press, 1988.

——. " 'Loopholes of Retreat': Architecture and Ideology in Harriet Jacobs's Incidents in the Life of a Slave Girl." In Henry Louis Gates Jr., ed., Reading Black, Reading Feminist: A Critical Anthology, 212–25. New York: Meridian, 1990.

——. Self-Discovery and Authority in Afro-American Narrative. Cambridge: Harvard University Press, 1987.

Smith, Venture. A Narrative of the Life and Adventures of Venture, A Native of Africa, But Resident Above Sixty Years in the United States of America, Related by Himself. In Arna Bontemps, ed., Five Black Lives, 3–34. 1897. Reprint, Middletown, CT: Wesleyan University Press, 1971.

Smith-Rosenberg, Carroll. "The Female World of Love and Ritual: Relations Between Women in Nineteenth-Century America." In Disorderly Conduct: Visions of Gender in Victorian America, 53–76. New York: Knopf, 1985.

Sobel, Mechal. The World They Made Together: Black and White Values in Eighteenth Century Virginia. Princeton: Princeton University Press, 1987.

Sollors, Werner. Beyond Ethnicity: Consent and Descent in American Culture. New York: Oxford University Press, 1986.

——. "Immigrants and Other Americans." In Emory Elliot, ed., The Columbia Literary History of the United States, 568–88. New York: Columbia University Press, 1988.

——. " 'Never Was Born': The Mulatto, An American Tragedy?" The Massachusetts Review 27, No. 2 (Summer 1986): 293–316.

—— and Maria Diedrich, eds. The Black Columbiad: Defining Moments in African American Literature and Culture. Cambridge: Harvard University Press, 1994.

Spengemann, William C. and L. R. Lundquist. "Autobiography and the American Myth." American Quarterly 17, No. 3 (Fall 1965): 501–19.

Spiller, Robert E., Willard Thorp, Thomas H. Johnson, and Henry Seidel Canby, eds. Literary History of the United States. Vol. 1. New York: Macmillan, 1948.

Spillers, Hortense. "Changing the Letter: The Yokes, the Jokes of Discourse, or, Mrs. Stowe, Mr. Reed." In Deborah E. McDowell and Arnold Rampersad, eds., Slavery and the Literary Imagination, 25–61. Baltimore: The Johns Hopkins University Press, 1989.

——. "Mama's Baby, Papa's Maybe: An American Grammar Book." Diacritics 17, no. 2 (Summer 1987): 65–81.

——. "Moving on Down the Line." American Quarterly 40, no. 1 (March 1988): 83–109.

Starling, Marion Wilson. The Slave Narrative: Its Place in American History. 2nd edition. Washington, DC: Howard University Press, 1988.

Stepto, Robert B. "Distrust of the Reader in Afro-American Narratives." In Sacvan Bercovitch, ed., Reconstructing American Literary History, 300–22. Cambridge: Harvard University Press, 1986.

——. From Behind the Veil: A Study of Afro-American Narrative. Urbana: University of Illinois Press, 1979.

——. "Narration, Authentication, and Authorial Control in Frederick Douglass' *Narrative* of 1845." In Dexter Fisher and Robert B. Stepto. eds., *Afro-American Literature: The Reconstruction of Instruction*, 178–91. New York: Modern Language Association, 1979.

——. "Sharing the Thunder: The Literary Exchanges of Harriet Beecher Stowe, Henry Bibb, and Frederick Douglass." In Eric J. Sundquist, ed., *New Essays on Uncle Tom's Cabin*, 135–53. New York: Cambridge University Press, 1986.

——. "Teaching Afro-American Literature: Survey or Tradition." In Robert Stepto and Dexter Fisher, eds., *Afro-American Literature: The Reconstruction of Instruction*, 8–24. New York: Modern Language Association, 1979.

Stone, Albert E. "Identity and Art in Frederick Douglass's *Narrative*." *CLA Journal* 17, no. 2 (December 1973): 192–213.

Stowe, Harriet Beecher. *A Key to Uncle Tom's Cabin; presenting the original facts and documents upon which the story is founded*. Boston: John P. Jewett, 1853.

——. *Uncle Tom's Cabin; or, Life Among the Lowly*. 2 vols. Boston: John P. Jewett, 1852.

Strong, Pauline Turner. "Captive Images." *Natural History*, December 1985: 51–56.

Stuckey, Sterling. *Slave Culture: Nationalist Theory and the Foundations of Black America*. New York: Oxford University Press, 1987.

Sundquist, Eric J., ed. *Frederick Douglass: New Literary and Historical Essays*. New York: Cambridge University Press, 1990.

——, ed. *New Essays on Stowe's Uncle Tom's Cabin*. New York: Cambridge University Press, 1986.

——. *To Wake the Nations: Race in the Making of American Literature*. Cambridge: Harvard University Press, 1993.

Tate, Claudia. *Domestic Allegories of Political Desire: The Black Heroine's Text at the Turn of the Century*. New York: Oxford University Press, 1992.

Teamoh, George. *God Made Man, Man Made the Slave: The Autobiography of George Teamoh*. F. Nash Boney, Richard L. Hume, and Rafia Zafar, eds. Macon, GA: Mercer University Press, 1992.

Thompson, Kathleen. Entry on Elizabeth Keckley. In Darlene Clark Hine, ed., *Black Women in America: A Historical Encyclopedia*, 672–73. Brooklyn, NY: Clarkson, 1994.

Todorov, Tzvetan. *The Conquest of America: The Question of the Other*. Trans. Richard Howard. New York: Harper & Row, 1984.

Tompkins, Jane. *Sensational Designs: The Cultural Work of American Fiction, 1790–1860*. New York: Oxford University Press, 1985.

Turner, Nat. *The Confessions of Nat Turner*. With Thomas R. Gray. In Henry R. Tragle, ed., *The Southampton Slave Revolt of 1831: A Compilation of Source Material*, 300–21. 1831. Reprint, Amherst: University of Massachusetts Press, 1971.

Turner, Victor. *The Ritual Process: Structure and Anti-Structure*. 1969. Reprint, Ithaca: Cornell University Press, 1977.

Tyler, Moses Coit. *The Literary History of the American Revolution: 1763–1783*. New York: G. P. Putnam's Sons, 1897.

Ulrich, Laurel Thatcher. "Captives." In *Good Wives: Image and Reality in the Lives of Women in Northern New England 1650–1750*, 202–14. New York: Knopf, 1982.

VanDerBeets, Richard, ed. *Held Captive by Indians: Selected Narratives, 1642–1836*. Knoxville: University of Tennessee Press, 1973.

Vaughan, Alden T. and Edward W. Clark, eds. *Puritans Among the Indians: Accounts of Captivity and Redemption, 1676–1724*. Cambridge: Harvard University Press, 1981.

Vlach, John Michael. *The Afro-American Tradition in Decorative Arts*. 1978. Reprint, Athens: University of Georgia Press, 1990.

Wagner, Jean. Introduction to *Black Poets of the United States: From Paul Laurence Dunbar to Langston Hughes*. Trans. Kenneth Douglas. Urbana: University of Illinois Press, 1973.

Walker, David. *Walker's Appeal, in Four Articles; Together with a Preamble, to the Colored Citizens of the World, but in particular, and very expressly, to those of the United States of America, written in Boston, state of Massachusetts, September 28, 1829. Third and Last Edition, with additional notes, corrections & c.* In Herbert Aptheker, ed., *"One Continual Cry": David Walker's Appeal to the Colored Citizens of the World (1829–1830), its setting and its meaning, together with the full text of the third, and last edition of the Appeal*, 61–147. New York: Humanities Press, 1965.

Walker, Jeffrey. "Joel Barlow." In James A. Levernier and Douglas R. Wilmes, eds., *American Writers Before 1800*, 100–2. Westport, CT: Greenwood Press, 1983.

Walker, Peter F. "Frederick Douglass: Orphan Slave." In *Moral Choices: Memory, Desire, and Imagination in Nineteenth Century Abolition*, 207–61. Baton Rouge: Louisiana State University Press, 1978.

Wardley, Lynn. "Relic, Fetish, Femmage: The Aesthetics of Sentiment in the Work of Stowe." In Shirley Samuels, ed., *The Culture of Sentiment*, 203–20. New York: Oxford University Press, 1992.

Warhol, Robyn. *Gendered Interventions: Narrative Discourse in the Victorian Novel*. New Brunswick, NJ: Rutgers University Press, 1989.

Warner, Michael. *The Letters of the Republic: Publication and the Public Sphere in Eighteenth-Century America*. Cambridge: Harvard University Press, 1990.

Warren, Joyce, ed. *The (Other) American Tradition: Nineteenth Century-Women Writers*. New Brunswick, NJ: Rutgers University Press.

Warren, Kenneth W. *Black and White Strangers: Race and American Literary Realism*. Chicago: University of Chicago Press, 1993.

Washington, John E. "Elizabeth Keckley: Companion and Confidante of Mrs. Lincoln." In *They Knew Lincoln*, 205–41. New York: E. P. Dutton, 1942.

Washington, Mary Helen. *Invented Lives: Narratives of Black Women, 1860–1960*. New York: Anchor Press, 1987.

Weber, Donald. *Rhetoric and History in Revolutionary New England*. New York: Oxford University Press, 1988.

Weiss, M. Lynn. "*Para Usted*: Richard Wright's *Pagan Spain*." In Werner Sollors and Maria Diedrich, eds., *The Black Columbiad: Defining Moments in African American Literature and Culture*, 212–25. Harvard English Studies 19. Cambridge: Harvard University Press, 1994.

Welter, Barbara. "The Cult of True Womanhood 1820–1860." In *Dimity Convictions: The American Woman in the Nineteenth Century*, 21–41. Athens: Ohio University Press, 1976.

Wharton, Martha L. " 'I Remember Hearing My [Mother] Tell . . .': Memory's Redeeming Power in Julia Foote's *A Brand Plucked from the Fire* [1879 and 1886]." A paper delivered at the Nineteenth-Century Women Writers Conference, Hartford, CT, June 2, 1996.

Wheatley, Phillis. *The Collected Works of Phillis Wheatley*. John C. Shields, ed. New York: Oxford University Press, 1988.

——. *The Poems of Phillis Wheatley*. Julian D. Mason Jr., ed. Revised and enlarged. Chapel Hill: University of North Carolina Press, 1989.

White, Barbara A. " 'Our Nig' and the She-Devil: New Information about Harriet Wilson and the 'Belmont' Family" *American Literature* 65, no. 1 (March 1993): 19–52.

White, Deborah Gray. *Ar'n't I A Woman? Female Slaves in the Plantation South.* New York: Norton, 1985.

Williams, John. *The Redeemed Captive Returned to Zion.* In Alden T. Vaughan and Edward W. Clark. eds., *Puritans Among the Indians: Accounts of Captivity and Redemption, 1676–1724,* 169–226. Cambridge: Harvard University Press, 1981.

Wilson, Harriet E. *Our Nig; or Sketches from the Life of a Free Black, in a Two-Story White House, North, Showing that Slavery's Shadows Fall Even There.* Henry Louis Gates Jr., ed. 1859. Reprint, New York: Vintage, 1983.

Wilson, R. Jackson. "A Note on the Text." In *The Autobiography of Benjamin Franklin.* New York: Random House, 1981.

Winthrop, John. "A Modell of Christian Charity. Written On Boarde the Arrabella, On the Attlantick Ocean." In *Winthrop Papers* Vol. 2, 1623–1630, 282–95. Boston: Massachusetts Historical Society, 1931.

Wright, Richard. *White Man, Listen!* 1957. Reprint, Westport, CT: Greenwood Press, 1978.

Yarborough, Richard. "The First Person in Afro-American Fiction." In Houston A. Baker Jr. and Patricia Redmond, eds. *Afro-American Literary Study in the 1990s,* 105–21. Chicago: University of Chicago Press, 1989.

——. "Strategies of Black Characterization in *Uncle Tom's Cabin* and the early Afro-American Novel." In Eric J. Sundquist, ed., *New Essays on Uncle Tom's Cabin.* 45–84. New York: Cambridge University Press, 1986.

Yellin, Jean Fagan. *The Intricate Knot.* New Haven: Yale University Press, 1972.

——. Introduction, chronology, and notes to Harriet Jacobs, *Incidents in the Life of a Slave Girl: Written by Herself.* Cambridge: Harvard University Press, 1987.

——. "Texts and Contexts of Harriet Jacobs's *Incidents in the Life of a Slave Girl: Written by Herself.*" In Charles T. Davis and Henry Louis Gates Jr., eds., *The Slave's Narrative,* 262–82. New York: Oxford University Press, 1985.

——. *Women and Sisters: The Antislavery Feminists in American Culture.* New Haven: Yale University Press, 1989.

Zafar, Rafia. "Capturing the Captivity: African Americans Among the Puritans." *MELUS* 17, no. 2 (Summer 1991–1992): 19–35.

——. "Franklinian Douglass: The Afro-American as Representative Man." In Eric J. Sundquist, ed., *Frederick Douglass: New Literary and Historical Essays,* 99–117. New York: Cambridge University Press, 1990.

——. "The Proof of the Pudding: Of Haggis, Hasty Pudding, and Transatlantic Influence." *Early American Literature* 31, no. 2 (1996): 133–49.

——. *White Call, Black Response: Adoption, Subversion, and Transformation in American Literature, 1760–1860.* Doctoral dissertation, Harvard University, 1989.

INDEX

༞

Craft, Ellen and William, 218*n*37
Crèvecoeur, J. Hector St. John de, 94
Cuguano, Ottabah, 92

Dean, Sharon G., 160
Devereux, George, 69
Delany, Martin R., 118
Delany sisters, the, 218*n*34
Dixon, Melvin, 119
double consciousness, 4, 25, 115, 152
Douglass, Frederick, 8, 9, 11–12, 13, 51,
55, 71, 74, 77, 78, 80, 87, 89–91, 95,
96–115, 123, 132, 158, 159, 173, 175,
187, 190; —works: *Life and Times*,
112; *My Bondage and My Freedom*,
111–12; *Narrative of the Life*, 90,
96–97, 98–115, 123, 151; "Self Made
Men," 112–13, 173; —family and
friends: Anna Murray Douglass
(wife), 108–9; Aunt Hester, 106; Bill,
fellow slave, 111–12; Caroline, fellow
slave, 112; father, as white man,
96–97, 106–7; *see also* Anthony,
Captain; grandmother, 96, 107, 123;
Harris brothers (friends), 111; Harris,
Henry, 104; Jenkins, Sandy, 110–11;
mother, 96–97; siblings, 96–97, 107
Du Bois, W. E. B., 4, 115, 152–53
duCille, Anne, 130, 133
Dumas, Alexander, 2, 191*n*1
Dunbar, Paul Laurence, 3–4, 152
Dustan, Hannah, 69, 73

elegy, 15, 27, 31
Ellison, Julie, 31, 34, 37
Ellison, Ralph, 87, 183
entrepreneurs, entrepreneurship, 157–58,
163–64, 167–68, 172–75, 180–82
Equiano, Olaudah, 56, 58, 59, 89–90,
91–95, 158, 174, 175, 186–87;
Interesting Narrative, 91–95; *see
also* Gustavus Vassa
Erkkila, Betsy, 20

Fabi, M. Guilia, 134
fashion, 153, 159, 163, 166–67, 180–81
Ferguson, Moira, 161
Fielding, Henry, 82
Fifteenth Amendment, 189

folklore, 5, 30, 110
food, 29–30, 48–49, 100, 102, 104–5
Foote, Julia, 65, 93, 204*n*79
Foreman, P. Gabrielle, 125, 153
Foster, Frances Smith, 3, 63–64, 180,
181, 182
Fourteenth Amendment, 188–89
Franklin, Benjamin, 89–91, 95–100,
102–16; *The Autobiography*, 89–90,
95–116; —family: Deborah Read
Franklin (wife), 108, 110; James
(brother), 100, 103–4, 105–6; Josiah
(father), 99–100, 104; —friends:
John Collins, 99, 109–10; James
Ralph, 109–10
free blacks, 52, 57, 61, 95, 163, 170
freedom, African American, 18–19, 22,
23–24, 25, 27, 35–36, 37–38, 90, 94,
107–8, 111, 113–14, 118, 147, 148,
171–75, 187
Freeland, William, 104, 110
French Revolution, the, 26

Garner, Margaret, 212*n*25
Gates, Henry Louis Jr., 5–6, 58, 145
Gatewood, Silas, 72
Gatewood, William, 74
gender, 34, 64, 89, 119, 120–21, 134,
152–53; *see also* masculinity
genre, adaptations and uses of, 5, 7–8, 10,
11, 13, 24, 25, 38, 41–52, 54, 69–72,
78, 95, 151–52, 154, 180, 185, 187
Gibson, Donald B., 215*n*67
Gilbert, Sandra and Susan Gubar, 119,
141–42
Gilroy, Paul, 63
Gray, Thomas, 69
Gronniosaw, James Albert Ukasaw, 43,
56, 58, 59, 92, 95
Gunning, Sandra, 3, 124, 136

Hallowell, A. Irving, 75
Halttunen, Karen, 153, 155–56, 161, 176
Hammon, Briton, 41, 54–56, 65, 69, 95,
187
Hanson, Elizabeth, 41, 49–51, 200*n*26;
"God's Mercy," 49–51
Harper, Frances, 189
Harper, Phillip Brian, 5